Kicking Up the Slope

Mark Whitby

First published in 2025.

ISBN: 9798291780183

Main cover image: with thanks to Atherton Collieries FC

All other photographs are from Kelly Jones or the author.

Contents

P91: July 2024

Winsford United v Northwich Victoria / Cheadle Town v Runcorn Linnets / Flint Town v Runcorn Linnets / Runcorn Linnets v Bolton Wanders U23s / Pilkington v Ramsbottom United

P97: August 2024

South Liverpool v Handsworth / Runcorn Linnets v Widnes / Wythenshawe Town v Runcorn Linnets / Runcorn Linnets v Hednesford Town / Witton Albion v Runcorn Linnets / Runcorn Linnets v Congleton Town

P106: September 2024

Avro v Runcorn Linnets / Lower Breck v Abbey Hey / Runcorn Linnets v Trafford / Bucket Hat FM / Runcorn Linnets v Mossley

P114: October 2024

Wythenshawe Town v Runcorn Linnets / Runcorn Linnets Ladies v Wirral Phoenix / Runcorn Linnets v Newcastle Town / Atherton Collieries v Runcorn Linnets / Northwich Victoria v Studley / Witton Albion v Runcorn Linnets / Runcorn Linnets v Nantwich Town Sandbach United v Barnton / City of Liverpool v Runcorn Linnets / Runcorn Linnets v Bootle

p128: November 2024

Runcorn Linnets v Chasetown / Runcorn Linnets v Kidsgrove Athletic / Runcorn Linnets Ladies v Wigan Athletic Ladies / Vauxhall Motors v Chasetown / Stalybridge Celtic v Runcorn Linnets / Bucket Hat FM

p136: December 2024

Runcorn Linnets v Ashton Town / Trafford v Runcorn Linnets / Runcorn Linnets v Vauxhall Motors / Runcorn Linnets v Hanley Town / Ashton Town v Maine Road / Runcorn Linnets v Wythenshawe / Bootle v Runcorn Linnets

#

‘A man can’t have no greater love,

Than to give ninety minutes to his friends.’

Sultans of Ping FC – *Give Him a Ball and a Yard of Grass*

Introduction

The north-west of England has long been established as a footballing hotbed. Half of the twelve original member clubs of the football league came from the region. That first league season saw Preston North End crowned champions with Everton the best supported side. By that point, Blackburn's Olympic and Rovers had already seized the FA Cup from the clutches of the southern amateur sides, beginning a march towards professionalism that quickly became unstoppable.

By 1900 Liverpool, Everton and both Manchester clubs (United were still known as Newton Heath) were all competing in the league. In those days, however, travel from the towns of Lancashire and Cheshire to the big cities wasn't easy. Although organised excursions to seaside towns like Blackpool had long been popular, regular rail travel was uncomfortable and dirty for those of limited means. Because of this, the teams in the big cities still drew supporters largely from their immediate communities and despite the increasing pull of rugby league in the area, there was enough interest in the round ball game in the smaller towns for the game to in the area between them. The Lancashire League came into existence in 1889 and several sides from the region became members over the next decade, including Prescot, Haydock, St Helens Town, St Helens Recreation and Warrington. Others would emerge in the first quarter of the 20th century, among them Runcorn, Rylands FC and Atherton Collieries.

When better infrastructure began to allow easier access to the bigger stadiums, it didn't mean bring an end to the development of football elsewhere. Manchester United's introduction of a halt station outside Old Trafford in the 1950s may have been the bedrock on which the club began to build its enormous support base, but the emergence of clubs like Ashton Town and Atherton LR in the 1950s is indicative of the continuing appeal of local, community-based football clubs.

The more recent surge in semi-professional clubs, which saw the likes of FC St Helens, Lower Breck and Widnes emerge, has shown that such an appeal continues to persist in the era of the Premier League and Champions League. Many of these clubs have benefited from the introduction of community facilities with artificial pitches which allow for use by multiple clubs and community organisations without the protection required by grass surfaces. Yet many are also the product of disillusionment with a professional game whose clubs have increasingly become franchises for the super-rich, moving far away from their community roots and in the process leaving those communities behind.

In the 33 miles between Old Trafford and Anfield, such clubs survive – and often thrive – despite much of the available footballing support draining away to either east or west. Travelling from north to south, you need to travel around 40 miles from Wigan to Crewe to find another Football League side. In between, these clubs carve out an existence despite most football fans in their local area already having an allegiance to those powerhouses at either end of the East Lancs Road.

Smaller clubs can either attempt to compete with that or, more plausibly, find a way to co-exist. Dual allegiances are common. In this book, for instance, we talk to Runcorn's Bren

Connolly, who is also a lifelong Everton fan, Vicki England of 1874 Northwich, who, like me, also supports Manchester United, and Liverpool fan Sam Phillips. Some younger fans, priced out of Premier League stadia, follow the fortunes of these major clubs via television while supporting their local teams, something which the gradual demise of Saturday 3pm football in higher levels of the game has enabled.

While supporting a bigger club brings brushes with success and glory, or at least a realistic chance of them, it brings other things too – media overkill, idle punditry, action replays from the kinds of angles that nobody ever needs to see football from...all of which are absent from this world, which is also one without VAR or goal line technology. With rare exceptions, football can be watched standing up, usually very close to the pitch. Weekend games rarely stray from the traditional 3pm kick off on a Saturday afternoon.

Players often greet spectators they know over the fence before the game and have a pint with them in the clubhouse after it. You can also stand with a pint and watch the game at most of these grounds - something that those who only frequent those lavish realms of the Champions League and Premier League will never know. The original community ideal of the football club, long sacrificed at higher levels of the game, lives on in these leagues. Young kids get in either very cheaply or for free, the clubs very much aware of the importance of building bonds and connections that begin early and, hopefully, remain for life. In this world, fans in the ground are still the lifeblood of a club, not the TV audience or corporate stakeholders: nurturing them is not just key to survival, it's the only way to survive.

Some of the issues that have adversely affected football at higher levels are not entirely absent here. Historic grounds have fallen to the property developer's ball and chain, including Runcorn's old Canal Street ground and Northwich Victoria's famous Drill Field. Clubs have been starved of money and died, sometimes to resurface at a lower level and sometimes just remain dead. It's a fragile existence.

But don't think you're entering a world of under-achievement. The axe of extinction may linger uncomfortably close to many, but these are clubs who, despite this, have endured and, to varying degrees, prospered. All the grounds I visit here host football at North-West Counties level (or equivalent) or above. An enormous amount of work goes into sustaining clubs at this level, both on the field and off it, and it is work that continues – with the vital assistance of volunteers who labour unseen on and between matchdays – and must continue, lest the clubs slide back to the county and district leagues from whence many of them came, or worse.

I've seen a club die at first hand. I began supporting the old Runcorn FC in the mid-eighties and, for a while, wrote match reports for a local paper. I watched them lose at Wembley three times, over several years building a reputation as one of the best clubs outside the football league. I then witnessed first-hand the decline, those trips to Wembley doomed to remain only as memories as a ground was bulldozed and a club began its slow march to extinction.

But sometimes death isn't the end, at least in football. Runcorn Linnets made a quick return from the ashes, the club taking its name from its predecessor's nickname. This book can be seen, I suppose, as a year in the life of a Runcorn supporter who happened to look around me to see football through the eyes of others who, like me, grew up in this area of the world, loved football and yearned for a match-day experience that the big grounds have, for various reasons, ceased to offer.

Within this eighteen-month period I do what I would have been doing anyway, following Runcorn Linnets home and away, sometimes to grounds within this area and sometimes outside it. I also visit every other ground in the area, finding clubs that had better experiences than Runcorn and others that endured much worse. Most, though, give their supporters the kind of volatile ride on the footballing rollercoaster common to football fans at any level.

Sometimes I found empathy, sometimes antipathy. There are rivalries and friendships; sometimes both. I found clubs struggling with form and clubs fighting to survive, while others thrived, expanded and dreamed of how far the wild ride of football might take them. Some clubs are well over a hundred years old while others have come into existence within the last two decades. At all of them I found devotion, solidarity and a rich sense of community.

Everything, frankly, that the game of football needs and is in danger of losing.

(Map is an approximation for illustrative purposes only)

Prologue: Runcorn FC

The ritual would have been familiar to many. Arrive at about 2.30 on a Saturday afternoon, park opposite the Linnets Club, make the short walk to the turnstiles situated below the flyover, pay, enter the Canal Street stadium, find my place on the terrace close to the home dugout and shout like an idiot for the rest of the afternoon. Sometimes I'd travel in by bus and have a few pints at the Navigation after the game.

Chronicler of the football grounds of Cheshire John Keohane isn't complimentary about Canal Street. 'A real mish-mash of stands, covers and bits of terracing, all of different ages and styles,' he calls it. While this isn't an entirely inaccurate description, I suppose you see a place differently when it's yours. Brian Howman, who began watching Runcorn as a child in the 1970s, accepts Canal Street wasn't exactly easy on the eye. 'A pre-war ground,' he concedes.

Brian has since moved to Dundee, is now a regular at Dens Park but is nostalgic about Canal Street and has fond memories of Runcorn, the games, the players and the pre-match routine. 'I remember match nights, going down Heath Road, and there'd be hundreds of people walking down the road to the football. And then we'd cross the road and down the steps. We'd have to queue to get in,' he says. 'You'd hear the old boys talking about the Cheshire League days when we'd take fifty coaches to watch us play Wrexham Reserves or whatever. But there was nothing else to do. Saturday was football day.'

Brian went to his first game in 1971. 'I was still in junior school. I remember we played Grimsby in the cup and my mum wouldn't let me go. We wore green and white stripes, that was the first kit then,' he remembers. 'In FA Trophy games, we'd get to play southern non-league teams. That was interesting.' The Trophy had only been introduced in 1969, a year after the formation of the Northern Premier League, in which Runcorn then played. 'I remember playing Wycombe and absolutely destroying them. There was always a bit of an edge there. I remember going to Bedford for an FA Trophy game and we'd take many hundreds away for these games. There were balloons and banners all over Bedford. We won with two breakaway goals.'

He can still reel off the names of the first eleven that won the Northern Premier League in 1976, singling out players like Barry Howard, who went on to be a club legend at Altrincham, and Barry Whitbread, later manager at Canal Street.

He recalls Johnny Worth from that team. 'He was six foot six and couldn't head the ball. He scored a hat-trick on his debut against Altrincham. We thought oh, he's gonna be something...but he kept getting sent off. He was just the perfect Runcorn player. He was scoring goals, won loads of penalties in the days before people won penalties, just by not letting people take the ball off him in the box till they kicked him.'

Bren Connolly, who now manages ground operations at Runcorn Linnets, was present at many of these occasions too. 'I used to watch Runcorn in the mid-seventies and eighties,' he tells me. 'I started skipping college on a Tuesday night if Runcorn were playing at home. I'd get the bus over from Widnes to Canal Street.'

Sam Phillips, now Head of Media at Runcorn Linnets, began supporting the club in the later years of Runcorn FC's existence. Sam's grandad played for the club in the 1950s so he was weaned on its heritage long before he first attended a match at the age of six. 'I'm pretty sure we played Hucknall Town,' he said, memories understandably fuzzy from being introduced at such an early age. 'I was lucky enough to see players like Spike Carter playing. It would have been the 96-97 season when I first started going, From then, I can't remember missing a game until 2014.' After briefly leaving the country to coach in America, Sam has since returned to launch the Bucket Hat FM radio station which transmits live commentary from Runcorn games, home and away.

Mark 'Spike' Carter has a strong claim to be Runcorn's greatest player, scoring 144 goals in 255 appearances between 1984 and 1991. Carter returned to Runcorn for another spell before hanging up his boots, including a stint as manager. Predictably, Brian names him in his long list of great Runcorn players. 'Carter should have had a better career,' he says. 'Back then, if you had a good job, you could earn more money than if you were playing third or fourth division.' Carter ran his own fruit and veg business so he opted to stay semi-professional with Runcorn before finally being tempted into the professional game at the late age of 31, a transition he made with some success, averaging close to a goal every two games with Barnet, Bury and Rochdale.

Later came Kenny McKenna, the kind of player who's loved by his club's fans but hated by everybody else. Brian recalls him checking to make sure the ref had his back turned before headbutting a Guiseley player. 'The ball had gone out to the right wing and Joe Connor had got it. McKenna and their centre half were running back and you could see McKenna look round, nobody looking, and he stuck the head on this guy at the same time as Joe Connor's getting fouled. So we've got a free kick on the right wing up by their box. McKenna comes up, the free kick comes over and the player who should be marking him is on the floor. Kenny McKenna heads it into the top corner.'

I remember a game at Telford when their central defender Steve Nelson had come up for a corner: in challenging for a loose ball, Nelson's boot had come off and he spent several minutes looking for it while play advanced up the other end of the pitch. McKenna had run off with it and dropped it in the centre circle.

Of course, arguably Runcorn's most famous ex-player wasn't even good enough to make more than a handful of appearances. 'I remember John Bishop taking a shot,' says Brian, 'and it not only went out for a throw, it went out for a throw behind where he shot from. Some people say he's not a very good comedian, but he's a better comedian than he was a footballer. But he's a good guy, for all that. His parents are lovely. They'd go and watch Eddie one week and John the next.'

Eddie Bishop, John's brother, was a far better player, a tough-tackling, combative midfielder. He played for Runcorn briefly after that combativeness led to him being shown the door by Altrincham when Tommy Docherty was manager there. 'I know players retaliate but Eddie had run twenty yards to headbutt a player,' Brian recalls. 'We signed him for Runcorn because he was a perfect Runcorn player.'

Brian's reeling the names off now. 'Stevie Joel...I used to work with his son.' Joel had been a promising player with Liverpool Reserves. It hadn't worked out and he'd ended up at Canal Street. He was one of the best long-thrown specialists I've seen. 'I remember Carl Thomas: he was a lovely lad, nice bloke. You'd be surprised by that if you'd seen him play. Don Page was a great player. Had his leg broken at Chester. Barrow went two feet over the ball, broke the boy's leg and you heard the snap in the stands.'

Then there was Ian Woan, later Sean Dyche's assistant at Burnley and Everton and a player who'd seemed a low-key signing when Runcorn brought him up from Newtown in the summer of 1989. After a series of thrilling performances on the left of midfield, league clubs were soon competing for his signature, Brian Clough's Nottingham Forest eventually winning the race at the eleventh hour, or even later, as legend has it.

'I was shown the transfer document,' says Brian, 'with Bournemouth crossed out and Nottingham Forest written above. And 60,000 or whatever was crossed out and 85,000 put in. Clough himself rang: "Has he signed? Oh, well we'll have him."' Brian manages a less than convincing Clough impersonation. 'Then they met at a motorway service station and the deal was struck'. Woan went on to play over 200 games for Forest in the top flight.

It was expected the money from the transfer would be used to fund what then looked a promising future for the club. We finished third at the end of the 1989-90 season with the best home record in the Conference: only poor away form – just three wins all season – prevented a serious tilt at the title. But soon Runcorn went from a team consistently in the top half of table to one with a more precarious existence. Two years later, we finished only three points clear of the relegation zone before another narrow escape the following season was followed by a brief resurgence in league form and the last of those three Wembley appearances in the FA Trophy Final, where we were defeated by Woking. Such brushes with better times offered only a temporary reprieve before relegation to the Northern Premier League in 1996 and the grim slide to extinction.

Where the ground once stood is now a housing estate. The Navigation isn't there either, having gone the way of many pubs, whose existence was entwined with a local community, the heartbeat of which was a local club.

Runcorn were eventually re-named Runcorn FC Halton and moved across the water to play at Widnes' Rugby League Ground. By that point it was clear the writing was on the wall and, unlike the graffiti that began to appear on the walls of the doomed Canal Street ground, it couldn't easily be washed away. 'The cost to the club per game to play here is at least £2500,' noted John Keohane, 'yet the average crowd is around 250 – do the maths yourself.'

The club justified the move to Widnes in the programme notes of the final game at Canal Street: 'the essence of a football club is not where it plays but the people who are part of the organisation'. Sam Phillips, still a child at the time, nonetheless has some fond memories from that period. 'The one that really sticks in my head was the Bristol Rovers game in the FA Cup, when we took them to extra time.' There's no question, though, that a large section of the club's traditional support base weren't happy with the move.

'I didn't go to watch Runcorn playing at Widnes,' says Brian Howman, 'and I didn't like the idea that we'd been called Runcorn Halton'. There were unmistakeable signs that Runcorn FC was Dead Team Walking and eventually the walking slowed to a halt.

An infamous sequence of events had led to the gradual demise of Runcorn FC, key moments being the fire that took the Linnets Club and robbed Runcorn of a major source of income and the collapse of a wall during an FA Cup game against Hull that led to urgent rebuilding work, partial closure and ticketing restrictions. In the same season, high winds took the roof off part of the ground and another fire burnt down the wooden stand.

By that point, football at that level had also changed a lot from when Brian first started supporting them, first with the creation of a national competition – the Alliance Premier League, which became the Conference and is now the National League – and the introduction of automatic promotion to the football league.

Brian believes another big factor in the club's eventual decline was that Runcorn's board didn't keep up with these changes. 'It was run by people with their eye on different things than running a successful small football club. We'd been in profit two years running, why not spend some of that, y'know? Back then, it was frustrating watching clubs who didn't have the recent history that we had overtaking us, because they were buying better players. So you start losing, it knocks a hundred off the crowd and then you say we've got to get a new manager, and even at that level it's not cheap. And then we get relegated, and if there are fewer people coming, how do you get back?'

It's a familiar downward spiral experienced by many clubs but Brian feels that, if the board had made the right decisions, it could all have been different. 'When they built the Halton Community Stadium (in Widnes), they wanted to build it in Runcorn, and the board at Runcorn said no. That should have been a red flag.

'I didn't go to the last game at Canal Street,' Brian recalls. 'I remember saying it'll be too much for me. Losing a football club is like a bereavement.'

By that point I'd stopped going myself. I'd like to say it was an emotional decision like Brian's, but in truth I can't remember why I stopped, or even specifically when.

I had a regular job by that point and had long since stopped reporting on Runcorn matches. Then I met my wife, got married and had children. Time drifted on, until I realised my son had reached an age when it seemed I must, if I was any kind of responsible father, introduce him to the world of live football. And that neatly coincided with Runcorn Linnets coming home.

By 2008, the supporter-run Runcorn Linnets, who'd spent their early years ground-sharing at Witton Albion, had moved to a new ground located behind the Halton Arms in Murdishaw. You parked near the pub, if you could, then walked around the back of it to a new stadium that was basic but neat and well-maintained. The Halton Arms went the way of The Navigation when the area around the ground was redeveloped. A new pub, the Queen of Hearts, has since taken its place, along with an Aldi, a Subway and a Vets4Pets.

Now, I park at the ground at around 2.30, often with my son Tim, flash my season ticket at the entrance and find my place on the terraces close to the home dugout. Then I shout like an idiot. Some things don't change.

January 2024

Something had to give. And eventually everything gave.

Monday 1 January

Wincham Park Stadium, Wincham

Northern Premier League West Division

Witton Albion 1 Runcorn Linnets 0

The rest of the country is waking with elbows bruised from the battle at the bar, or else reflecting on how Jools Holland's new year extravaganza isn't quite what it was. Close to where I live, a guy hangs out of his far door, fast asleep, his body suspended by a seatbelt which is all that prevents the rudest of new year awakenings. In the rest of the world, half-hearted resolutions made at the stroke of midnight are already being broken.

And me? I have my eye on other disappointments.

Travelling south, the post-industrial landscape straddling the Mersey has long given way to the green fields of mid-Cheshire but at Witton Albion's ground – in Wincham, just outside Northwich – you wouldn't know it: beneath an unmistakeably dark Northern January sky, lurk an asphalt mixing plant and the site of the old salt works.

Northwich's association with salt goes back to Roman times, when the presence of brine springs led to the establishment of a settlement as a cross point for the River Weaver. Much later, seventeenth century entrepreneurs seeking coal accidentally discovered the area to be rich in rock salt and turned their attention in its direction instead, the town of Northwich and village of Wincham being major centres for salt mining until excessive extraction began to cause the ground to collapse and in the early 19th century attention switched to nearby Winsford instead. Collapsing grounds would later become an all too familiar feature of this part of the world.

Despite the early 'Salt Boys' nickname of Northwich Vics, the football clubs in the area all emerged long after the salt extractors had moved on. Northwich Victoria were founded in 1874

and quickly became Cheshire's most dominant club, winning the first six Cheshire Senior Cup tournaments following the competition's introduction in 1880.

Northwich's other club, Witton Albion, were founded in 1887, four years after Winsford United were established. Barnton FC, in a village to the north of Northwich are relative babies, having come into existence just after the second world war.

Without a 'big' club in the area, football in mid-Cheshire had the ground all to itself, so to speak, and Northwich Victoria became founding members of Division Two of the Football League when it was introduced in 1892. The great Billy Meredith, arguably football's first superstar, played for them, though he, like other top players, were quickly tempted away by bigger clubs (he played for both Manchester teams) and Northwich found professional football difficult to maintain. They resigned from the league just two years later to become, for much of the next century, one of the country's most eminent non-league clubs.

Neither Witton nor Winsford experienced such flirtations with the professional leagues. Witton became founder members of the Cheshire League in 1920 and remained there until 1979 when they gained promotion to the Northern Premier League. Throughout this period, Mid-Cheshire remained a vibrant area for non-league football. However, the presence of four clubs at roughly the same level in such proximity left each of them fighting for the attention of a relatively small population. In his book *The Card*, Chester supporter Dave Hill, when visiting Witton Albion for an FA Trophy game notes, 'There seem to be more football clubs per capita than is strictly necessary,' Partly because of this, none of the three clubs who once called Northwich home now plays its home games in the town.

Witton were the first to make the decision to decamp. 'In 30 years' time, people will still be referring to Wincham Park as Witton's new ground,' forecast Kerry Miller in his excellent book *The History Of Non-League Football Grounds of Great Britain*. Well over 30 years later, he was right: we still do.

It may be no more than a quirk of the fixture list, but Wincham Park is the perfect place to start this odyssey. It's probably my favourite away ground. Home to a small but lovingly maintained Non-League Football Museum, the stadium, built some way from the club's previous home in Northwich town centre, has managed what few new grounds have achieved in the decades since: to produce a modern ground that retains the character of the old one. You can still feel the ghost of the old Central Ground, on the site of which there's now a Sainsbury's, breathing through the concrete here. Or perhaps that's just the post-new year flatulence.

Received terrace wisdom at this level has it that New Year's Day games can hinge on which of the sides overdid the celebrations most the night before. The players, unlike their well-paid professional counterparts, get little monetary reward for putting off the festivities until the close season. Perhaps with that in mind, four of the league's sides opted to bring their matches forward, to the Saturday. Some of the performances in Runcorn shirts today have me thinking it may have been a good idea if we'd sought a similar arrangement.

As the Linnets' early landlords when the new club was in its infancy, there remains a good relationship with Witton. The always excellent Witton programme – long established as one of the best in the country, and for my money probably the best – recalls an infamous FA Cup tie in the fifties, when a goal from Witton was allowed to stand despite Runcorn's protests that the ball had entered the goal via a hole in the side netting (if you ever wondered why the referee's assistants faff about checking the nets before each half, this is why). Runcorn stormed off and refused to continue. They received a hefty fine and the game was awarded to Witton.

Linnets go into today's game second in the league, following a win over promotion rivals Prescot Cables on Boxing Day but, as has been the way for much of the season, inconsistency looks likely to thwart any serious title ambitions in a league from which only the champions are guaranteed promotion. The story of this game has an irritatingly familiar plot. Despite dominating possession for long periods, Runcorn create few clear-cut chances and the one sustained period of Witton pressure, just after half-time, brings the match-winning goal.

Prior to their move to Wincham Park in the early nineties, I visited Witton's old ground in Northwich a lot, usually popping into the excellent Omega Records on the way. I recall buying The Pixies' magnificent *Surfer Rosa* there, among other magnificent additions to my vinyl collection. With that in mind I'm pleased to note that the musical selection at the ground is better than you get at most, highlights being Radiohead's *High and Dry,* and *Golden Brown* by The Stranglers. My son Tim, a frequent partner in crime on these forays, insists that Gordon Brown would have won the 2010 election had he adopted the latter as a theme tune. I suggest that employing a song about heroin to set the theme of your campaign would have been asking for trouble. He says he got trouble anyway. Touché, I think, gazing into the pissing down rain as another speculative cross finds the hands of the Witton keeper.

Attendance: 767

Saturday 6 January

APEC Taxis Stadium

Northern Premier League West Division

Runcorn Linnets 1 Kidsgrove Athletic 0

We'd had five days to digest that disappointing performance at Witton. I've become familiar with this Runcorn side's inconsistency, and the consistency of football in general, but it still felt difficult to square the performance in the Boxing Day win against Prescot with that limp display at Wincham Park. Now we're in Runcorn, for the first home game of 2024.

Alan joins us today. He introduced me to Runcorn in 1985. A few years ago I encouraged him to come and see the new club, who've been playing here since 2010, following four years of ground-sharing at Witton. Mike Bayly, wrote in his book *Changing Ends* just before the opening of the new stadium, that it had been 'derided in some quarters for its bland soulless architecture.' But that was at the beginning when it was little more than a football ground with a wall around it. Now, with a small clubhouse and covered areas on every side of the crowd, the APEC, while unlikely to win any design awards, is neat, functional and, for a long time now, has felt like home. If someone feels the need for a more picturesque setting, they can always check out Halton Castle after the game.

When I mention going to Witton's ground on New Year's Day, Alan recollects that we were both there when Witton played Cheltenham Town in 1992, a game I have long since forgotten. Alan has a memory for such things. Those memories are imprinted in the programmes of every football match he's ever been to, going back to the early sixties, so he's now furious that Runcorn have announced they'll no longer publish a physical programme. There is a free virtual one you can access on match days but he says it's not the same and I understand what he means. Inevitably, clubs at this level must make choices and determine priorities and if the club's survival comes down to things like dispensing with the expense and effort required to put out a programme for every home game, I'm fine with that. But then, unlike him, I never kept and stored away my programmes in neat piles, the pages of each suffused with memories. His collection reaches back to the sixties.

For me, it's hard to argue that such considerations trump survival and success on the pitch and today Runcorn's win comes courtesy of a single Olly Molloy goal in the first half. We lost experienced striker Jamie Rainford to a bad injury before the season started and our other top striker Ryan Brooke has missed a lot of the season through injury, so the signing of Molloy from Charnock Richard made a big difference. He's among the league's top scorers, averaging better than a goal every two games.

In a close, competitive match we have chances to extend our lead, most of which are thwarted by an extrovert Kidsgrove keeper. He and one of the assistant refs have some sort of row when they go off the pitch at half-time, the liner repeatedly telling him to shut up, but they walk out in the second half smiling and chatting together. Indeed, some think they've gone too far, because, when Runcorn's Jacques Walsh is sent off for a second yellow late in the game, the liner and keeper watch on from a few yards away, their arms round each other – the relationship appears to be accelerating quickly to second base, not exactly a good look in terms of demonstrating neutrality to an incensed home crowd.

Anyway, Runcorn hang on for an important three points and stay third in the league while Kidsgrove, runaway leaders early in the season, now loiter in a congested mid-table along with, it seems, almost everybody else.

Attendance: 607

Tuesday 9 January

Townfield Lane, Barnton

Mid-Cheshire Senior Cup Semi-Final

1874 Northwich 1 Northwich Victoria 3

Fraught relationships between clubs in local areas are not unusual; there is animosity, spite, jealousy and raw hatred, historical enmity going back years, often resulting from games few supporters alive can even remember. There are chasms which can only be filled by the desire for retribution or restorative justice, which never comes or, at best, does so only fleetingly. There is envy, scorn and ridicule.

And there is Northwich, 'the most dysfunctional football town in the country,' according to Simon Hughes in his book *On the Brink*.

Once one of the best clubs outside the football league, Northwich Victoria now finds itself broken, split between two rival clubs, neither of whom even play in Northwich anymore. Tonight they're facing off at a bitterly cold Townfield Lane in an encounter that will mean little to most of the footballing world but which, to fans in Northwich, means everything.

Quite how Northwich got to this point takes some unravelling. Northwich Victoria used to play at Drill Field, once the oldest ground to host continuous football in the world. Even the reasons for them losing the ground smack of fortune administering a smiling blow across their glum faces: told by the Conference that the ground wouldn't be big enough for them to remain in the league, Northwich flogged their historic stadium to Wain Homes only for the league to change its mind and decide a stadium of its size would have been fine after all.

Witton Albion, for they are part of this story too, played at the other end of the town in those days. The lack of a relationship between the two clubs meant no agreement on playing on alternative Saturdays so both clubs often played on the same day, scattering an increasingly meagre fan base (Northwich only has a population of around 20,000 even now) between them.

Something had to give. And eventually everything gave.

Witton moved out of town to Wincham Park at the end of the eighties. Northwich Vics stayed put but stumbled from one financial crisis to another until the famous Drill Field was eventually sold. Northwich followed Witton's lead rather more closely than was probably wise, plonking their new ground – the Victoria Stadium – right next to Witton's. Albion having placed a sensible distance between the two clubs, they were now so close to each other that visiting supporters often found themselves trying to gain entry to the wrong ground.

Following their eventual eviction from that stadium, Vics agreed to a groundshare with Witton. Some might say an earlier arrangement of this kind would have avoided a whole lot of trouble. By that point, however, it was far too late and many disillusioned Vics fans had already gone, establishing their own club 1874 Northwich, named after the year in which the original club was founded.

That presented existing Northwich fans with a difficult decision. Imagine a wall going up with members of your family on each side: you're forced to decide which side to go on, knowing it's going to be a decision that will cement allegiances for the rest of your life.

'I watched Vics from the age of seven,' says Vicki England, secretary of 1874 Northwich. Her family was so devoted to Northwich Vics her dad named her after them. 'So I grew up Vics.'

So, when the great separation occurred, how did she make her decision?

'The thinking was that Vics wouldn't survive,' she says. 'I was wobbling because this is the club that I'd always loved.' Vics were going through a nomadic existence at the time, playing home games wherever they could. 'We were playing at Leek one Friday night against Hednesford and we found the NPL were chucking Vics out of the league and I think that kind of made our minds up. At that point 1874 hadn't been created. There was a meeting, and in fact I did the minutes between the football club, the supporters' trust, et cetera, to see whether there was any common ground, but it was clear that there wasn't.'

As Vicki tells her story, you get a real sense of the emotional turmoil that she and her fellow supporters experienced. It's something that few football fans will ever have to go through and understandably many open wounds remain. 'I've got friends that stayed with it,' she says. 'There are people on the Vics side who do understand why we did what we did. People will say they don't see how we can walk out on our club, but we created a club in the image of what we loved.

'I felt that my Vics died. The Vics that I'd followed all those years, it felt like it had died because of what had gone on with it. You did have that closure with the old Runcorn. Bad as it was, I suppose that's helped Linnets going forward because you haven't got this over-hang of...why are you creating a new club when your club's still going? I understand why they're saying it. If it had been more clear-cut and all the supporters had taken it forward, I think we'd be in a lot better shape.'

Although not one of the initiators of the move to create 1874, once she'd decided which way to jump she quickly became closely involved.

'We had the vote in November 2012 to form the new club. The guys on the board started to look at creating the club and I joined a month or two later. I've been club secretary since March 2013.'

Forward momentum has been in short supply for both clubs of late. At the time of this match, 1874 are bottom of Northern Premier League West Division with Northwich Vics struggling a tier below in the Midland League (in the world of regional leagues boundaries sometimes get drawn in unlikely places). 1874 host the match at their temporary home at Barnton FC while Vics are currently ground sharing at Winsford: it's a scenario a section of supporters on each side blames the other for. Barnton's ground at Townfield Lane has one of the lowest surrounding fences I've ever seen at a football ground. It would be easy to climb over and get in for free, or to watch from an upstairs window of a nearby house. I see no evidence of anyone attempting either. It's absolutely freezing – a night only for diehard fans and idiot neutrals like me and Tim.

As if there isn't enough bad feeling around, the Mid-Cheshire Senior Cup exists for clubs in the local area (all five of them) to get together on an annual basis and stir the pot a bit more. Alongside the established county cup competitions these 'district' cups exist around the country but clubs above county level usually don't take them as seriously as the sides in this area do. The Vics manager Steve Pickup is certainly fired up and he's booked early in the game for constant haranguing of the ref. Following the yellow card, he turns to the fans standing near the dugout and moans to them instead, both about the ref and his own players' constant inability to get the ball into the final third.

Despite his side's underdog status in this game, he can see 1874 are there for the taking and, in an entertaining second half, his team manage to produce that killer ball in the final third and more, exploiting uncertainty in the Vics defence to open the scoring before finishing off a fine passing move to snatch a second soon after. 1874 get back into the game and, at 2-1, have the visitors struggling to get out of their own half before a goal on the break seals the tie 3-1.

'We're the club that wouldn't die' sing the joyous travelling fans. Perhaps so, but they've been on life support since the mid-nineties and some might conclude that a sensible course of action would be for the clubs to kiss and make up. Judging by the level of barely concealed animosity circling the ground, there seems little chance of that happening any time soon.

Attendance: 315

Saturday 13 January

Halton Stadium, Widnes

Northern Premier League West

Widnes 4 Mossley 0

'The ball is round,' wrote Sepp Herberger, an apparently profound statement of the obvious. Imagine my consternation, then, when the first thing they did at my school was toss us an oval-shaped item to play with. I looked around me. No one else seemed uncomfortable with the idea. Not for the first time in my younger years, I felt alienated and confused, especially when everybody else on the school field started chucking this egg-shaped thing to each other, seeming to know what to do with it.

Yet not one of those kids tossing this alien object about was wearing a rugby league kit. To a boy, everyone wore a replica football top: Liverpool shirts predominated, with Manchester United and Everton well-represented, alongside a single Wolverhampton Wanderers top (there was always some kid in a Wolves top, for some reason). Not the expensive, sponsor-laden designer objects of today; this was the seventies, when you could get many seasons' wear out of a single shirt providing that when you 'grew into it' you didn't grow too much.

This was Old South Lancashire, an area where rugby league players seemed to live on every street, but where the glamour of the big football clubs of Liverpool and Manchester still threw everything else into shade.

The Old South Lancashire rugby league belt was home to several powerhouses of the game: Wigan, St Helens, Warrington, Leigh and Widnes, where I live. Clubs in these towns were all founder members of the Northern Union at the end of the 19th century, joining their counterparts across the Pennines to break away from the Rugby Union fat cats in the south, to forge a new code in the north of England.

Runcorn, in North Cheshire, initially joined the Northern Union before folding in 1918. They were the first champions of the Lancashire League in 1895 and played at Canal Street until the First World War, at which point the pitch was rotated to stretch from north to south and the ground sold to new owners who wouldn't allow rugby to be played on it, a policy that led to the birth of Runcorn FC.

Rugby League returned to Canal Street, not entirely successfully, with the emergence of Runcorn Highfield in the 1980s. It's worth noting, perhaps, that in the augural season of 1895-96, Runcorn finished third, above all the powerhouses-to-be. Runcorn Highfield, however, are best known for a record-breaking run of 61 consecutive defeats between 1989 and 1991.

The ground where Widnes play is an all-seater arena built on the site of the famous Naughton Park Rugby League ground. Widnes RLFC built a ground fit for the top-level club they were, only to tumble from that level pretty much as soon as it was built. They won their last Rugby League Championship in 1989, something that looks unlikely ever to happen again.

I walk to the ground, which is just twenty minutes from my house. Yes, I live in Widnes but support Runcorn. There are some who consider this curious, as there's a local hostility between the two towns that's embedded in their histories. Widnes was originally a Viking settlement and Runcorn was founded by the King of Mercia as a base from which to guard against a potential invasion from across the Mersey. They were enemies from the very beginning.

Now, both occupy the borough of Halton and have done since 1974. I was at primary school when the new borough was created and the teacher told us: 'Today you're in Lancashire but tomorrow you will be living in Cheshire.' This generated some furrowing of the brows: was the entire community about to be gathered up and plonked on the other side? This was mass deportation on a huge scale: why was nobody protesting?

I'm not the only Widnes-based Linnets fan. A 'WA8 Linnets' flag is a permanent fixture of the Shed, the popular end at the APEC. When I was seeking a local club Runcorn had one and Widnes didn't, at least not one playing above district level. That situation continued until 2012 when a team called the Dragons took up residence at the rugby league stadium, renaming themselves in the process. You don't switch football team allegiances – not if you're a real fan – so the idea of becoming a Widnes fan didn't even occur to me. Besides, from the off the whole Widnes FC project seemed unconvincing and, despite their current healthy league position, still does.

The stadium is currently the largest outside the football league and the small crowd, bolstered by visiting Mossley fans, is scattered thinly across one side of it. Widnes still has the feel of a rugby town that really yearns for the glory days of Rugby League to return, with football more like a passing fad that is desperately trying to kid itself it's more than that. Playing on an artificial pitch also seems wrong, as it always does, yet somehow appropriate: an artificial pitch for an artificial club.

The spat between the King of Mercia and the Viking community may have died down, but there remain local tensions between Runcorn and Widnes which I find quite tiresome. Both towns suffered from the demise of the local chemical industry and the shoehorning of both into the Halton unitary authority has meant that any spare cash that might be around (there has been very little) has led to allegations of favouritism from one side or the other. As you would expect, the emergence of a football club in Widnes has been drawn into this rivalry to a limited degree, but to me it seems fabricated, a rivalry almost constructed for rivalry's sake.

Sam Phillips agrees. 'Rivalry is something that's missing for me,' he says when I mention the old days of Runcorn and the rivalries we had with teams like Altrincham. 'You want to beat Widnes, but there are no games where you think at the start of the season, "That's a game we want to win."' Proper football rivalries can take years to develop, fuelled by memorable games or infamous incidents on the pitch or in the stands and this one just hasn't got that history.

The Widnes manager is Michael Ellison, former player and manager of Runcorn Linnets. Ello was well-liked at Runcorn and is doing a good job at Widnes, who are in mid-table this season in a league where mid-table could be said to stretch from second to next to bottom: everyone between Leek, enjoying a growing lead at the top, and 1874 Northwich, adrift at the other end. Widnes should have been relegated last season but were rescued because Skelmersdale were demoted instead due to a 'shite ground' ruling. The Widnes ground is anything but shite, but the experience of being in it is. The atmosphere is close to non-existent.

Even when Widnes take control of what turns out to be an unexpectedly one-sided game, the crowd just isn't big enough, or close enough, to create any kind of atmosphere. Ello is active on the sidelines as usual, yelling and bouncing around, though less so after Widnes take the lead, and control of the game, through an excellent Olly Wright shot from long range. They begin to dominate what I'd expected to be an even encounter, running up four goals, including two from ex-Runcorn player James Steele, even having the luxury of missing a second half penalty.

Widnes look well-equipped to survive and even thrive under Ello, but will that mean more of the local community will come to find out what's going on? Few people I speak to around here even know Widnes has a football team and some even seem baffled by the very concept, as if the town's name and the round ball game are so disconnected that the whole idea literally makes no sense.

I spend the whole game with one earplug in, listening to commentary from Bucket Hat FM, Runcorn's matchday radio service. Runcorn are playing at Newcastle Town and lose 1-0, another disappointing result against the kind of team we should be beating if we have designs on promotion this season.

Hosted by Sam Phillips and Jack Walsh, the idea for Bucket Hat FM came about when football returned after the Covid lockdown but supporters still weren't allowed to attend matches. 'Obviously I didn't want to miss any Runcorn games so I approached the club and asked if it would be possible to come along and do a live radio broadcast. People can't go to the games,' he reasoned, 'so it might be a good way to keep them involved with the club.' The club agreed and Bucket FM was born, quickly gathering an audience of Runcorn fans who, like me today, can't be at the game for whatever reason. Then-chairman Dave Jones accompanied him on that first broadcast, a game against Atherton Collieries, he recalls. 'We just had a laptop and a microphone and talked about whatever was happening on the pitch.

'Now it's me and Jack Walsh. We've got a researcher who does all our research throughout the week. He collects all the stats on the opposing team, which players to watch, recent fixtures and stuff. We've now got headphones and mixer boxes to raise the quality as much as we possibly can. For the play-offs, at Workington (last season), it was a poignant moment for me and Jack because it was the point that made us realise that we've actually come really far with this. Our highest listenership in the Workington game was 596.' The audience for that Atherton game, he recalls, had peaked at 12.

It's an example of how football at this level presents opportunities for supporters to get involved and use their own skills and initiative to make a difference. This couldn't happen at a big club, a fan having the simple idea of a radio broadcast, taking it to the club, putting it into practice and growing it to the point where the radio audience for Bucket Hat FM on a Saturday afternoon dwarfs the attendance of many Northern Premier League crowds, including the one at the Halton Stadium today.

Maybe Widnes need something like this too but looking around me, even in the presence of a resounding victory like this, I don't sense any prospect of it happening.

Attendance: 175

Wednesday 17 January

I should be in St Helens watching Pilkington FC v Charnock Richard but it snowed on Monday night and the Pilks' ground is still iced up. Non-league stadia, even those with artificial pitches, are not impervious to the weather in the way your modern Premier League grounds are.

Set against a scale of human suffering, I realise there are worse things we can encounter than missing a football game, but I hate it when I think I'm going and then can't. A more measured perspective is to take the good with the bad and say to the Premier League, 'I'll see your undersoil heating and raise you standing at games, paying on the gate and the absence of away games at the other end of the country stuck away at 8pm on a Monday night.' On balance, I still think we get the better of the deal.

Saturday 20 January

Deva Stadium, Chester

National League North

Chester 2 Bishop's Stortford 0

Although the thaw is underway, the frost that's lingered since Monday sees off Runcorn's game against Bootle, along with most other football in the area. Fortunately, the Chester game survives so we head down the M56 to the historic Roman city, or at least an industrial area on the England-Wales border close to it. The ground straddles the border, which caused some problems when post-lockdown restrictions in England and Wales differed.

'We went into a meeting expecting it to be a conciliatory discussion to try and find a way forward,' says Chester vice-chairman Jim Green. 'But we were presented with a letter on behalf of North Wales Police and Flintshire council warning us that, in their eyes, we had breached Covid regulations.' The club were forced to postpone the next home game and the problem was only resolved when restrictions in the two nations became more closely aligned several weeks later.

Runcorn fans, or at least those of my age, have fond memories of Chester's old Sealand Road ground, a ground situated firmly in England where we famously won an FA Cup First Round tie when Chester were still a football league club. 'I was working in Frodsham,' says Brian Howman. 'The foreman was a joiner called John Williams and he'd been a Chester fan all his life. He was a horrible bastard, the kind of fan who thinks anyone in the non-league is shit. He was saying what Chester were gonna do to Runcorn...of course, we won. I always used to get in early – I was the nearest person to the factory so I had a key – and I doctored his notebook so that months after he'd be going through his notes and he'd see...Spike Carter? After that it'd be "Morning John" and he'd be "Morning...stuffy cunt."'

Now Chester are a 'shit' non-league team themselves. Not long ago, the re-formed club was climbing back up the pyramid but the relentless rise has since been stalled and the road back to League Two, if it ever gets there, is proving to be long and arduous with more potholes than the A41.

Not that the road in the other direction was any easier. Chester's fall out of the league followed years of mismanagement. Fred Atkins describes the 1999-2000 season, when Chester were relegated from the football league, as 'one of the most inept campaigns in Football League history' and, this being football, it's up against some stiff competition.

And yet, following that ignominious decline under a shadowy American owner called Terry Smith, things managed to get even worse. Stephen Vaughan, a boxer who'd previously overseen the decline of Barrow, did take Chester back in into the football league but Vaughan's goal of promotion to the Championship within five years proved as fanciful as his promise of shrewd financial management. The debts the club accrued eventually saw them face a 25-point penalty and inevitable relegation. This time they weren't bouncing back.

The rogue's gallery became complete when Morell Maison entered as Director of Football. Maison arrived from Halesowen Town, a club half a million quid in debt. At that point, Chester fans gave up on the club's board, bought the lease on the Deva Stadium from the local council and started their own club. I went to watch them twice in the season after their re-birth and found a buoyant supporter-owned club with a constitution that prevented them ever getting into debt again. They won both of those games on the way to three successive promotions.

In their heads, you feel, Chester remain a football league club in waiting. Go backstage into the restaurant and boardroom and you find a hall of fame comprising players who represented the club with distinction during their years in the football league, the likes of Ronnie Hughes, Stuart Rimmer and, naturally, Ian Rush.

It's a world away from Widnes FC, in a stadium where the only recognised heroes are rugby league players. Chester do have one thing in common with Widnes though: a former Runcorn Linnets manager. Calum McIntyre is now in charge at the Deva, having arrived at Runcorn to replace Ello in 2021. It's fair to say a large chunk of the Linnets support were disappointed at Ello's departure so Calum had some winning over to do. He achieved that quickly, developing a team that reached the play-offs at the end of that season, something that's now regarded as a minimum performance level but then felt like a massive step forward.

Sam Phillips believes Calum's tenure saddled Runcorn with expectations they've since been unable to fulfil, in terms of the style of play at least. 'It's been difficult for Runcorn managers following Calum McIntyre. A lot of Runcorn fans over the last five years came in when Calum came in. Under Calum, they were treated to fast, entertaining, attacking football. Anyone who follows that is going to find it difficult. It was exhilarating to watch.'

Calum left the club that summer, returning to Chester where he'd previously coached the youth team. A young manager with immense potential, he was bound to step up to something bigger before long and generally Runcorn fans understood his departure and continue to wish him well. Today, I look forward to seeing the easy-on-the-eye football he'd brought to Runcorn played two levels higher up, presumably with better players. Chester are just outside the play-off places going into this game so, despite some patchy form of late, my expectations are high.

Sadly, Iwan Murray, who Calum brought to Chester with him, isn't playing. 'The best player I've seen playing for Runcorn Linnets,' Sam Phillips calls him and it's hard to disagree. McIntyre the manager and Murray the player are examples of a truth non-league football fans must accept: if they're that good, they're not going to be around for long. I can't help wondering if Iwan might have brought some much-needed finesse to what turns out to be a very dull game.

Hang on, you might say, *isn't Bishop's Stortford in the south?*

That's right. Hertfordshire.

Fuck are they doing in the National League North then?

That was a question they asked too, though I expect they formulated it slightly differently. Where lines get drawn between the southern and northern divisions depends on the teams you have once the dust settles following all the promotions and relegations. Basically, there were enough sides to the south of Bishop Stortford to force them to go into the northern division with long distance treks to places even further away than Chester, such as South Shields. They weren't happy but, judging by their results so far this season, it's a problem they won't have for long. They're the bottom of the league, having won only five games, though one of those did come against Chester back in August.

Incidentally, this kind of geographical weirdness is nothing new in football's regional leagues. Bradford Park Avenue, for example, spent a full season in the Southern League in 1907-1908. At around the same time, the Western League, intended for teams in spitting distance of the Bristol Channel, was won by the likes of Spurs, West Ham and Millwall.

Here, Chester are clearly the better side, but the football is laboured and predictable. The fans around me in the East Stand are making their dissatisfaction known in an increasingly animated manner as we go into half-time goalless, the home side having done little to test the Bishop goalkeeper, who has a kind of endearing, Neville Southall binman chic about him.

The game descends into an error-strewn contest and never really recovers. When Chester take the lead in the second half, it comes via a speculative shot blocked by a defender which drops fortuitously into the penalty area, eventually finding its way to Glendon, who scores.

There's no easing of the Chester jitters, though, and Bishop almost grab an unlikely equaliser when some comedy defending leads to the visitors hitting the post. When they win a free kick deep into injury time the keeper comes up, only for the ball to be headed cleanly away to set up a Chester break. With the keeper still some way from the half-way line, Norton ambles forward and rolls the ball into an empty net. The win leaves Chester fourth in the league, firmly in the play-off places, but they'll have to play a lot better than this to stay there.

That second goal brings the second biggest cheer of the afternoon. The biggest came at half-time when it was announced Wrexham were losing at Newport. I was in the toilets at the time and a weird, loud cheer rose from the cubicles, accompanied by a toilet seat being repeatedly banged down. Chester fans always hated Wrexham, well before everybody else did.

Attendance 1988

Tuesday 23 January

Storm Jocelyn, which sounds like the name of a home improvement guru, and the heavy rain that comes with it means the Irlam v Barnoldswick Town game I'd planned to go to in the North West Counties League is off. I stay at home, taking in match updates from the National League North where, it seems, Chester are far more convincing in their 2-0 win at Chorley.

Saturday 27 January

Bucket Hat FM

The weather's stopped mucking with my schedule now but a lack of available transport stops me from getting to the Vauxhall Motors v Runcorn match. I consider walking down the road to watch Widnes v 1874 Northwich but decide I'd rather give my full attention to what's happening in Runcorn's game, so I opt to spend a rare Saturday afternoon at home listening to the commentary on Bucket Hat FM.

Bucket Hat FM, like other similar stations that have sprung up around non-league football, is an enormously valuable resource for anyone who can't get to the match. As a Runcorn fan in the eighties and nineties, I'd often have to wait until well after an away game had finished to find out the score and any further details wouldn't be discovered until a match report appeared in the local paper later that week, if one did appear.

Eventually I decided I couldn't live like this and began going to almost every away game in person, soon combining this with writing reports for the Runcorn World myself. When Halton Community Radio acquired a temporary licence, I phoned in a report after the 1994 Woking v Runcorn FA Trophy Final at Wembley, using a public telephone from inside the ground: that was about as close as you could get in those days to up-to-the-minute coverage. The guys presenting the show had no interest in football and just wanted to get back to playing Nirvana or The Lemonheads or whatever and I could hear them sniggering as I told the world how devastated we were by this third Wembley defeat. 'Yeah...we're pretty devastated too,' one of them said, before the two of them burst out laughing.

Bucket Hat FM presenters Sam Phillips and Jack Walsh don't snigger at Runcorn defeats and do a great job conveying the sights, sounds and, yes, sometimes the smells of the match-going fan. They're on top form today. Jack has developed a line in off-the-wall comments and partial non-sequiturs that generate a listening experience akin to down-to-earth version of classic-era Test Match Special.

'My dream job when I was a kid was to be a radio commentator,' admits Sam, 'so when this opportunity came around, I thought it's a good chance for me to do the thing that I've always dreamed of for the team I support.'

But there is no attempt to imitate John Motson or David Coleman, thankfully. Their quirky style combines with an approach that manages to be partisan without becoming overly biased. Even more impressive, perhaps, is how well they've managed to achieve a high broadcasting standard – they're easily the equal of most local radio commentators in terms of professionalism, and better than most – without sacrificing the feel of two guys chatting while they watch the game.

Some will no doubt allege favouritism on my part in this assessment. However, I would like it recognised that I'm a bit of a picky bastard and my natural inclination would be to be over-fussy about standards when it comes to my own club. To win me over, they must be doing something right. Mike Bayly, on encountering Chelmsford City's fan commentary, noted, 'It sounds like a teenager reluctantly reading out his English essay to a full classroom.' To be fair to the Chelmsford fan, when presenting on the radio this is a more difficult pitfall to avoid than many people realise.

'We always said we just want to be accessible for the normal fan,' says Sam. 'We wanted to be like two mates – in the pub – talking about the match. We want it to be professional in the sense of bringing the game to people so they can picture what's happening on the pitch and I think sometimes I'll make something sound better than it was – Jack always pulls me up about this but it's just to try and make the listeners at home get a picture. But we'll never lose that approach of two friends in a pub, because that's what makes it.'

After a drab first half, there's a lot to report on for Sam and Jack in the second, Runcorn eventually securing a 4-2 victory with goals from both central defenders – O'Mahoney and Kay – and a clincher from Molloy, after an eight-minute cameo from James Hooper, who comes on as sub,, claims the goal with his first touch and is then carried off after being clattered into the fence.

'He looks like a mummy,' observes Jack, gazing down at Hooper as he takes his place on the Runcorn bench. Elsewhere he speculates on the Vauxhall players' fondness for Meat and Potato Pies and talks about the many 'celebrities' he's bumped into at Asda in Runcorn, most of which are non-league footballers. One contributor to the 'chat' which runs parallel to the broadcast says he once had a late-night drinking session with Sam Allardyce, before Big Sam was eventually carted off to bed at 5.30 after he began 'chundering'.

They also keep us up to date with other scores around the league. Widnes thump 1874 Northwich 5-0. Sam and Jack agree that 1874 are probably going down, something which Jack says he is sad about. Many will empathise with this sentiment. Although Runcorn and Northwich – both before and after the split – have regularly played each other down the years,

I've never been aware of any real animosity between the two clubs. Many years ago, on Saturdays when for whatever reason Runcorn didn't have a game, I'd head to the Drill Field to see Northwich Vics play so they became something of a second Conference team for me in those days.

'We have a great relationship with Runcorn,' says Vicki England. 'In that season when we were preparing to start, we visited a few clubs. I came to watch Linnets a couple of times. Many clubs helped us but Linnets were fantastic.'

It's something they'll miss next season, she tells me, knowing that, like Northwich Vics, they're likely to be playing in the Midland League where they won't get anything like the same number of visiting fans they get now. There may be local rivalries at this level of the game, but they're tempered by the knowledge, among regular fans anyway, that we really do need each other to survive.

February 2024

There's a row of seats facing the other way...

Saturday 3 February

APEC Taxis Stadium, Runcorn

Runcorn Linnets 0 Trafford 0

Northern Premier League West Division

It's been a frustrating theme of this season: Runcorn squandering chances and dropping points against teams we should be beating. Booth saves Doyle's penalty in the first half: had that gone in, you feel we'd have secured a comfortable win. As it is, the save seems to fuel Booth's perception of himself as Gordon Banks and, whenever Runcorn manage to pierce the organised Trafford defence, he's there to tidy up and, on a couple of occasions, make truly spectacular saves. We gather in the Shed End to applaud the keeper off at the end: it's well-deserved even though the idea of celebrating somebody for ruining your weekend may seem faintly irrational.

The Murdishaw Massive are in there with us...somewhere.

We know them by their flags. Their online presence conceals their faces: balaclava-covered heads and flak jackets.

The Massive are Runcorn's ultras. When not serenading the on-pitch heroics of the yellow and green, they're online fighting the corner of people in the community who've been left holding onto the shittiest end of a particularly shitty stick.

Murdishaw, the area of the town in which Runcorn Linnets are based, came into being in the 1970s as part of the New Town development. But it's what the development left behind that frames the Massive's existence. Thatcher's neoliberalism came hot on its heels and those promised business opportunities moved south, leaving nothing to replace the dying chemical industry which poured unfiltered filth on the heads of residents across the borough even as it was, bit by bit, departing the scene. And that was part of the problem because the whole rationale for the New Town development was to position itself close to established industry, and particularly the ICI plants. By the time the New Town came into being, ICI was rapidly beginning to downsize, leading to massive unemployment in the town and a huge hole in those 'established industry' calculations on which the New Town Development was based.

This scenario left Halton, for a period in the early eighties, with the worst unemployment rate in the north-west. Worse, for a while, even than inner-city areas of Liverpool or Manchester. And New Town areas like Murdishaw harboured levels of socio-economic misery that dwarfed much of the rest of an impoverished borough.

At the time, Runcorn played in old Runcorn ('proper Runcorn' a Canal Street regular once told me when I used that term). Suspicion and animosity existed between this community and the new town areas that further divided an already divided community.

'I thought it was one of the downfalls of the original football club,' says Brian Howman. 'It didn't manage to find its place as part of the community. Runcorn New Town people didn't want to watch them in big enough numbers, and it was run by people with their eye on different things than running a small, successful football club.'

Now, Linnets are helping to bridge that divide. The focus is on Runcorn as a single community, with the club heavily involved in local initiatives ranging from support for the local Food Bank, to collecting toys for disadvantaged kids at Christmas. There's a sense of a club understanding its role among a town's people and using that position productively.

'We've had our work in the community recognised at the Halton Business Awards,' says Bren Connolly. 'We obviously are in a deprived area and, for us, it's vitally important we do what we can to help the community.'

For members of that community, there's a welcome at the club to anyone who wishes to get involved on a personal level. The case of Kelly Jones is instructive. 'I started coming as a fan and just got to know people, really. I started working on the bar and got more involved that way. I spoke to Tracy Daley first, spoke to Alan Jones (Club President) and Bren. They said they wanted help with the newsletter and I do that sort of thing at work so I was happy to do that. And then, I was asked to help the Under-21s with their social media originally, and then I was asked if I wanted to be the official secretary.' Recently, she's been voted onto the board with specific responsibilities for administration and fan engagement.

The newsletter, emailed out to season ticket holders and registered fans, is one of the mechanisms the club is using to improve communication with its supporters. 'Most people won't know exactly what goes on behind the scenes at the club,' says Bren, 'and we've tried to publicise that in the newsletter that Kelly Jones is now doing a great job on. On each edition of the newsletter, we've gone into what's a typical Monday, what's a typical Tuesday…'

Whatever barometer we use to judge 'success' in football, in a sense clubs like Runcorn achieve something significant just by being here. During the Co-vid pandemic, the club teamed up with the local Queen of Hearts pub to distribute food packages to isolated members of the community. In addition to those Christmas toy appeals, there have been Easter egg drop-offs fronted by club mascot Ron Corn.

It can be a frustrating experience watching them on the pitch at times, though. There's no doubt we have one of the strongest squads in the league (we thrashed leaders Leek 5-0 earlier in the season) but every time it seems we're poised to put together a run of results, the wheels don't so much come off as appear to have been replaced with square ones. Manager Billy Paynter tries several different attacking permutations today – bringing on the recovering Ryan Brooke and exciting young prospect Adam Moseley, while trying the talented Will Saxon on both the right and in the number 10 role – but we only manage to make the wall of white kits look more like Real Madrid than a side third from bottom of the league.

Perhaps a better comparison would be the white shirts of 70s Leeds, minus the thuggery. I wish Trafford *were* more like Leeds so I could hate them. I wish they'd fouled us off the park, that they'd time-wasted like a French aristocrat on the steps of the guillotine.

But in truth Trafford are a likeable bunch who defend well and get what they came for – a valuable point in their fight against relegation.

As a result, the gap we had over fourth place is narrowing with Witton Albion now only two points behind us. They've played two more games but many of the sides in the pack just behind them haven't and some even have a game in hand. We should be challenging Leek and Prescot for the one automatic promotion place but, because of too many results like this, we're taking more glances at the rear-view mirror than a school bus driver with Gary Glitter on his back seat.

1874 Northwich, of course, can only look upwards, but they snatch a valuable draw at Mossley courtesy of an equaliser from ex-Runcorn player, and former Fijian youth international (seriously), Oliver McFadyen. For Vicki England, it's one of the few highlights of what's turning into a horrible season. 'Mossley's always a really tough place to play,' she reflects later. 'We were at the bare bones with players and we got this draw and I felt like we'd won the FA Cup.'

Attendance: 639

Tuesday 6 February

Gorsey Lane, Warrington

Liverpool Senior Cup Quarter-Final

Warrington Rylands 1906 1 Tranmere Rovers 2

This feels wrong. Rylands' ground is a serviceable, if basic, footballing arena which appears to have had some kind of extra-terrestrial visitation. A persistent blue light emanates from the 'members lounge' on one side of the ground. The standard concrete dugouts, often a fixture of grounds at this level, have been abducted and replaced by those modern arching things which are set back from the pitch area, leaving a mammoth technical area encroaching on what might have been used for more terracing. Where we stand, a series of horizontal Rylands badges have been hammered into the fence. 'A hyper-branded hellscape,' Tim calls it.

Like Widnes, Warrington is very much a rugby league town. If you watch a Premier League match in a Warrington pub, you'll likely do so in the company of Liverpool and Manchester United fans, who have historically split the town's residents' football allegiances between them. It is also easily the biggest town in the area covered by this book. With a population of over 200,000, Warrington is bigger than cities like York, Oxford and Preston.

In 2016 Paul Stretford, agent of Wayne Rooney and Harry Maguire, looked at the then Rylands FC, who had languished in the Warrington & District, Mid-Cheshire and other leagues since their formation in 1906, and fancied that he might do what Gary Neville and his chums had achieved at Salford City: exploit the potential of a large population and establish a football club good enough to aspire to promotion to the football league.

Following Stretford's intervention, the club joined the North West Counties League Southern Division in 2018 and began a rise through the leagues that currently sees them riding high in the Northern Premier League's Premier Division.

However, the fans have still not arrived in great numbers: in terms of support, Rylands still languish well behind Warrington Town, who themselves have historically struggled to tempt locals away from their rugby league fixation. Not only that but the ground, wedged between housing estates in a built-up area of the town, is hardly built to accommodate a growing support base. Parking here is a nightmare.

At the time of visiting, the club's website claims in a list of 'facts' that it is Warrington's most successful club, which is highly debatable bordering on plainly untrue. It also claims they were denied promotion to the Northern Premier League due to the Covid pandemic a few years ago, also a bit of a stretch as only the champions were guaranteed promotion and they were eight points behind leaders 1874 Northwich at the time of the abandonment, having played a game more.

There are some facts that don't appear on the website: they have one of the lowest average attendances in their league, for one, and tonight, despite it only being a fiver on the gate, this Liverpool Senior Cup match against professional opponents draws an even smaller crowd than the 500 or so they regularly attract to league games, though I've never actually managed to track down tonight's confirmed attendance.

Admittedly the crowds are an improvement on what they attracted when Rylands were in Runcorn's division a couple of years ago. Now that Stretford seems to have stopped pumping money in, though, it's hard to see them continuing their upward ascent for much longer, although for now they're occupying a healthy position in the play-off places and still gazing upwards at the relatively rich pastures of National League North.

I notice after the game that Rylands Twitter doesn't even mention the sending off that reduces the home team to ten men in the second half. It follows a bad challenge which leads to an old-fashioned 21-man brawl (convention decrees there is always one goalkeeper who doesn't get involved). By that point Tranmere – who aren't fielding their first team in this competition – appear well in control having scored twice in the first half, through a penalty and a classy move that results in a fine finish from Norris. Ten-man Rylands unexpectedly begin to make a game of it, though, and pull a goal back through Cockerlin's header from a free kick. They then continue to create chances and look far more organised defensively than they did with eleven on the pitch.

The last half hour is an enjoyable tactical battle: it's no surprise that Rovers run out winners but it's a far closer game than had seemed likely at the time of the sending-off and their ability to organise so adeptly for the fightback perhaps shows why Rylands are doing so well in their league. Yet, for all the team's endeavour, there feels something fake about the whole experience and, snaking our way out of the almost impossibly tight car park after the game, it quickly become easy to forget that a football g exists, hidden among the terraced streets, and easy to believe that one day it won't, at least not here.

Wednesday 7 February

Townfield Lane, Barnton

Mid-Cheshire Senior Cup Round One

Barnton 1 Winsford United 2

This is more like it. OK, Barnton's ground – as I've already hinted – is a bit untidy but give me that over the soulless incongruity of Rylands any day. Last time we were here it was for that Northwich derby in the Mid-Cheshire Senior Cup. This time, it's the same competition and a chance to see the ground's permanent residents in action against the permanent residents of the ground at which the other Northwich team play. Because there are only five teams in this competition, these are the only teams who didn't get a bye in the first round - the winners will play Witton Albion in the other semi-final and the winner of that will go on to face Northwich Vics in the final.

Bizarrely, kick off is delayed fifteen minutes due to problems on the Runcorn-Widnes bridge. That's the way me and Tim came but surely few other fans, if any, are travelling south. Winsford doesn't lie in that direction and, unless there's some enclave of Barnton FC ultras hiding away in Widnes, it feels like they delayed the game just for us. Which can't be true, obviously. And anyway, we're still there in time for the original kick off time. It's possible some of the players are travelling down, of course, but they all seem to be out there for the warm off. The ref? In that case, why not just announce that the ref was delayed without bringing the Mersey Gateway into it?

The game, when it eventually starts, is a feisty encounter which Winsford come from behind, deservedly, to win. There's an edge to the tackles throughout, emblematic of the ancient rivalries that invariably rise to the surface in this competition.

Winsford think they've been awarded a penalty after five minutes. In fact, they *are* awarded a penalty only for the referee, curiously, to change his mind after several minutes of deliberation. From our position, there's no doubt the Barnton keeper took Woods down after the ball had gone but he protests vociferously, following the ref as he goes to consult the assistant on the other side of the pitch who evidently recommends he changes his decision. As a free kick is awarded to Barnton outside the box, it appears this is because of an offside in the build-up, but I certainly see one and, unless I missed it, the assistant wasn't flagging for it. My puzzlement is shared by the Winsford manager, who is going mental.

Officials certainly don't help themselves in such circumstances and when a Barnton player is booked for calling the other assistant a 'fucking clown' late in the game, it's easy to emphasise to a degree: his side have been the beneficiaries of such clowning, though, but have rarely looked like capitalising on it.

Winsford run out deserving winners, forced to come from behind after Ferreira nods in a cross at the far post to break the deadlock in the second half. Winsford respond well and five minutes later they're level with their own far post header courtesy of Aikenhead. Ten minutes from time they grab a scrambled winner to set up a semi-final with Witton the following weekend, Witton's Northern Premier League commitments being forced to take a back seat to this competition. I told you they take it seriously.

Attendance: 102

Saturday 10 February

APEC Taxis Stadium, Runcorn

Northern Premier League West Division

Runcorn Linnets 5 Clitheroe 1

Sometimes it all comes together. Will Saxon's goal to open Runcorn's scoring, a masterfully placed shot from the edge of the box, looks a goal of the season contender, only for it to be bettered by Ollie Molloy who, in the second half, drives forward from just inside the Clitheroe half to unleash a thirty-yard screamer into the roof of the net. Between them there's a sublime passing move which ends with Saxon squaring for Mackenzie O'Neill to finish at the far post. Saxon, on fire, adds his second and Eden Gumbs comes off the bench to grab Runcorn's fifth. He's then sent off, along with Teague of Clitheroe, after the second mass brawl of the game. Clitheroe have basically lost their heads and Runcorn players are not exactly shrinking violets when the over-the-top tackles start flying in.

It had all looked very different in the first half hour. Clitheroe were on top, exploiting the kind of defensive mix-up we've seen too often this season to open the scoring via the mercurial Sefton Gonzalez, a non-league legend who's in the running for the golden boot and just doesn't miss chances like that. I'm still thinking of the points dropped against Trafford last week and beginning to become convinced we're going to blow promotion even before the play-offs this season. After Saxon's equaliser, Gonzalez is through again and is only denied by a magnificent goal line clearance. Had that restored the Clitheroe lead, you sense the outcome may well have been different.

It's a cliché that fine margins are what it's all about in football but nonetheless very true. Often managers are sacked after a bad run of results fuelled by a few near misses, an unlucky deflection or two, a dodgy refereeing decision...confidence becomes low in the dressing room, acrimony grows, players start blaming each other and suddenly everyone's feeling sorry for themselves, or wishing they were somewhere else, or both. Or maybe a head gets in the way of a goal-bound shot, you go on to secure a huge victory and suddenly everything looks great.

Prescot Cables lose 3-0 at Newcastle Town so Runcorn are now only one point off second place. A noisy Shed cheers the Runcorn players off, all convinced that we're back in the hunt, not just for a play-off place, but the championship itself.

Elsewhere, Winsford take Witton Albion to penalties in the Mid-Cheshire Senior Cup semi-final but manage to miss three of them and the opportunity for a bit of local giant-killing fades with each one.

Attendance 531

Tuesday 13 February

Silver Street, Irlam

North West Counties League Premier Division

Irlam 0 Wythenshawe 1

'It would help if it stopped raining!' Irlam's frustrated club secretary Warren Dodd told *Salford Now* in November. 'The corner of our pitch at the top end is a high spot, above the level of the pitch, and as such the water runs down to the pitch side.'

Many clubs will be familiar with the kind of drainage problems Irlam have had to endure this season, leaving them with an already significant fixture backlog. Tonight, fear that the game will fall victim to the weather again combine with the allure of the Champions League knockout stages to stifle any prospect of a large attendance, despite the visit of high-flying Wythenshawe.

Wary of Irlam's well-documented weather difficulties, I almost decide to head to Prescot, where Cables are playing Leek Town in the top of the table encounter in Runcorn's League. I want them to draw, though, which experience tells me can make for a hard watch. So we take a chance on Irlam, even though the rain shows no sign of stopping as we drive east down the M62.

Teams from West Manchester, who exist in the long shadow cast by Manchester United, have relatively short histories. Clubs with deeper roots reside on the east or to the south of Manchester: Mossley were founded in 1903, Stalybridge Celtic in 1905 and West Didsbury & Chorlton (then known as Christ Church FC) in 1908. On this side of the city centre, Trafford, who play in Flixton, didn't come into existence until 1990, while Irlam FC emerged in 2006, although their roots as the works team Mitchell & Shackleton FC, originally from Eccles, go much deeper. Salford City, who are of course now a league club, only came into being in 1989, though a parent club – Salford Central – had been knocking about the local leagues since before the second world war.

Irlam's rivals today share a nickname – The Ammies – with Salford, indicative of the two clubs' amateur roots. Fans of their local rivals Wythenshawe Town claim they aren't entitled to their official name, pointing out that their ground is in Gatley. It's the kind of thing, inconsequential to most outsiders, that can fuel a fierce longstanding rivalry and this season both the Ammies and Town are slugging it out at the top of their league, providing unlikely competition for Bury FC, who are attempting to fight their way back into the football league with resources that dwarf other North West Counties League clubs: their average attendance this season of over 3000 is, incidentally, better than Salford's.

Irlam's Silver Street ground lacks the incongruous adornments of Rylands and has a neatness that Barnton lacks. I like it here. There's a small training pitch at the far end of the ground, which answers my question as to why, behind one of the goals, there's a row of seats facing the other way. It's raining again, but it's the kind of constant drizzle which, while annoying, thankfully never puts the match at risk. There's not much cover at Silver Street, though, so unless you want to huddle with the bulk of the home support in the sheltered terracing at one end of the ground it's out with the brollies.

Irlam are already drifting towards a mid-table finish this season while Wythenshawe's promotion hopes fuel a hunger and determination to get a result out of this. You sense, and they probably do, that Bury are unlikely to drop too many points and are in that late-season championship-challenging mindset where a draw must be regarded as two points lost rather than a point gained.

The contrast in styles makes it an intriguing contest: Irlam are direct and combative while Wythenshawe look to keep it on the ground and pass through midfield. Their manager constantly yells at them to take control of the game in a tight first half, waving his arms about while screaming at his charges that he wants to hear more talk on the pitch. In the second half, the penny seems to drop and Wythenshawe gradually assume the upper hand, the captain Hevingham an influential presence in the middle of the park, allowing the Wythenshawe Guardiola to take a back seat.

The pressure eventually forces a handball in the Irlam box and Dickov's penalty sends the keeper the wrong way. It's enough to secure a win that leaves Wythenshawe in third place, with neighbours Wythenshawe Town second behind Bury, a remarkable position for both at this stage of the season. Wythenshawe have the games in hand to make up the points on Bury and it would be a hell of an achievement if they were to do so. On this evidence, they have enough to hold their own at Runcorn's level.

Speaking of which, Leek secure a 1-0 win at Prescot, giving them a probably unassailable ten-point lead at the top. Realistically both Prescot and Runcorn are now battling for the second-place finish that would mean a home game in the play-off semi-final and, potentially, the final.

Attendance: 165

Saturday 17 February

Bucket Hat FM

Once again, life gets in the way of the plan I had to travel to see Runcorn, who are away at Stalybridge Celtic, so it's Sam and Jack on Bucket Hat FM again. Jack has a cold. Sam says he sounds like Barry White but to me he sounds like, well, Jack...with a cold. However, the cartoon image of Barry White from the Simpsons' 'Whacking Day' episode stays with me throughout the broadcast. I'm willing Jack to utter the words, 'I love the sexy slither of a lady snake' or break into 'Can't Get Enough of Your Love, Babe' but he never does.

Runcorn secure an important 1-0 win via an audacious first half lob from central defender Sean O'Mahoney. It means an opportunity for Runcorn to post on Twitter the bizarre GIF of a cowboy O'Mahoney swirling a lasso. Prescot Cables can only draw at home to Hanley Town so we leapfrog them into second place. Leek are surprisingly held by Vauxhall Motors and there is mirth in the studio when Jack announces, presumably into his handkerchief, that Leek's Carr has scored against Vauxhall. This still leaves a nine-point gap for Runcorn to make up if we continue to harbour championship ambitions. And a trip to Leek is on the horizon...

Tuesday 20 February

APEC Taxis Stadium, Runcorn

Liverpool Senior Cup Quarter-Final

Runcorn Linnets 0 City of Liverpool 2

'Me and Peter (Furmedge) started looking at why Liverpool didn't have a non-league football team,' Paul Manning, City of Liverpool's co-founder told Johnny Phillips in an interview for the Football Pink, explaining their reasons for starting the club. A strange observation as, when City of Liverpool were formed in 2015, the city had recently witnessed an explosion of such teams. Lower Breck were founded in 2010. Litherland REMYCA, whose roots in Seaforth go back to 1959, settled in North Liverpool in 2013, while AFC Liverpool had been established in 2008. It might be pointed out that AFC don't play in Liverpool, but then, despite many efforts to do so, nor do City of Liverpool.

To launch anything with any success, you need to have a degree of market awareness and non-league football is no exception. City of Liverpool were based on delusion from the very beginning, a lack of understanding that the field of play they were entering was not just less empty than Manning and Furmedge seemed to think, but pretty much saturated. Despite the positive future Phillips anticipated in the article, City of Liverpool's problem was always going to be that they were trying to fit themselves into a gap that didn't exist.

Though drawn away, we play at home because CoL don't currently have a ground. In fact, they've never had a ground but now a dispute with Bootle, where they were tenants, has escalated to the point where their Sefton landlords have evicted them, leaving them looking for somewhere to play on a game-by-game basis.

Not for clubs at this level the fancy legalese of a carefully drafted Premier League statement, though Bootle's opening gambit in the war of words was admittedly restrained enough, referring to a 'material disagreement' before CoL responded with a fiery retort which, while it didn't contain the words 'stick your material disagreement up your arse' had a tonal undercurrent which suggested as much, lambasting Bootle's 'ludicrous allegation' and their 'crocodile tears' over the matter. 'We refuse to be bullied' they finished, falling only marginally short, you feel, of a glove-slap and the invitation to sort out their differences with flintlocks as the sun rose over the Liver Building.

An Everton season-ticket holder who'd become disillusioned with Premier League football, Bren Connolly's journey back to non-league football began with a trip to watch City of Liverpool. 'I really enjoyed just being able to stand, chat with people and have a pint.' Eventually, though, he found his way back home. 'I went down to Pavilions to watch the Runcorn derby. Linnets won 5-0 and I sort of got hooked again. Not long after that there were a couple of appeals that went out for help with some pitch work and it sort of grew from there, really. I carried on helping and then a few years back decided to put myself forward for the board. I'm down here three or four days a week plus match days, of course.'

Bren believes it's the reason why many people are attracted to football at this level, a chance to become directly involved in the running of a club, enticing for those looking for something more substantial than observing from a distance the gloss and hype of big-time football.

Both these supporter-run clubs are, in a sense, embodiments of that vision, though they've had very different experiences. While Linnets are well-established within the local community, CoL continue to battle Liverpool City Council for the right to construct a home stadium. Furmedge has even gone as far as standing in local council elections for a new party, Beacon Liverpool, indicative of the somewhat adversarial relationship they have with the council and that they're unwilling to back down in their aim to embed the club in the city's footballing culture.

City of Liverpool normally play in purple, symbolising their aim of bringing Liverpool and Everton supporters together in one club, the one unique selling point the club had on its formation and one that has admittedly allowed them to build a sturdy fanbase, despite their nomadic existence. Runcorn have a particularly unappealing purple away kit but there seems no reason to expect to see it paraded tonight. Wrong. We arrive to find City of Liverpool are wearing an all-orange kit and Runcorn are sporting the abomination, daubed in blotches of purple and lilac like something Rosko tore up and threw in the bin, thought better of, took out and flushed down the toilet.

The performance befits such monstrous livery. Runcorn were beaten finalists in this competition last season but won't get a chance to repeat the disappointment of that penalty shoot-out defeat to Marine as City of Liverpool show a desire and purpose that we're unable to match, deservedly winning with two second half goals.

After first looking at potential sites in Wavertree, Speke and Tuebrook and drawing a blank, City of Liverpool have been pursuing the prospect of a ground within the Fazakerley area of the city. With that idea seemingly as distant a prospect as any reconciliation with Bootle, they enter the semi-finals of the Liverpool Senior Cup alongside three other teams who also play outside the city – Tranmere from Birkenhead, Marine from Crosby and the winners of Prescot Cables (Knowsley) and Bootle (Sefton) whose game tonight was postponed. A Bootle v City of Liverpool semi-final or final might be fun.

Attendance: 317

Friday 23 February

Jericho Lane, Liverpool

North West Counties League First Division North

South Liverpool 4 Ashton Athletic 0

'There are two teams in Liverpool,' Bill Shankly was once credited with saying. 'Liverpool and Liverpool Reserves.'

It was, of course, a tongue in cheek broadside at the expense of Everton, emphasising his team's dominance over their city rivals. Leaving aside reserve teams, youth teams and the enormous number of Sunday League teams in the city, there were in fact three teams in Liverpool at that time: Liverpool, Everton and South Liverpool.

South Liverpool in their current guise were reborn in 1991. Like City of Liverpool, they're now a fan-owned club. Their continued existence post-1991 was something else Manning and Furmedge overlooked in their market analysis, or lack of it. Indeed, in the interview cited earlier, Johnny Phillips talks of 'the city being without a non-league side...since the demise of South Liverpool in the 1990s.' Although you can argue that any publicity for football at this level is good, a degree of research would be nice, especially when said publicity flagrantly disregards the work of so many who strove to keep a historic side like South Liverpool alive.

The original club were formed in 1935 and quickly established themselves among the powerhouses of pre-war non-league football, later kickstarting the careers of future Liverpool FC players Jimmy Case and John Aldridge.

I last went to see them at their Holly Park ground in 1990, after which the club hobbled on for a few more months before ceasing to exist following a clubhouse fire, the last of three fires that, along with several spates of vandalism, finally finished off a historic ground, reputedly the first to host a game under permanent floodlights. Like Runcorn, they were resurrected quickly by a loyal support base and have since relocated to Aigburth. In their original guise, South Liverpool once entertained genuine hopes of election to the football league, believing, not without credence in those days, that Liverpool could support three professional clubs. Applications were submitted and rejected on ten separate occasions.

'In the post-war years,' Barry Howman notes, 'South Liverpool were complaining that, if crowds went below 4000, they were going to have problems.' He also recalls them bringing 400 fans to Canal Street, 'when their home crowds were about 400.'

When Mike Blackstone visited Jericho Lane in 2003 for his book *The Brown Sauce Is Off*, South were still fighting to get out of the Liverpool Combination. Admission was free and, he reports, 'the playing area was enclosed by a rope and metal posts...there was no covered accommodation for spectators.' Both club and ground have progressed since then. You now pay to get in and the guy taking the money is thanking everybody for coming as they move through the entrance, which is via the clubhouse. There's a proper metal fence around the ground and sheltered seating.

South currently sit in the play-off positions of North West Counties First Division North, so hopes of a next step up the pyramid don't seem too far-fetched. Ashton Athletic, struggling in the lower half of the table, are a team South should beat if they are in with a realistic shout of taking such a step. However, South have had a couple of bad results recently, including a 3-0 reverse at relegation-threatened Shelley.

It's an artificial pitch but I'm in a charitable mood because I know South Liverpool's history and how they ended up here. Without really intending to, I find myself rooting for them.

They don't let me, or any of their fans, down. South are two up within twelve minutes with a couple of delightfully worked goals. First, the impressive Elliot Owen is put through with a beautifully timed pass down the right wing and his cross finds Oscar Billington, who puts them ahead. A move on the other side of the pitch finishes with James Cottrell dispatching in a similarly clinical manner. There are some chances for Ashton in a lively match but South always look the better team and add two more goals, from Hough and Merrifield, in the later stages.

The win leaves South in third place. They're well behind leaders FC St Helens, who look a secure bet for the championship and it's a congested field for those play-off places, with the six teams immediately below them within eight points and all with games in hand. It could be an interesting end to the season.

We walk out into the pitch-black night. Nearby is Otterspool Prom, legendary local destination for the hopelessly romantic or pissed off with life or both. But, away from the floodlights, nothing can be seen, nor can the lapping of the Mersey be heard, only the post-match conversations behind us disappearing into the Liverpool night.

Attendance: 123

Saturday 24 February

APEC Taxis Stadium, Runcorn

Northern Premier League West Division

Runcorn Linnets 3 Hednesford Town 0

Non-league football is a 'survival of the fittest sport,' former Scarborough player Gary Cohen told Aaron Moore for his book Field of Dreams and Broken Fences. This is true in more ways than one. Survival isn't assured purely on ability: the team with the best players can meet a sticky end if the rest of the set-up isn't right. Being fittest to survive is dependent on a whole range of off-field factors: the stewardship of the board, the quality and work-rate of its volunteers, maintenance of the pitch, financial management...the list is a long one.

Just up the road, Runcorn Town's game against Ilkley Town has been called off due to a waterlogged pitch, something that hardly ever happens at the APEC. The ground staff do a fantastic job here, one of the many tasks carried out by figures whose contributions rarely get seen by most fans, let alone acknowledged.

Often who does what at a club is dependent on what volunteers come forward and what skill set they have or are prepared to acquire. 'We've now got Tracy Daley who's come in as a volunteer coordinator,' Bren tells me, 'and Tracy has picked up quite a few of the responsibilities I had previously. For example, I used to do a lot of the shopping for the tea bar and the bar but we've now recruited somebody who covers the tea bar and they have that responsibility.' It allows Bren to focus more on ensuring everything is in place so things run smoothly on match day: 'coordinating the stewards and the staff, making sure we're fully staffed.' It's a big responsibility: he shows me the long list of voluntary staff. These are people who have lives and responsibilities outside the club and, if a couple of them don't turn up for whatever reason, it can leave the operation very stretched.

It's almost important to make supporters are aware of what they can do to enable things to run as smoothly as possible. For example, there's been a big push to get people to use the bins, which limits the amount of litter-picking necessary during and after a game. It's working: Runcorn's is one of the tidiest grounds I've been to. But those bins still need emptying. 'A couple of volunteers have come forward and tend to tidy up after the games,' Bren tells me, 'but 15 bins need dragging to the skip and emptying. It does take an awful lot of work and we're grateful to the people who do it.'

Then there are the kits. 'The first team are playing on a Saturday. They're training on a Tuesday and Thursday. Each time there's kit that needs to be washed, dried, hung up, Paul Tandy does most of that work now and does a great job.' That's without even mentioning the demands of the youth and women's teams.

The club house, although it's a good source of income, also needs to be staffed, tidied and stocked. 'We've had a lot of events and, although that's great for raising money, there's an awful lot of work for people like Ange and Paul who tend to run those events. There are bins to empty in the clubhouse. There's lots of cleaning to do.'

Without Bren and others, clubs like Runcorn Linnets just wouldn't be able to continue. He mentions Paul Tandy ('fantastic guy') as an example of someone who devotes days of his free time to ensuring the club continues to function, ('he almost lives here'), but there are several others to whom the rest of us owe a huge debt: Bren's fellow Evertonian Paul Riley and the 'fabulously committed' Ange Murphy are among those he names. 'We're fortunate to have a number of people who just get stuck in and do what's necessary.'

It's people like this, whose contributions are replicated across the footballing pyramid, who make it possible for football at this level to continue.

It's all-consuming at times,' Vicki England admits, reflecting on her role at 1874 Northwich. 'I do football work before I go to my paid work and then come back, do family stuff and then I'm back on it. I work a couple of hours a day, if not more, doing something for the football club. And then, leading up to a home game...you're just doing something all the time. Sometimes you can be up to one o'clock in the morning doing football work and then I might go to training or match-day and all the players come out and you think, this is why we do it.

'It's the whole experience. You're closer...our players get to know supporters on first-name terms afterwards in the clubhouse. You get to know those players. You're not going to get to know Bruno Fernandes or anyone like that, but you've got a real affinity with players that are pulling that yellow shirt on, or us. The support that you give Linnets or I give '74 means so much more.'

Today, my Linnets play a team who have, in the recent past, played and indeed thrived at a higher level. FA Trophy winners as recently as 2004, Hednesford were relegated from National League North in 2016 and dropped out of the NPL Premier Division last season. Now, despite enjoying some of the best attendances in the league, they're favourites to go down with 1874, although they beat Runcorn when the sides met at Hednesford earlier in the season.

This time there's no problem. Although Hednesford compete well in the early exchanges, after Runcorn open the scoring through a Tony Kay header from a corner there's only going to be one winner and the margin of victory could and should be greater, especially after Hednesford go down to ten men in the second half. The keeper Boucher deserves credit for keeping the margin of defeat reasonably respectable but there's also some wayward finishing from Runcorn. O'Neill looks to have spurned one such opportunity before eventually scrambling it home to double Runcorn's lead and Molloy grabs a third to secure a comfortable victory.

As expected, the loyal Hednesford fans are here in good numbers, travelling up from Staffordshire: currently only Clitheroe and Chasetown have larger average attendances in this league. They've had a grim couple of seasons but continue to support their side well and presumably will continue to do so in the Midland League next season, assuming that's where they end up.

It calls to mind the period of decline of the original Runcorn in the nineties where, from a side regularly in the top half of the Conference (now the National League) we began to flirt with relegation before jumping in with both feet.

The expectations change but the love doesn't. Anticipation still builds before a match even though for Hednesford fans it is no doubt now tinged with a gloomy realism. I've been where those Hednesford Town fans are and all fans who follow a club at this level have a sense of 'There but for the grace of God...' lurking obstinately behind the passion and bravado.

Attendance: 645

Tuesday 27 February

Ericstan Park, Wythenshawe

North West Counties League Premier Division

Wythenshawe Town 4 Litherland REMYCA 0

We ignore the temptation of a journey south to Winsford United v Ashville and head to the most easterly ground in the geographical region covered in this book. Not as far as Wythenshawe's ground, which stands outside our self-imposed boundary, but to Wythenshawe Town, whose longitude lies slightly to the west of Old Trafford. Wythenshawe was once savagely described by Manchester City keeper Tony Coton as 'the kind of place where pit-bulls walk around in packs for their own safety.' It hangs on to the south-west of Manchester, looks out at Cheshire, towards the green fields and footballers' mansions of Wilmslow, and says, 'Not for us.' Happy Mondays and New Order pound from the pre-match speakers.

While we're here the other Wythenshawe club (if you accept that they *are* a Wythenshawe club, which Town fans typically don't) are scheduled to play at leaders Bury. There's still a three-team battle going on at the top for promotion to the Northern Premier League West Division. I would love the two Wythenshawe teams – or indeed anyone else – to edge Bury out and keep them away from the NPL next season (I'm assuming for the moment that Runcorn won't have escaped by then to a higher flight ourselves). We've been here before, when Macclesfield briefly stopped off in Runcorn's league on their journey back up the pyramid. Bury, I fear, will do the same, bringing big crowds but with an upward momentum nobody else can live with, leaving the rest of us to complete for the play-off places.

As it happens, the Bury-Wythenshawe game is postponed, as indeed is the Winsford-Ashville match, after an afternoon of steady rain. Here at Ericstan Park, though, the pitch is in good condition, clearly benefiting from a slight slope rising to a gradual mound in the middle of the pitch. Nothing pronounced, but presumably enough to help with drainage.

There's also a huge scaffold with netting protecting the Aldi at one end of the ground from any stray balls, though one does manage to get over it and clobber a Peugeot and I make a mental note never to park my car there during a match, should I ever venture this way again.

The ground is clearly a work in progress and the word 'progress' is one that's been used a lot around these parts in recent years. Town didn't enter the North West Counties League until

2019 and manager Steve Kinsey, who took the job when still in his twenties, steered them to promotion to the Premier Division before stepping down at the end of the season. Last summer, the club were left with no manager and very few players on their books, so a massive rebuilding job was required, something that was carried out with such effectiveness they now find themselves, under his replacement Rory Fallon, close to fulfilling Kinsey's original aim of taking the club into the Northern Premier League.

Tonight, they don't miss the opportunity to close the gap on the top two, scoring twice in each half. Central striker Tom Bentham gets two of the Town goals, the first in the second minute and the second a thunderous drive late in the game after a well-timed run gets him in behind a rapidly tiring Litherland defence.

But it would be wrong to dwell too much on individuals here. Wythenshawe Town are an impressive team unit. Like their local rivals when we saw them earlier in the month, they look well-equipped to compete at the next level up. The fact that both teams are giving a club as big as Bury a fight at the top end of the league testifies to that.

This win puts Town level on points with the leaders having played two games more. Wythenshawe are well-placed in third, with two games in hand of Bury. Having seen both Wythenshawe clubs in action it seems clear that Bury, despite their history, resources and big crowds, will have a fight on their hands to achieve the promotion that many at the start of the season looked upon as inevitable.

Attendance: 160

March 2024

'Make it make sense!'

Friday 1 March

Windleshaw Sports

North West Counties League First Division North

FC St Helens 1 Daisy Hill 0

There is a mood of defiant independence about St Helens that is pronounced even by the standards of the rugby league belt. Its continued fixation on the oval ball game despite awkwardly rubbing shoulders with Liverpool remains a proud symbol of that, which is one reason why football's efforts to take off here have historically been subdued. A single triumph in the 1987 FA Vase for St Helens Town – where long ago the nascent careers of Manchester United players Bill Foulkes and John Connelly were nurtured – failed to give that team the upward propulsion that had briefly been promised. When their ground was eventually sold off in 2002, a series of groundshares accompanied a steep decline culminating, in 2015, in dramatic relegation from the North West Counties League, where they'd been members since 1982.

FC St Helens, where we are this evening, were only founded in 2014 and their rapid progress contrasts sharply with the slow decline of their local rivals. Could they do what proved beyond St Helens Town and take a football club from the town to the rarified heights of the Northern Premier League? Last year they finished third in the North West Counties League North Division in their first season, and this year they're runaway leaders, almost certain to be promoted and join another St Helens side, Pilkington, in the NWCL Premier Division. Their Windleshaw Sports ground has historical significance as the original home of the rugby team back in the nineteenth century and the site of the first rugby encounter between perennial rivals St Helens and Wigan.

But we're here for the football and it's a ground-hop day.

Ground-hop days are where, in theory at least, hordes of football supporters descend on a ground to 'cop' it, drink beer and sometimes trade memorabilia with other football supporters. Groundhoppers aren't a phenomenon unique to non-league football but, as Mike Bayly puts it, they tend to stand out in these surroundings 'like a jigsaw piece blatantly placed in the wrong box.' Except on days like this there are loads of them, so it's more like a whole load of mixed-up pieces from different jigsaws. Given the completist tendencies of many groundhoppers – 'trainspotters with a football fixation,' Bayly calls them – they'd probably find this simile deeply troubling.

Though I visit a lot of different football grounds, I've never considered myself a groundhopper. As Bayly concedes, not all of them fit easy categorisation but their creed seems to me one of high seriousness where visiting football grounds in far off places is something you must build your life around, not just do as a mere hobby. I met one when travelling back from London on the train once. He'd been to Welling United to tick it off his list and carried, in the seemingly obligatory plastic bag, an enormous folder containing documents and write-ups of his travels, which he meticulously updated by hand after every trip. I can't see him here this evening. Given the size of that folder, he probably ticked off all the grounds in this ground-hop long ago, or capsized under its weight to die the ultimate groundhopper death.

Hang on. If you don't consider yourself a groundhopper, what's the book about then?

Well, I suppose it's about...a supporter of Runcorn Linnets exploring the culture of football in the local area. Nothing more than that.

By hopping from ground to ground.

Yeah, but a groundhopper would be going all over the country watching games, possibly even abroad. I'm keeping to a small part of the north-west of England.

Maybe you're just a particularly shit groundhopper.

No, it's just that I lack the...um...completist tendencies that a true groundhopper has.

You take smaller hops.

I suppose so.

So that makes you...more of a grasshopper than a groundhopper.

If you like.

The real groundhoppers who are here have got a whole weekend of this, whereas tomorrow I'll be off the groundhopping treadmill, if I were ever truly on it, and back to following Runcorn. Four games are scheduled for the ground-hop tomorrow, the first starting at 11am, all in convenient distance of each other, with two more on Sunday. The groundhoppers have the opportunity, if they so wish – and my guess is most of them do – to take in seven matches at different grounds over a frenzied weekend of hopping activity, quaffing and scoffing their way through club bars in the process.

I find myself surrounded by men in winter coats – it's a cold night – and various shades of bobble hat. I pick out a Sparta Prague one but the accents around me reveal that many of those present are from the local area. A woman walks by with a City of Liverpool FC scarf on, walking a large dog – there are possibly more dogs here than I've ever seen at a football ground – and she's dyed her hair purple, presumably out of devotion to her team rather than because of a drunken visit to the hairdressers. The dog is similarly attired in a purple doggy coat.

The groundhopper fraternity certainly swell the crowd, though much of the atmosphere comes from the kids behind the goal who bounce up and down, chant and yell abuse in the direction of the Daisy Hill keeper Morgan Newns, who does well to prevent St Helens from running away with it in the early stages. Daisy Hill are dangerously close to the relegation zone and the gap in quality is clear from the off. The home team have enough chances to inflict a hammering but a combination of poor finishing and good goalkeeping from Newns – including a penalty save – keeps the scores level until Hall scruffily heads home after a bouncing ball in the area manages for once to elude the keeper's hands.

But it's only 1-0 at half time and in the second half the visitors make more of a game of it. There are chances at both ends and the atmosphere becomes fevered, and tempers on the pitch fraught, as the game reaches a tense climax. The manager and assistant in the St Helens dugout are yelling and waving their arms in the direction of the nearby liner, who retains an impressive calm, rightly so as, contrary to the vexed pronouncements of the St Helens coaching staff, I can't recall a single bad decision from the officials all game. That's the kind of perspective only neutrality can give you in the heat of a football match, the result of which may have massive implications for both sides and those emotionally invested in their fortunes, while the rest of us – me, Tim and the groundhoppers – will just move on to the next game.

At one point the questioning of the ref and liner gets a bit bizarre. 'Make it make sense!' yells a desperate St Helens defender. It's unclear exactly what he wants to happen, unless the ref happens to be a trained counsellor and can help with a problem that appears, for this player, to have transcended his immediate surroundings to re-cast itself as full-blown existential angst.

In the end, St Helens – who still carve out the better chances and continue to miss them – see out the game and take another step towards the Premier Division. By now, I note, several of the ground-hoppers have left. There's a Groundhop Police group on social media who enforce a groundhopping code, outing 'fake' or 'cheating' groundhoppers, and I'm sure leaving a game ten minutes early contravenes it.

Attendance: 504

Saturday 2 March

Harrison Park, Leek

Northern Premier League West Division

Leek Town 3 Runcorn Linnets 0

The first time I visited Leek Town's ground was to see the old Runcorn with Cousin Andy (aka The Big Man) in an FA Trophy tie in January 1991. Andy now lives in Australia so understandably it's hard for him to Runcorn matches these days but that afternoon he arrived hungry and craving pies. This was not unusual. We called at a nearby shop where he declared his interest to the shop assistant. 'We got some lovely pies' she told him and sold him one. Munching on the pie on our way to the ground, The Big Man mocked her appraisal of the pie's qualities, declaring it 'fucking disgusting' and hurling it to a nearby dog. The dog seemed OK with it.

It was a memorable game, which is perhaps why such small details of the day stand out. A cracking encounter finished 3-3 after one of the longest periods of injury time I can remember – though that may have something to do with the knife-edge on which the game was poised. I chat to a Leek Town one before the game and recount details of that game, of which he has no recollection, but appears to be living the drama enough to be horrified when I reveal the eventual outcome – a win for us in the replay at Canal Street.

Since then, Leek and their ground have survived while Runcorn have returned from the dead. We've tormented them for the last two years, beating them in the semi-finals of the play-offs in both seasons. Last November we produced our best football of the season to demolishing them 5-0. Since then, though, they've gone 16 games unbeaten in the league – winning 14 – and are now nine points clear at the top.

Runcorn have brought two coachloads of supporters to this one and the match is all-ticket. There's been a good behaviour warning from the Runcorn chairman too, after random dickheads set off flares during the high-octane encounters referred to above, causing damage to Leek's artificial pitch and costing the club money it could scarcely afford to fork out. It's the first time I've travelled by coach with Runcorn Linnets. I used to do it regularly with the old team: in those days it was often long journeys to the south-east and places like Sutton, Maidstone and Dartford but nowadays we don't go much further than Leek.

There's an optimistic mood on the way there which has not so much dissipated on the way home as been completely annihilated. Runcorn are woeful in the first half and, against a good Leek Town bolstered by the confidence of that unbeaten run, we're lucky to go in only a goal down. The pint of Bass I had in the Dyers Arms before the game requests an escape route at half-time so I venture into the dingy bogs on that side of the ground. 'Careful you don't grab hold of someone else's' advises the Runcorn fan coming out as I go in, to find it pitch black in there and several other blokes stumbling about, struggling to find something against which to pee.

I emerge blinking from the toilets that time forgot just as the teams are coming out. Runcorn look rejuvenated in the early stages of the second half after a tactical adjustment at half-time and there are opportunities to level, plus a blatant handball in the area that isn't spotted by the ref. The Leek fan next to me is yelling abuse at the protesting Runcorn players so I tell him that, with decisions like that, it's not surprising they're top of the league. He tells me to fuck off, though strangely this comes out sounding wounded rather than aggressive. I put an arm around him – he's about a foot smaller than me – and tell him I was only joking. A spot of, for me, unfamiliar male bonding occurs and we chat for the rest of the match, he keeping his celebrations discreet as the Runcorn defence falls to pieces in front of us.

The normally reliable Sean O'Mahoney fails to stop a run down the Leek right which ends with a cross and a doubling of the home lead. The third goal is comedy defending but nobody in the Runcorn contingent is laughing: we ludicrously play the ball around our own box until the inevitable happens.

The Leek fan even seems a bit embarrassed for me – which is the last thing I need. Seriously, I'd rather him be jumping up and down, pointing in my face and joining in the chorus of '3-0 in yer big day out' which is piping up from the home supporters. Sympathy from a rival supporter is about the worst thing you can endure as a football fan. It's not in evidence around the rest of the ground: celebration tinged with relief seems to be the predominant reaction to their easy win: they really wanted to avoid the play-offs this season – and more specifically to avoid us in the play-offs – and now only the most calamitous of run-ins can prevent them from going up automatically.

Some people I know who only support bigger teams assume that football at this is somehow less meaningful, that you don't experience the same levels of disappointment and despair when witnessing a heavy defeat. They're completely wrong. As I walk back to the coach, there's a hole the shape of hell where my soul should be. I'm not even sure what that means but it's hard to put into words exactly what you feel after something like this. The only real difference at this level is you don't have to endure the endless reminders from media about the debacle: in the eyes of the world, your misery can at least be allowed to maintain a low profile. But the hollowness is just as deep, the pain every bit as acute, the loss in some ways even more accentuated by the knowledge that, beyond these two coaches and the Linnets fans who will have been listening to Sam and Jack's commentary, nobody really cares.

On the coach back there's a mixed mood. There's a fear of defeat in the play-offs for a third successive season, though results elsewhere today mean that seemingly healthy gap above those below us has been eroded and Bootle, who we play next week, will be level with us if we lose to them. Could we even fail to make the play-offs? There's a complaint about the ref and that missed handball, though generally I think we're all aware we got what our performance deserved. Some are unhappy with manager Billy Paynter and certain players: there's disappointment that exciting youngster Adam Moseley remained on the bench and didn't get a chance to run at the Leek defenders the way he terrorised the Hednesford left back last Saturday. If we do miss out on promotion this year, someone offers, it's going to be more difficult next year with the presence of a big club like Bury in the league and the probability that some of our best players will move up to a higher level without us...

But mostly there's defiance, a belief in your side that you must have if you support any club: otherwise, what's the point? There are young kids on the coach for whom this experience, though not a pleasant one, will be a life lesson. Specifically, that you wake up on days like this filled with hope and optimism, then end it feeling like a turd being slowly flushed into the cesspit of life. Then you wake up the next morning and feel that way all over again. Then the next match comes and the energy and optimism – blind or otherwise – return with it.

It embeds something important in your character as you navigate an otherwise fickle, constantly changing world. That sense of loyalty, of belief, somehow survives in football even when it's destroyed in other areas of life. By next Saturday the inhabitants of this coach will arrive at the APEC revived, bullish and certain that this year is the year we're going to do it. Because that's what you do.

Attendance: 973

Tuesday 5 March

Cantilever Park, Warrington

National League North

Warrington Town 0 Southport 3

There is a book about the history of Warrington Town FC called *From London Road to London Town*, written by an old mate of mine called Mike Wheeler. charting the club's 'rise' from its foundations just after the second world war to an eventual appearance at Wembley in the FA Vase Final in 1987, where they lost to St Helens Town, a rare occasion where followers of the round ball game in those oval ball strongholds got to visit the old Twin Towers. Mike followed both with a ferocity that sometimes tipped into deranged fanaticism. Warrington RLFC fans tell of his wading into hundred of St Helens supporters on his own, punching the air and yelling 'Wire! Wire! Wire!' at the top of his voice. And Mike had a loud voice.

It's a shame his book stopped there because their subsequent history has been far more interesting and would, I expect, make a far more interesting read should someone – not Mike – wish to write it.

At the end of the season of the 1986-87 season, Warrington were promoted to Division One of the North West Counties League and entered the Northern Premier League shortly afterwards, eventually stumbling back to the North West Counties and being demoted to the Second Division for the usual reason of their ground being shite. They sorted the ground out and eventually climbed back to the Northern Premier League Division One North and in 2015-16 experienced one of those season-long highs that every football fan longs for and some never experience in a lifetime, winning the league by 15 points and scoring over 100 goals in the process.

Despite the dominance of the oval ball game here, the rugby league team have been crowned champions on only three occasions, all in a ten-year period after the Second World War. As such, they lag well behind powerhouses Wigan and St Helens in terms of historical achievements, despite having a much larger population than either.

Their failure to generate a bigger football team is easier to understand. The town lies pretty much half-way between Liverpool and Manchester and to watch a Liverpool v United match in a Warrington pub is akin to standing in the middle of one of those Xmas Day games in World War One, only without the truce being called. I once ventured into one of its many fine pubs on such a matchday to find it segregated, literally split down the middle with United fans on one side and Liverpool on the other.

Recently, Warrington Town have experienced something of a golden period, securing promotion to National League North via the play-offs last season after narrowly missing out the year before. Average attendances now hover above the 1000 mark, hardly remarkable for a town with a population of 175,000 but even ten years ago crowds frequently dipped below 200. When Mike Blackstone visited the ground back in 2003, he reports that the programmes sold out because a larger than anticipated crowd of 253 had turned up for a Third-Round Qualifying game in the FA Cup. Prior to that, their biggest attendance that season had been 110. Long before this game starts, it's clear tonight's crowd exceeds 1000 by some distance, due partly to the presence of a large away contingent but also, you sense, because of optimism building in the local area about where his Warrington Town team might be heading.

I first saw Southport play in the mid-seventies when they were still a football league team. Back then, Warrington were still competing in the Mid-Cheshire League. Now, the latter are just outside the play-off places in National League North, higher in the non-league pyramid than they've ever been. Southport, meanwhile, are dangerously close to being drawn into a relegation battle so it's a big game for both teams, for very different reasons.

Both the home crowd and the travelling Southport fans are certainly pumped up but the bullishness among the Warrington support begins to dissipate when it becomes clear that defeating the well-organised and disciplined visitors is not going to be straightforward. I speak to a group of Southport fans who tell me they are nowhere near as bad as their league position suggests and that's apparent from what's happening on the pitch where Warrington are struggling to get their speedy forwards in behind a resilient back four. Southport have a disciplined game plan and look dangerous on the break, duly taking the lead through Bennett after 12 minutes, then doubling it with a Carver goal to go in two up at the break.

The home fans behind the goal Warrington are attacking in the first half have been noisy throughout the half: their chants often refer to the team as 'Wire', the old nickname for Warrington Rugby League Club before the Super League abomination 'Wolves' replaced it. Despite the performance tonight, there is a sense of something growing here, a football club's rising profile drawing on the energy of a community to fill a void that few realised was there.

'It's taken it away from its roots,' says Carl Gleavey, bassist of legendary Widnes band Zen Baseballbat, about the Super League's re-branding and rule changes. 'People are becoming more distant from it.' The most recent attempt to 'expand the game' is to play matches in Las Vegas. Carl now lives in Warrington and has witnessed the Americanisation of rugby league first hand, as a long and proud history was simply swept aside as the Wire became the Wolves while in Widnes the Chemics became the Vikings.

'Wakefield Trinity changed their name to Wakefield Wildcats, but they've changed it back again,' Carl points out, suggesting that those historical attachments might not be as easy to dispose of as those who run the game would like.

Whether Warrington Town are truly offering a viable long-term alternative to rugby league in the town may depend on whether the club continues its upward momentum. Of course, one of the changes that happened to rugby league was to play it in the summer, allowing anyone with a fondness for both sports to enjoy both. However divorced from its heritage it might be, it's worth noting that Warrington Wolves still have an average attendance of over 10,000.

But there's something different here, an energy here that wasn't there when I last saw Warrington Town about six years ago. The crowd is around double what Runcorn attract but I feel the same sense of community bond, particularly among young fans priced out of arenas like Old Trafford or Anfield and for whom rugby league perhaps doesn't exert the cultural pull it once did. Their chants make it clear how much they hate Rylands too.

Then, at half-time, things tip over. From where I'm standing, it seems a group of Southport fans have tried to enter the Warrington 'end'. This is not necessarily a declaration of war: in non-league football fans regularly change ends at half-time but the Warrington fans here are not willing to yield ground they clearly regard as 'theirs' and fighting ensues. There's a large security presence at the stadium – much greater than at other grounds I've been to this season – yet this potential flashpoint area is unguarded and it takes the hi-vis guys some time to arrive, by which point a Southport fan has been lifted and dumped over the perimeter fence.

The idea that violent incidents never happen in non-league football is a myth. They don't happen often and the opportunities offered by a lack of segregation to speak to, drink and compare stories with rival fans are worth protecting. But the intensity of the matchday experience is pronounced at any level of football. The relatively small numbers involved make such incidents less likely, while the lack of media attention means that occasional explosive altercations don't get reported to the wider world. This has the beneficial effect of not twitching the antennae of those in the local vicinity who may be drawn by the promise of a toxic atmosphere. The infrequent incidents I've witnessed would certainly have received wider exposure had they occurred in a Premier League stadium.

When it comes down to it, every football team has its share of dickhead followers and the bigger the crowd, the greater the chance of those dickheads coming together for a spate of organised stupidity. Ten years ago, Warrington would have been unlikely to experience something like this. Five arseholes in a crowd of 250 is unlikely to have much effect: quadruple the number and 20 arseholes may well feel emboldened to start something.

The tension following the incident lingers throughout the rest of the game. Clearly there are fans on both sides who feel they have unfinished business, but stewards are now patrolling the war zone and their presence is enough to deter a resumption of hostilities. On the pitch, the Southport keeper makes a couple of good saves but Warrington struggle to exert any sustained pressure and Southport secure the win with a scrambled third goal from Anson.

They needed it too. Fellow strugglers Darlington have secured an unlikely victory over second-placed Scunthorpe. Defeat for Southport would have left them in the relegation places and even after this win they sit only two points above the danger zone. News comes through that Rylands have won at FC United, making it an all-round terrible night for the home supporters. Should Warrington fail to go up and Rylands get promoted via the play-offs – a distinct possibility – the two teams would be together in this league next season for the first time and Warrington would be forced to fight for local eminence at close quarters. In such circumstances, there might be a need for even greater numbers of security personnel.

Leaving the ground, there's a feeling that the events of the night might not be over. A lot of young Warrington fans are hanging around, some of them making it clear what their intentions are. Police reinforcements are turning up and for once I'm glad we've had to park quite a way from the ground. I know fans of my age who regard the days of football hooliganism as a kind of golden age but to me violence at football matches was at best an irritant and at worst sickening.

Raw emotional attachment to a football club can be a great thing but when it's bolstered by the fake bravado of hundreds of like-minded fans at your back, that's when police costs begin to rise and those who've supported the club through less auspicious times begin to ask whether it's still for them. A rise through the leagues comes at a price, and not just a monetary one.

Attendance 1421

Saturday 9 March

APEC Stadium, Runcorn

Northern Premier League West Division

Runcorn Linnets 0 Bootle 1

Yesterday it was announced that John Williams had passed away at the age of 88. John was the Runcorn manager when I started going to Canal Street in the mid-eighties: before that, he'd led Runcorn to the title in what was then the Alliance Premier League (forerunner of the Conference and National League) and took them to Wembley for the first time, in the FA Trophy defeat to Altrincham. He'll always be remembered with respect and affection at Runcorn and there's a heartfelt minute's applause before the game.

Alan says he preferred it back then, citing again the availability of a physical programme as one reason. We were also at the top level of the non-league game in those days and could approach each season with the realistic possibility of a good run in both the FA Trophy and the old Bob Lord Trophy, plus a genuine chance of advancing to the First Round Proper of the FA Cup: we hosted teams like Wigan and Crewe and I visited league grounds like Wrexham's Racecourse Ground and Chester's Sealand Road, where we achieved memorable giant-killing victories, and Scunthorpe's Old Show Ground, where we gave them a hell of a fright before losing to a late goal. 'We should have won that,' says Brian Howman, shaking his head.

I can understand Alan's viewpoint, but I don't agree. I love the community club Runcorn has become and the whole idea of a supporter-run club made real. And, unlike the old Runcorn, where you genuinely couldn't see how the club might progress further – realistically, there was no way we'd have attracted the crowds to sustain a club in the Football League – here there is still capacity to grow, expand and improve.

How far we can realistically progress is a matter of debate among Runcorn fans. 'I believe the aim should be to get back to the National League,' says Sam Phillips. I'm not sure how viable this is, pointing to how much the National League has changed since those days: most of its clubs are professional now, including a lot of ex-football league clubs.

'There's plenty of room for us to expand,' Sam argues. 'We've got some big aspirations. We've seen even in the last few years the development of the ground. I think we need another 50 seats to fully meet the ground grading of the next league.' Most importantly, he believes, the people who run the club are the right people. 'There are some good football people at the back of our club, people who understand football, people who've been in and around football for a number of years in different roles.'

Bren Connolly agrees, rejecting the allegations of some Runcorn fans that the club isn't ambitious, agreeing with Sam's view of the levels we can aspire to. 'It's certainly the aim,' he says. 'It's disappointing to hear people say we don't want to get promoted because it'll mean extra money required. But we wouldn't be here most days of the week if we weren't ambitious. Our chairman, Peter Cartledge, is massively committed and massively ambitious for the club.

We want to see the club move forward so, yeah, the aim absolutely is for promotion, but one step at a time.'

He talks about plans for LED floodlights which would help to reduce electricity bills. 'And we're looking at the possibility of building another stand. That's one for the future. The priority at the moment is bringing the red brick changing room inside the perimeter fence. We're not going to generate the income necessary,' he admits, 'so we're relying on grants for things like these. But there are very few grants that will give you 100%, so we're looking at generating some of the income ourselves. We're hoping we can get 75% funding, which is a massive help of course.'

But those grants aren't easy to come by. They're even more thin on the ground now than they were when the club was formed, with more clubs fighting for ever more scarce resources. 'In the meantime, we're doing what we can with the money we have and there have been donations from sponsors like Webbs such as the tea bar, paid for by Adam Janes of Webbs in honour of his dad Tex, a massive Runcorn fan. For the hospitality suite, Paul Riley has been out and spoken to some of our sponsors and we've managed to get that paid for with very little input financially from the club. A lot of the improvements we've made have been self-financed or sponsor-financed and obviously we're really grateful for that. Other sponsors have provided funding but, realistically, we'll need at least some of those grant applications to come through.'

If not, even Sam doubts whether we'll be able to move to those levels as a purely supporter-run club. 'It would be very difficult for us to get into the National League without some form of financial backer,' he admits.

But the experience of other clubs has been instructive. Not long ago, for instance, it was felt to be only a matter of time before FC United established themselves at least at the top tier of the non-league pyramid. At the time, other supporter-run clubs looked enviously on their ability to attract high crowds but progress has long since stalled and, having invested heavily in anticipation of such progress, they're now heavily in debt.

Sam is fully aware of the pitfalls, mentioning the example of FC Fylde whose progress through the leagues was halted when their financial backer abruptly pulled out. It's not the only example of a club who've allowed themselves to be lured into such arrangements by the promise of short-term success. 'And that's the fear,' he says. 'We want to last but we want to progress.' It's a doubled-edged sword and many involved with football at this level have found themselves on the wrong end of its blade. In 2019, for instance, even prior to the Covid pandemic which exacerbated many such problems, the figures showed clubs in the National League making a cumulative loss of £16 million. The cost of getting to the National League is high and sustaining a presence at that level carries an even bigger price tag.

'You can do it with fan ownership,' is Brian Howman's view. 'But getting back to where Runcorn were, in the top tier of non-league, that needs *very very* good fan ownership.'

He's aware, of course, of the danger of bringing in outside money. 'Nobody who ever has that much money ever says "Do what you want with it." They'll always want to have some control.'

Aside from these considerations, progress will also of course require performances on the pitch. We've seen a few good ones against today's opponents down the years. Although the Leek game starkly revealed Runcorn's self-implosive tendencies, the away win at Bootle earlier in the season was one of those occasions where we had a hint of what this side could become should we get some consistent forward momentum. It was the bet Runcorn away performance I've witnessed this season.

Today's performance isn't at the same level, to put it mildly. A Burkey goal gives the visitors the lead after just two minutes and for the rest of the game Runcorn struggle, and ultimately fail, to get back on terms. There are two good saves in the first half from the Bootle keeper but few opportunities beside those and an equaliser always looked beyond. We succumb to a second successive defeat, allowing Bootle to draw level with us on points. 180 minutes without a goal and the very real possibility of failure to make the play-offs is staring us in the face.

Prescot draw at Kidsgrove, so Leek, after a predictable victory at 1874 Northwich, now enjoy a 15-point lead at the top.

Attendance: 651

Tuesday 12 March

Vidimor Community Ground, Runcorn

North West Counties League Division One North

Runcorn Town 0 Ilkley Town 3

When Runcorn Linnets won the North West Counties League in 2018, Runcorn Town finished in a respectable third place and gate-crashed the celebrations by beating us on the last day of the season. In a Halton 1-2-3, Town finished just three points behind Widnes in second. There were no play-offs in those days, otherwise Town might well have joined us in the NPL.

Since then, Town have gone into reverse, suffering relegation from the North West Counties Premier Division and now languishing in the lower half of Division One North. Last season, they finished next to bottom, escaping relegation into the county leagues only after a long and anxious wait while the long-winded and complex mathematical contortions used to decide these things were conducted. When the two sides met in the Liverpool Senior Cup earlier this season, Linnets ran out 7-0 winners.

Runcorn Town were formerly Mond Rangers, the works team from the ICI factory where my dad was employed for years: he tells me he picked up the injury that ended his career as an amateur footballer on this pitch. They decided to re-name themselves Runcorn Town in 2005 and set about getting themselves into the North West Counties League, which they achieved in 2010 when they installed the floodlights under which we'll be watching the game tonight.

It's a drive down an unlit narrow road to get to the ground, parking in the dark car park of the old Pavilions club then walking down a further unlit passage towards the giant incinerator, rising like some metallic Kilimanjaro above the ground, except it's nothing like a mountain and, surrounded by other industrial structures, in the dark it looks more like something out of

Bladerunner, eerie coloured lights appearing out of nowhere against the night sky. It's one of the few remaining reminders of the area's past, where the chemical industry nursed the local population from cradle to grave, filling its lungs with shit in the process. The provision of recreational facilities for its workers was what gave the town this ground.

It's something that David Proudlove, when he visited for his *Work & Play* book, portrayed almost romantically, referring to the looming industrial structures as an 'incredible backdrop...The giant concrete chimney of the neighbouring incinerator and other industrial structures tower over the place...that view across to Weston Point remains and gives the impression of a football club still rooted within an industrial community: you work over there, and play over here.'

There's a good match programme here too. Those like Alan who lament the loss of a physical Runcorn programme may well question why, if a much smaller club can produce one, we can't. And they may have a point. The one for tonight shows the originally scheduled date of 24 February, when this match was postponed.

At one point during the first half, I rescue the ball from within a pile of thorns as Tim looks on with a smug grin. There's hardly anyone else standing nearby so one of us has to do it and Tim shows no sign of making a move in that direction. Later, a spinning ball drops out of the sky towards him. This is pay-back, I figure, only for him to take it in his arms with the aplomb of an Indian boundary fielder in the recent Test series against England, then hurl it back almost in one movement.

Away from this off-pitch battle of nerves, Runcorn Town attack down the slope in the first half, though not as often as their number 9 Mamadou Djabi might hope: he's largely isolated in attack and his attempted layoffs frequently fail to find a colleague. Djabi is working hard for no reward but keeps persevering, his efforts, like the rest of his team-mates, appearing less and less likely to bear fruit as the game progresses. Ilkley are playing it around comfortably and the only surprise is that it takes them till first half injury time to score the opener through Dean.

With the slope in their favour in the second half, Ilkley always look likely to add to their lead. Gonzalez Mele finds the net from close range before Croft crashes a third in off the bar to give the visitors what you sense will have been one of their most comfortable games this season.

It's a hard night for the home side and, as a club, Runcorn Town now look far from the outfit that gave their local rivals such a scrap just six years ago and, for a time, kept alive the possibility of a Halton triumvirate in the Northern Premier League.

Attendance: 99

Saturday 16 March

APEC Taxis Stadium

Northern Premier League West Division

Runcorn Linnets 2 Avro FC 1

Runcorn Linnets enter the season's final stages with a minimum of eight games left to save our season. To make it more than eight it'll mean beating several teams who are, like us, all still in the mix for a play-off place. Currently, anyone between 2nd and 15th knows a good run from here means they could accompany Leek on the road to the Northern Premier League next season.

Avro, a side from Oldham who were promoted last season, are among them. They currently sit in 11th place but should they walk away with the points today and win their game in hand, they'll be just five points behind Runcorn. And any dropped points today would allow a whole bunch of clubs in between to further narrow a gap that's been closing in the last few weeks.

Thankfully Runcorn look renewed and up for the fight that a physical Avro side look determined to give us. Ryan Brooke, starting up front ahead of Ollie Molloy, deservedly gives us the lead from close range but the game tightens after that, becoming scrappy, the midfield at times resembling more a reenactment of the Somme than a game of football. The ref flashes yellow after yellow, mostly in the direction of Runcorn players who, being Runcorn players, don't shirk the aggressive challenges of their opponents. The resulting unrefined tussle begins to play to the strengths of Avro and they equalise just before half-time.

Despite what some fans around me seem to feel, it's unlikely a club like Avro have the resources to bribe the referee in any meaningful way or would bother to do so merely to give themselves an outside chance of reaching the play-offs. It's more that Avro are skilled at staying just this side of the permitted threshold and are good at provoking the opposition into crossing the line.

Billy Paynter makes the decision to bring on Molloy for Will Saxon at half-time. Saxon is our most creative player but he's finding no room in that crowded midfield and is on the receiving end of some rough challenges. He's already had a yellow and you can see him picking up another for retaliating or protesting too vehemently to the card-happy ref.

Molloy, meanwhile, is the sort of player who will ensure some brown streaks will be on defenders' shorts in the Avro laundry basket at the end of the day and he duly enters the melee with relish, though the real turning point comes when Adam Moseley is introduced. He immediately gives us more balance and begins to find space on the right, tormenting two Avro defenders as he enters the penalty area, then twisting inside to draw the foul that brings a penalty to Runcorn. I immediately think back to Doyle's miss against Trafford but this time it's Sean O'Mahoney who steps up and makes no mistake.

Many Runcorn fans would like to see Moseley starting more regularly. They also worry that, if he doesn't get regular football, he'll move on. I think that's inevitable at some point anyway.

He certainly has the potential to play above Northern Premier League standard and I'm just glad we get to keep the lad for a while before the inevitable happens. Sam Phillips thinks we'll see him playing at this level for a few years yet. 'We've got to hope it's with us,' he says. 'Then in two or three years he'll have developed into the player he's going to be.'

At this stage of his career, Sam is more realistic about what Adam can contribute. 'You're looking at him,' he says, 'and you think, no, he doesn't look that player at the moment but it's because football's a team game and you've got to have what's around you.' And that means not just the players on the pitch, but the right approach from the coaching staff too. 'He's only 19. Let him enjoy it.' Introduced at this stage of today's game, he's certainly doing that. Runcorn have fought and won the right to play football and Billy Paynter has timed the introduction of his most naturally gifted player perfectly.

You feel a Adam Moseley in this form could make a real difference at the business end of the season, which we're suddenly looking forward to again with anticipation rather than just hope. Prescot lose at Leek and defeat for Bootle means we're three points clear of the rest of that huge play-off pack. You sense a huge lift in the mood at the APEC this afternoon: a feeling that sustains football fans at any level. Belief.

Attendance: 609

Saturday 23 March

The Lower Angel, Warrington

It's Non-League Football Day, that Saturday of the year when we're supposed to put our big club affiliations aside (mainly because it's an international break so they aren't playing) and head to our local non-league ground for pies, pints and a spot of good-natured banter with the opposition.

Thing is, though, I hang around such grounds on most Saturdays, so I don't feel in any way awkward that I'm in the Lower Angel in Warrington having a pint with Carl and Gary Gleavey. I couldn't get to Clitheroe for Runcorn's game, so I decide to resume our discussion about football, rugby and anything else that comes up over a few beers.

Last time I was here, much of the talk around the bar concerned Luke Littler, the teenage darts sensation who had reached the final of the PDC World Championship. The media were clear he was from Warrington but the guys around the bar were disputing this and an animated conversation took place with some claiming he was from St Helens, Runcorn or Widnes. In these parts, such distinctions are important. To Sky Sports that won't make much difference, but to many of the blokes around the bar it's huge enough to fuel a discussion lasting several hours. Actually, pretty much anything can fuel a discussion of that length at the Angel: just before Christmas I came in here to find them talking about *Treasure Island*: three pints later I left and they were still discussing it, accompanied by regular rounds of 'Ah, Jim lad!'

Within days of Littler ascending to the ranks of darts nobility, they had a 'Luke Bittler' ale on tap here. It was stupendously awful. In the view of the regulars, Littler had now have moved from cherished local lad made good to national property and that meant he'd crossed a line. 'He's a United fan too,' grumbled a Liverpool supporter at the bar.

The North-West of England is the area where industry gave the country its lungs, only for the profits to disappear into other parts of England leaving only foul air for those lungs to splutter on. It's where the pioneers of rugby league were ostracised by their Rugby Union overlords. And. of course, it's an area in which big time footballers may start their careers, and may even occasionally finish them, but can never reap any real rewards without moving elsewhere. Roger Hunt began playing football in Warrington before winning the league and cup with Liverpool and a World Cup with England. Ted McDougall kicked a ball about on the ICI Rec a stone's throw from my house in Widnes before going on to score 256 league goals in the football league. In Widnes and Warrington, only rugby league heroes stay local and, it seems, remain local heroes. If the rest of the world wants Luke Littler, they're saying around this bar, they're welcome to him. Yet at one time, even in the close season, pretty much all the talk in this bar would have been about rugby.

Has darts now become the new Rugby League?

Carl seems horrified by the idea. 'Rugby League's in our blood. I always think of Rugby League as the last working-class sport. I suppose we can say that about non-league football: it still has its working-class roots. But rugby league clubs now struggle more than some non-league football teams. There are the Super League clubs, and then you've got the next tier which has some big clubs in like Bradford and Widnes. But in football, you have the FA Cup and through that people still know those non-league teams. People are still aware of those teams, of that tier of the game.'

I was growing up in Widnes during a golden period for the rugby league team. Their frequent trips to Wembley for the Challenge Cup Final would lead to most of the town decamping to London for the day. The place would become a ghost town, shops shut, some pubs staying open only to tempt the few left behind with a live broadcast of the game.

I remember some Widnes fans mocking me when I suggested going to Wembley to watch Runcorn in the FA Trophy Final was a parallel experience: some parts of old Runcorn would book their own coaches and have the whole street heading down there. For the Wycombe and Woking finals, I went in this way, staying overnight on Brian's sofa and heading down there on a coach filled with fans who lives a stone's throw from Canal Street. 'Widnes are at the top of their sport,' those rugby fans would tell me. 'Runcorn aren't.'

Yet in those days both teams were semi-professional. Eric Hughes, who played for Widnes in the seventies, taught at my school. I'd frequently pass Widnes players in the street or drink in the same pubs. Andy Gregory, before he moved to Wigan, lived a hundred yards or so from where I do now. For years, semi-professional careers in both rugby league and football could give people a good living standard when combined with a regular occupation, something that a club would be only too willing to help you secure if you were good enough.

'I was talking to an old boy and he told me something that sounds ridiculous until you actually pull the bones out of it,' says Brian Howman. 'This would be in the eighties and he must have been in his eighties. He said, "You know, son, I used to play for Runcorn." And he explained that he signed for Runcorn from Arsenal, for more money. I thought, OK, this should be fun.

But there was the maximum wage then...we were talking back in the twenties, I would think, possibly 1930s. He played for Arsenal Reserves, but he came to Runcorn, which was owned by the Highfield Tannery, so he got a job at the Tannery, which was already more than he was earning at Arsenal Reserves, and then he got a few bob playing for Runcorn.

'Same with rugby league players. Jim Mills came up from South Wales and got a job in Bass. When Bass closed, the foreman had a job round the corner from us. He told me the arrangement with Jim was he used to go to work every morning and he'd just ask him what he wanted to do that day. He's a fucking hero in Widnes, Jim Mills. So these part-time players get a good job, which isn't really a job, and then they get a part-time wage as well.'

Now, of course, the top level of the non-league game is mostly professional, while the top level of rugby league has been given a Sky Sports makeover designed, it seems, to remove any residue of the sport's working-class roots. At Runcorn Linnets' level of the game, I would argue that it's very much a part of the appeal that no such makeover is ever likely to happen.

The discussion moves on to Carl and Gary recalling Runcorn's FA Cup tie called Burnley in 1981. 'We were arrested,' they tell me. They weren't in Canal Street that day, for a game which Runcorn lost 2-1, but had gathered with some other lads on the flyover from which you could get a good view of the action below. 'The police turned up and just arrested us all,' Gary laughs.

Between conversations and visits to the bar, I'm checking for score updates on my phone, where I find that Olly Molloy's goal in the first half is cancelled out by a Clitheroe second half equaliser for what those present inform me was a fair share in the points. Although leaders Leek are surprisingly held to a draw by lowly Hednesford, Prescot and Bootle both win which means they're again breathing uncomfortably down Runcorn's necks.

Sunday 24 March

APEC Taxis Stadium, Runcorn

Cheshire Women's County Cup Semi-Final

Runcorn Linnets Ladies 6 Nantwich T. Women 2

What do the following places have in common: Chester, Garston, Leigh, Northwich, Runcorn, St Helens, Warrington, Widnes and Winsford?

Yes, they all lie within the geographical area covered by this book but they're also places that were hosting women's football matches over a hundred years ago.

There were certainly many more. These are just the places for which we have documentary evidence of women's football games happening, as helpfully collated by women's football historian R.S. Titford. The north-west of England was an early hotbed of women's football and, even during the ban, teams like Manchester Corinthians and Fodens, from Sandbach, continued to promote women's involvement in the game despite the constant threat of official sanctions by the FA.

Given the fullness of my football-watching schedule, it's often difficult to fit in games featuring the Runcorn women's team but this one seemed a good place to start. There'll be no Runcorn men's team in the Cheshire Senior Cup Final this season, but Runcorn Linnets Ladies stand on the threshold of the women's version of the competition.

At the time of this game taking place, there's still limited coverage of the women's team on the club website and, as an infrequent visitor to their games, I'm still struggling to familiarise myself with the names of the players scoring the goals that take Runcorn to an impressive 4-0 lead at half-time. Runcorn are above mid-table in the North West Women's Regional League South Division while Nantwich play a level below in the Cheshire Women's League, so on paper this should be an easy passport to the final for the home team. Despite that, the visitors make a decent game of in the second half, pulling two goals back before Runcorn eventually finish off the resistance with a couple of late goals.

There are around 100 fans present. It's free to get in and I wonder whether it would be better to charge something to contribute towards running costs. Unlike some other teams at this level, it's not pay-to-play: the club properly supports its women's team with kits and other expenses and they get to play on the home ground, which isn't always the case at any level of women's football.

'It's being spoken about,' Kelly Jones tells me when I ask about the possibility of charging on the door to cover some of these expenses. It's never as simple as that, of course. We'd need to have someone on the turnstiles, for a start, and it's frequently the case that a women's game at the APEC follows on the heels of an academy fixture, so there's nothing to stop someone just hanging around afterwards to watch both games, as some do. I can see a case for someone holding a bucket at the gate where we come in though.

As women's football at this level becomes more competitive, these are issues that need to be wrestled with, yet there are other concerns that won't be so easily addressed. While many football fans moan about the standard of refereeing, at least at NPL and NWCL level they have proper assistants running the line. Here, the shortage of officials is all too evident: although the games have to have a ref, usually a couple of people from the two clubs involved offer a token presence on the lines, which often amounts to just standing around with flags tucked under their arms.

As such, it's often left to the ref to make decisions on offsides from a position on the pitch where no one can make an accurate judgement. The increasing levels of abuse such decisions often generate, from both from the dugout and the terraces, is another indication that women's football at this level is growing in intensity and it needs a proper refereeing set-up to meet its increasing demands. That's part of the wider shortage of referees though and, sadly, the more abuse the officials get, the less chance there is that this shortage will be addressed.

Tuesday 26 March

Moss Lane Stadium, Altrincham

National League Premier Division

Altrincham 4 Wealdstone 1

'The Robins aren't bobbins,' sang the late, great Frank Sidebottom. And with good reason. Altrincham can claim to be among the greatest of all non-league sides, certainly among the most well-known. Much of their fame comes from their FA Cup giant-killing exploits: in the period between 1965 and 1995, during which they took the scalps of 16 league clubs in the competition, including First Division Birmingham City in 1986. Prior to that, in the days when promotion to the league was still not automatic, they'd once narrowly failed to be elected, trailing Rochdale by just one vote because the representatives from Luton and Grimsby, who'd been expected to support Altrincham, didn't turn up, the former held up in traffic, the latter, allegedly, in the bar.

During that time, Runcorn considered Altrincham our main rivals. 'There was always an edge,' says Brian Howman, recalling contests between the two as far back as the seventies. 'We never had the FA Cup achievement that Altrincham, or even Northwich Vics, did,' he rues. If we're honest, we perhaps felt in their shade in other ways too. After Runcorn won the Alliance Premier League at the first time of asking, Alty won it for the next two years. Brian's hero Barry Howard was in that Altrincham side and, for that reason, is more well-known as an Alty player. We beat them in the Cheshire Senior Cup Final in 1985, only to lose to them at Wembley in the FA Trophy Final the following season.

Following that Wembley final, any tensions that may have lain dormant were cranked up. My abiding memory of the day was of our coach departing Wembley to the farewell greeting of a flabby Altrincham arse mooning us, but that wasn't what caused the inflammation of hostilities. John King, legendary Alty manager, announced that he was quitting after the final and Altrincham pinched John Williams from us to take his place. He took with him Runcorn central defenders Bobby Fraser and Graeme Jones, who'd formed an imperious defensive partnership that season. Captain Ossie Smith soon followed.

We were furious. Then it was Alty's turn to be furious when King, rather than disappearing into the sunset, his Altrincham legacy forever intact, announced he was joining Runcorn as John Williams' replacement, bringing with him left-back Peter Densmore and scourge of league defences in some of those FA Cup runs Gary Anderson, a player whose red face, tongue often clenched between teeth, was the visual epitome of the player who gives everything in every game. By the end of the next season, a case could be made for Runcorn having benefited more from the switch, especially as Alty fans never really saw the best of John Williams, while Jones failed to take his Runcorn player of the year form with him down the M56. Alty finished above

Runcorn, but only by two points, and we again secured a sweet victory over them in the Cheshire Senior Cup Final.

Since then, it's fair to say our paths have diverged, with Runcorn's by some distance the less pleasant one. John King eventually went back to Altrincham and almost won the Conference – and promotion to the football league – before both clubs entered a fallow period. Runcorn's, of course, was far more fallow and included the loss of our ground and eventual extinction; Altrincham fell out of the Conference but have since regained their position in what is now the National League and are still at their Moss Lane ground. While they once rubbed shoulders with Runcorn and Northwich in the Conference, they're now easily the highest placed club in the area covered by this book and go into this game just outside the play-off places, another tilt at promotion to the football league very much in their sights. Runcorn finished in the top four twice in the late eighties: such an achievement now brings the chance of a play-off final at Wembley and advancement to the league, if your ground is up to it. The truth is Canal Street never would have been.

'Canal Street still looked like a pre-war ground,' recalls Brian Howman. Which had been fine until automatic promotion came in and changed everything. This was inevitable, he thinks, believing Runcorn lacked the forward thinking necessary to survive in this new, competitive era. 'It needed to be done; it just needed to be done differently. It's easy to say in hindsight but it was just a beckon to anyone who wanted to get a bit more money. If it was done for entirely sporting reasons, then yeah, but what in football is?' Back then Runcorn were one of a quartet of Cheshire clubs playing at the top level of semi-professional football, along with Alty, Northwich Vics and Macclesfield. 'Altrincham have come out of it,' reflects Brian, 'but the rest of us? We've all died at least once.'

Altrincham and Wealdstone are among a minority of clubs playing at this level who were once regular opponents for Runcorn in the old Conference years. Many of the clubs in there now are former league clubs - such as Scunthorpe United, Southend United and Chesterfield – while others who have since climbed to this level, the likes of Solihull Moors, a club only founded in 2007, Boreham Wood, who in 'our day' were yo-yoing between divisions in the Isthmian League, and Forest Green Rovers, then in the Midland Division of the Southern League and now a team who have been to League Two and back.

Chesterfield were officially confirmed champions on Saturday, having dominated the league this season. They go back into the Football League, having last season missed out somewhat unfortunately on penalties to Notts County in the play-off – a memorable match at which I was present. We had the best of all worlds at that one: able to appreciate a good game of football from a neutral point of view, in the Notts County end so we could leach off the good vibes and, without scarfs or any other identifiable fan attire, able to get into the Spoons near-Wembley that had been declared Chesterfield-only for the day. Remarkably for a pub in London, they had on special offer Market Porter for just 99p a pint.

Wealdstone, the first club ever to do the 'non-league double' of league and FA Trophy and ancient stamping ground of one Vinnie Jones, are currently involved in a potential relegation bunfight featuring as many as eleven teams all anxious to avoid the other relegation places alongside already doomed Oxford City.

Altrincham's is the 'away' ground I've visited more than any other and it has altered very little down the years: there's a certain defiance about this humble stadium remaining proudly intact while so much of the football world has changed around it. The only evidence of modernisation lies in the small but horribly tacked-on 'fan zone' on one side of the ground.

Altrincham, like many clubs in the National League, are now full-time. I recall in the eighties many assuming automatic relegation from the league would lead to league clubs having to go semi-professional, but the reverse has happened. I talk to Tim about the old days and he wonders why Altrincham and their ground were able to survive in that brave new world when others were not. I've often wondered it too. Some will point to the wealthy surroundings here, where Manchester meets the 'Football Wives of Cheshire' territory of Wilmslow. Altrincham was established as early as the mid-nineteenth century as an attractive place for Manchester's new middle class to head. There was once a 'rival' club here, Linotype, founded by the company of the same name. The firm went out of business in the seventies so the club, then in the Mid-Cheshire League, merged with Cheadle Heath Nomads, eight miles or so to the east of here.

But not every middle-class suburban club is able to sustain itself as Alty have. There is the competition of established middle class sports for a start – Sale Rugby Union Club is just up the road – and there's the not inconsiderable obstacle of Old Trafford being a short drive or, nowadays, tram ride away. If this bit of Cheshire/Greater Manchester really is the wealthiest patch in the north of England, as I've heard claimed, it's hard to imagine much of that wealth ever coming through the Altrincham turnstiles.

I put ancient rivalries aside and admit to a certain respect for what Altrincham have managed to achieve here. It's unquestionably helped that Altrincham are one of the few non-league clubs to establish themselves, through their FA Cup endeavours, as a national 'name' but the club have remained community-focused, living resolutely within their means, refusing to mortgage their futures for the chance of league football once denied to them by a combination of London traffic and whatever that bloke from Grimsby was drinking. Runcorn Linnets played them as recently as last season, succumbing to a thorough 4-0 drubbing at the APEC in the Cheshire Senior Cup, reminding us of the yawning gap between where Runcorn used to be and where we are now.

Moss Lane is the first ground I've come to during the writing of this book where this is some sort of segregation in place. I say 'some sort' because the away fans are coming in through the same turnstiles as everyone else. 37 have travelled up from the south-east and those who gravitate towards one end of the ground are haphazardly penned in there, though it's clear when Wealdstone open the scoring that others are spread around the ground. Despite their lowly position, Wealdstone have started the better of the two sides, testing the Alty keeper several times before eventually Barker's low drive finds a way past him.

It seems to wake Altrincham up and they're level within minutes, Newby's finish ensuring they go in level before an entirely different Alty emerge after the break. I mean, they're the same players but a simple tweak to their game plan sees them pressing higher up the field, denying Wealdstone the space they enjoyed in the early stages. They dominate the half, taking the lead through a thundering volley from Wilson before a beautifully crafted move started by Osborne's wonderful pass sets up a cross from Mooney on the right for Banks to finish at the near post. Linney later adds a deserved fourth and Altrincham, following a disappointing defeat to Gateshead here on Saturday, end the night back in the play-off positions. News that Southend have won at Solihull Moors, who sit above them in the league, adds to the joy of the home supporters.

Wealdstone, meanwhile, still have work to do to remain in the National League next season. They're three points above the relegation places with games in hand and their application in the first half hour of this match suggests they can do it, though they'll be hoping for some help from Altrincham, who next travel to Kidderminster Harriers on Good Friday, another of the six clubs still at this level with whom the old Runcorn regularly crossed swords. Our 8-3 win over Harriers in the 1985-86 Bob Lord Trophy remains the biggest scoreline I've ever seen in a football match.

Attendance: 1740

Friday 29 March

APEC Taxis Stadium

Northern Premier League West Division

Runcorn Linnets 0 Nantwich Town 0

It's not to be taken seriously, of course, but this morning Witton Albion's Twitter account predicts the scores of all the remaining games and how the play-off places will shape up at the end of them. They pretty much base them on current league positions, so they assume Runcorn will win today's game and the rest of our games, except for a predicted defeat at Prescot on Monday. Eventually we'll finish third, Witton's calculations say, and face Bootle in a play-off semi-final.

As I'm sure they're aware, football doesn't work out as neatly as that and certainly not in this league where, except for runaway leaders Leek and relegation certainties 1874 Northwich, it seems anyone can beat anyone else. As football fans, we can get angry about the inconsistency of our teams, but the truth is that inconsistency is football's default mode.

The difference between success and failure in football rests on tight margins: a scuffed shot, a slip in the area, a borderline refereeing decision...every football fan wants his or her team to be among the small elite around the country who achieve the holy grail of consistency, as long as it's the Leek rather than 1874 kind, and even those teams will slip up occasionally. A good run of form can be as illusory as a bad one: managers can be sacked when the latter follows the former when all that has really happened is the exposing of, or papering over of cracks before the law of averages asserts itself.

It's one reason why so many involved in football – players as well as fans – are so superstitious. There's a lot that's fortuitous in football, more than many like to admit, and the wearing of 'lucky scarves' or putting your boots on in a certain order give an illusion of control that the rational side of your brain will tell you is just not there. TV commentators and pundits, when explaining how a game went, tend to construct a retrospective narrative, changing their view of a team's performance when a deflected shot squeezes past into the net against the run of play. 'They've been terrible today' suddenly changes to 'They did well to hang in there and it paid off.' All that really happened was they scored a flukey winner and next week they may well concede one, for those same pundits to conclude 'What's frustrating about this team is their inconsistency....' No one likes to admit it, but so much of what happens on a football pitch is nothing more than luck. The more successful sides manage to minimise the impact of fortune – as you can with better players, superior tactics or just working harder – but even they never manage to eliminate it entirely.

On our way to the ground, we pass Halton Stadium, as we always do. Queues are already forming ahead of the Good Friday Rugby League game between Widnes and Swinton. Tellingly, however, the queues are all forming along one side of the ground, a tell-table sign that it's only partly open. When Naughton Park was here, it was often a place to avoid today because a Good Friday would invariably mean a derby with Warrington, St Helens or another big club and the ground would be swarming, nearby streets packed with parked cars, fans of both sides spilling out into the street from Leggies and the Albion at either end of the ground. It's another unmistakeable sign of decline..

This has always been a traditional day for Rugby League but no football matches in Runcorn's league were initially scheduled for today. Runcorn and three other clubs, however, have successfully negotiated to bring Saturday's matches forward, presumably to give them an extra day's break ahead of the Easter Monday fixtures.

The decision is vindicated by an above average crowd, bolstered by a good number of Nantwich fans who also have hopes of their club making the play-offs. In that respect, they possibly need the win even more than Runcorn do.

With so much at stake, it's perhaps understandable that it's a scrappy, closely fought affair with the emphasis on risk management rather than adventurous attacking football. Though Runcorn marginally have the best of a second half after a first in which it's hard to recall a serious effort on goal, a draw is a fair result at the end of a nervy and easily forgettable match.

At the end, players and fans troop towards the exit knowing that Bootle are one up against Trafford which means we'll be back in third place tonight, fourth place tomorrow if Prescot win at Clitheroe, but there's late drama – a Trafford equaliser five minutes into injury time keeps

Bootle behind us in the table. Those Witton predictions are already well wide of the mark. Fortune hasn't smiled on anyone today: as it so often does, it's departed the ground with a sly wink.

Attendance: 847

Saturday 30 March

Crilly Park, Atherton

North West Counties League Division One North

Atherton LR 4 Holker Old Boys 1

In many ways Leigh, about four miles south of Atherton, is the archetypal Rugby League town. Wigan and St Helens fans may well choke on their beer at the very suggestion but in those towns football clubs have at least laid down roots, relatively successfully in the case of Wigan. In Leigh, aside from one notable period from 1995 when Horwich RMI left the outskirts of Bolton to move in there, it's remained pretty much exclusive rugby league territory. And when Horwich arrived, Andrew Longmore in *The Independent* summed up the consternation of locals with elegant succinctness: 'Unsigned boundaries were crossed. Horwich is football; Leigh is rugby league.'

Leigh RMI, as they became known, ground-shared with the Leigh Centurions Rugby League team, and, to the surprise of many, went on something of an adventure, progressing to the National League in just five years. The heady experiences of those promotion years didn't last though and, only eight years after reaching the pinnacle of the non-league game, they found themselves playing in front of crowds of under 300, changed their name to Leigh Genesis and eventually gave up on the whole idea of selling football to a town where numerous pubs compete to demonstrate their credentials as the foremost rugby league boozer. The Centurion and Leopards' Den (formerly the Britannia) compete fiercely for the crown, but even the local Spoons – the Thomas Burke – has rugby league memorabilia plastered all over its walls.

'It's reassuring,' nods Carl Gleavey, recalling our earlier discussions of the drive to separate rugby league from its historical roots. 'Leigh can be seen as one of the game's success stories.' He's talking about rugby league, of course, not that brief, exhilarating venture into the world of the round ball. Despite having Wigan close by, Leigh RLFC have retained their place among rugby league's elite, even winning the Challenge Cup in 2023, and that may be at least partly due to their success in keeping football out of town for any kind of prolonged period. The rugby club has been in existence since 1878. Leigh RMI lasted a mere 13 years.

Leigh Genesis soon moved to Atherton, ground-sharing with the wonderfully named Atherton Laburnum Rovers, where we are today. They continued to decline and, after relegation from the Northern Premier League, opted not to go into the North West Counties League, opting instead to join the South Lancashire Counties League. Today, they're in Division Two of the Manchester League. The greater sadness in all this, though, is the demise of Horwich RMI, forced out of their historic home as Bolton Wanderers and their faceless new stadium moved in.

It's fair to say Genesis were no more likely to thrive in Atherton than if they'd somehow managed to remain in Leigh. Football took root here a long time ago and the town has two well-established clubs. Atherton Collieries were founded in 1916 while our hosts today have origins dating back to 1956. They took their name from the Laburnum Playing Fields, their original home in the shadow of Laburnum Mill, part of the large nineteenth century cotton spinning complex in the town.

Up to yesterday, Rovers still retained a slight mathematical chance of winning the league, but FC St Helens' victory over Runcorn Town means they've secured the title. Now it's all about remaining at the head of the play-off pack and today they face visitors who themselves are nipping at the heels of that pack.

There are other games of interest today. Not only are Runcorn Linnets' rivals Prescot Cables travelling to Clitheroe, five of the six games taking place in the Northern Premier League West Division feature teams with a serious interest in the battle for the play-offs.

Elsewhere, Wythenshawe Town's neighbours Wythenshawe visit Bury in a potential promotion decider in the North West Counties Premier League. Town are currently top but don't play today and both teams facing off at Gigg Lane have the games in hand needed to overhaul their lead Meanwhile, up the road from here Atherton Collieries face Basford as they battle to avoid the drop from the Northern Premier League Premier Division. It's a day for extreme multi-tasking, of somehow navigating updates on our phones while keeping both eyes on the match.

Rovers are offering free entry to anyone with Premier League or Football League season tickets today. My Runcorn one doesn't count but I wouldn't want to deny them the six quid entrance fee anyway. I'm not sure how many take them up on the offer. I see a couple of guys in Manchester United shirts on this warm and sunny Easter Saturday, but most of the crowd seem to be LR regulars with a smattering of Holker fans who've made it down from Barrow.

Unusually, we opt to sit. There is a raised stand which gives a better vantage point than standing at the fence. The area of the pitch nearest to us is heavily sanded and clearly a bit the worse for wear after a punishing season. LR play the ball around well, though their passing game becomes notably more difficult to execute in this part of the pitch. They are a team in form and look it and it's no surprise when they take the lead after just 10 minutes via a lethal, dipping effort from Rawsthorn that the keeper reacts to far too late.

Holker are seeking a more direct route to goal and find one when a long pass puts Dawson through to bring the away side level. Despite soaking up a lot of pressure, it looks like they'll go in all-square at half-time but a minute from the break Hunter restores the LR lead.

It's been a cracking first half and you feel Holker could still make an impact until, just after the hour mark, it all falls apart. Rawsthorn gets his second of the game to make it 3-1 and, within minutes, Dawson is sent off for a bad tackle. From there it's just a matter of how many LR get. Just one, it turns out. Rawsthorn heads in three minutes from time to secure his hat-trick before receiving a red card himself after a touchline altercation in injury time.

The win leaves Atherton LR in second place and third place South Liverpool also win to strengthen the two sides' play-off aims. Holker leave with their own ambitions severely dented but will be travelling down the M6 again on Wednesday night for a game at Runcorn Town still with an outside chance of being involved.

There's drama at the end of the Bury-Wythenshawe game in the North West Counties Premier Division: in front of over 4000 fans, Wythenshawe equalise with a penalty deep in injury time, leaving the two Wythenshawe sides to face each other on Easter Monday in what, for some reason, is known as 'El Civico': the winner, if there is one, will be in prime position for the championship and that automatic promotion place.

Attendance: 120

April 2024

It's a good thing Pep Guardiola doesn't manage Charnock Richard…

Monday 1 April

Joseph Russell Stadium, Prescot

Northern Premier League West Division

Prescot Cables 2 Runcorn Linnets 2

In a quirk of the fixture list, all four sides in the play-off positions face each other today and, in the Northern Premier League's Premier Division, the situation is replicated with Macclesfield travelling to Hyde and Rylands facing Marine. The evicted City of Liverpool, you feel, are playing for more than just the three points against former landlords Bootle, but inevitably our interests are focused on this one, where Runcorn visit Prescot knowing a win will take us ahead of them with, on paper, an easier run-in.

Prescot Cables are a long-established club, formed in 1884, adding the suffix due to links to British Insulated Cables, the town's major employer at the time. Although the current capacity of the stadium is a little over 2000, a record attendance of 8122 was recorded in 1932. After a successful period in the 1950s, during which they reached the First Round of the FA Cup twice, they entered a difficult period after losing the main stand to a fire in 1960, at one point falling into the Mid-Cheshire League before, over time, ground improvements were made that allowed them to join the North West Counties League in 1982. It's the story of both a club, and a ground, refusing to die and you feel the spirit that kept them alive oozing through in a stadium full of character as Cables, like us, have the scent of promotion via the play-offs in their nostrils.

In recent years, any success has come in the Liverpool Senior Cup, which they won in 2017 and 2018. Soon after, they were threatened with expulsion from the league until Knowsley Council came to the rescue, purchasing the ground and granting the club a 99-year lease. Despite that security, they only avoided a relegation play-off by the skin of their teeth in 2022, so this season's involvement in the battle for the play-offs has, from the perspective of the rest of the league, come as something of a surprise.

The sunny Easter weekend weather has disappeared and there's been heavy rain overnight. News comes through that the City of Liverpool-Bootle clash has been called off. There's a pitch inspection at Prescot too and, as the rain continues to fall during the morning, I begin to fear the unthinkable – an Easter Monday with no football - until finally the announcement arrives that the game will go ahead.

We arrive in plenty of time for this one with umbrellas in hand, walking past a gaggle of Prescot kids behind one goal. One of them informs us we're going to get 'smoked'. When the game starts, they begin bouncing around a bit like those kids at the FC St Helens game only less vigorously. Then again, it's not as cold.

The rain's still falling, though, and the pitch doesn't look in great condition. Despite this, the two sides manage to produce a hugely entertaining game of football, an experience only rendered less pleasurable by the disembodied transatlantic voice that for some reason Prescot use for their announcements, complete with exaggerated proclamations in the kind of drawl that belongs firmly in American sports and should they there, where I can't hear it. Having been forced to endure that horrible purple kit again against Nantwich, it's good to see us back in yellow and green, with Prescot changing instead into their faded pale blue and grey affair that looks like it's been rescued from a skip.

Sartorial observations aside, it's hard to argue that a draw isn't a fair result but there's some disappointment that Runcorn, who lead twice, fail to hang on for the win.

The first goal comes from a penalty decision following a clear handball by the Prescot defender. O'Mahoney dispatches the spot-kick firmly into the top corner but the Runcorn players protest that it was deliberate handball to prevent a goal and should have been a red. The ref's decision is yellow. Prescot equalise before half time then O'Mahoney restores Runcorn's lead again with a header from a corner before Smith drills in a shot from the edge of the box to equalise again. Later, footage of a reckless Jacques Welsh challenge, for which he receives a yellow card, appears online with the suggestion that it should have been a red. I'm standing right next to the tackle and it clearly isn't a sending-off offence, though I wouldn't go as far as other Runcorn observers, who say it isn't even a foul. As is often the case in football, being a partisan fan can leave you in a frenzy of perceived injustice that only adds to your other frustrations, and frankly there are enough of those already. I may be in the minority on this but I reckon the ref gets both contentious decisions right. The muddy pitch makes tackles like the Welsh one look far worse than they really are. Most fans will tell you they don't want to see unnecessary red cards ruining the game, until the offence occurs against their team and the howls for a sending off begin.

The game against Prescot on Boxing Day was the best I've seen at the APEC this season and, despite the conditions, this one, helped by the ref keeping it 11v11, probably matches it. Elsewhere, are today crowned champions, while Witton Albion comfortably see off old rivals Northwich Victoria, confirming their relegation.

In El Civico, Wythenshawe Town come from behind to beat Wythenshawe in front of 1200 fans, meaning automatic promotion is now in the hands of the former. Rylands beat Marine 3-0 and sit second in the Northern Premier League Premier Division. In a game that attracts 4500 spectators, Altrincham beat Oldham Athletic 1-0 and are now fourth, looking a very good bet for the play-offs.

But all of this is overshadowed by the terrible news that came in overnight from Winsford United, whose player Ross Aikenhead has died at the age of just 24. We saw Ross score for Winsford at Barnton earlier in the season and the same two teams play there in the league today, the players requesting that the game goes ahead to honour his memory. They lose 4-2 but the scoreline is incidental: a truly terrible season for Winsford, who still sit in the relegation places and risk relegation to the county leagues, is ending in an unimaginably horrible way. It's a cliché to say these things put football into perspective, but that doesn't make it any less true.

Attendance: 1203

Saturday 6 April

APEC Taxis Stadium, Runcorn

Northern Premier League West Division

Runcorn 2 Mossley 0

We hammered Mossley 3-0 at their place in the autumn but the nerve ends are raw for their visit today. Defeat in this one would find us in serious arse-twitching territory.

Last time I saw Mossley was that surprise walloping at Widnes. Since then, they've limped to an unimpressive position in the lower half of the table: safe from relegation and playing out the remainder of a disappointing season. They always bring a good following, though, and it's no different today. I've ended up volunteering to scan in the season tickets at the gate adjacent to the main turnstile today and can see the Mossley faithful arriving there, with the relaxed yet bored demeanours of fans performing a role that was laid out for them earlier in their lives and is now, in the absence of anything else, ritualistic. I know it well.

The game is played in a swirling wind. My bucket hat flies off my head twice, until I decide I'd better shove it in my pocket lest it end up causing mayhem on the field of play. I have visions of Billy Paynter giving an interview at the end of the season: 'I think we still believed, you know, until that game against Mossley when the hat blew across Brookie's face when he was about to tap in from close range...'

Thankfully, there's no hat or any other impediment in view when Brookie, looking more like the Ryan Brooke of old today, heads Runcorn into the lead. The wind means any chance of seeing a decent game of football is unlikely, but a Runcorn win is assured when Anthony Kay hooks a stray ball into the net from the edge of the box just after half-time. From there, Runcorn control the game, Doyle and recent recruit from Hednesford Thompson forming a promising partnership in midfield, to run out deserved winners.

Billy Paynter is clearly determined to ensure we stay focused and, after bringing on Molloy to join Brooke in attack, he loudly informs them that, if they can't play together, they'll 'go on the fucking wing'. As threats go it's not exactly Joe Pesci in *Goodfellas* but it does suggest the idea of them playing as a double spearhead has been considered and, now that Brookie looks as sharp as ever again, you wonder what havoc the two of them could wreak on opposing defences if we can get it to work.

There's good news from Prescot: Hednesford's resurgence is probably happening too late to save them from relegation but they come away with a point, which means Runcorn lead Prescot by +1 goal difference going into the last three games.

Attendance: 585

Tuesday 9 April

Wincham Park, Wincham

Mid-Cheshire Senior Cup Final

Witton Albion 2 Northwich Victoria 1

The rain gets steadily worse throughout the morning. It's the time of the year when many clubs, who've succumbed to deluge after frozen pitch after deluge during the winter months, are attempting to play catch-up, often in vain. The North West Counties League is supposed to finish the weekend after next with play-offs scheduled for the following weekend, but in the Premier Division, one club, Colne, still have nine games to play. The league has extended the season by for another week, but even with that it's a packed programme of matches and Colne, should they win most of them, could cause a logistical problem by qualifying for the play-offs on the date when the play-off semi-finals are being played. Or, if this weather keeps up, sometime in June.

In the same league, Barnoldswick and Ramsbottom still have six to fit in and are scheduled to play each other tonight but, as the clock ticks past midday, it's announced that this is another match that's bitten the dust. Charnock Richard and Isle of Man have eight more and seven more to play respectively and I don't need to go into what logistical problems may befall the latter in attempting to get them played in the next eleven days, or even the next eighteen.

It's given rise again to a discussion about whether leagues at this level should play through the summer, adopting a Scandinavian timetable to minimise the potential for winter weather running amok through league programmes in this way. I can see one potential benefit: another three months in the year in which I can watch football matches, and if the alternative is more of those improving but still wrong artificial pitches then I'm raising my hand in favour of summer football should anyone ask me, which they won't.

Witton announce a pitch inspection for 3.45 and my hopes aren't high until, in early afternoon, we begin to see sunlight peeking through what earlier was just a wall of ominous grey cloud. A further inspection is scheduled for 6 o'clock and in the intervening hours the hard wind drives away the clouds like Olly Molloy brushing off an opposition central defender and sunlight begins to bathe this corner of England. The match is on.

I admit to having no real interest in who wins the Mid-Cheshire Senior Cup, aside from a slight favouring of underdogs Northwich Vics. That they *are* underdogs when for so many years they held dominion over Albion in the mid-Cheshire pecking order is one of many kicks to the gut their fans now take on a regular basis. Tonight delivers another.

These two teams are the original Northwich rivals. Local animosity between them was compounded, Brian Howman recalls, in the early days of the Northern Premier League. 'Witton were really pissed off that when the Northern Premier League was founded, it was a one club-one town rule. Witton Albion stayed in the Cheshire League and Northwich Vics came up.' Worse than that, it was widely rumoured that Vics were influential in establishing this policy. Witton had been members of the Cheshire League since it was founded in 1920 right up to 1979, when they were finally allowed to be promoted to the NPL in the year that Vics went up into the Alliance Premier League.

We make the most of the occasion – it's a final, after all - visiting the museum before the game starts, browsing the packed-in memorabilia and musing that other grounds could easily do this: devote a corner of the place to honouring the strange obsession held by most of us who visit these parts. It's great browsing through the pennants and programmes of yesteryear but the highlight for me is a photograph of Witton's mascot Willy. For me, the best mascots always look a bit deranged with the potential to make the children they're supposed to entertain recoil in terror. Willy looks like some Frankenstein experiment involving Jimmy Savile and Eddie Large and has surely had a starring role in a many a Northwich child's nightmares down the years. 7/10 for design but a solid 10 for bed-wetting potential.

I look towards the gathered Vics fans. They retain the defiance of that heady win over 1874 in the semi-final, but there's something about them that tells you these are people who've had the stuffing knocked out of them over and over again: the civil war that erupted within their club, subsequent relegation from the Northern Premier League and, this year, relative exile into the Midland League where they're playing clubs they have no historical relationship or rivalry with. I suppose they're getting to see quite a few new grounds, but that modest thrill will have been tempered by losing at almost all of them. They currently sit in the bottom three, that win over 1874 a rare triumph in yet another depressing season. Then again, visiting any club with a ground anywhere is a constant reminder that their club, who once boasted one of the most iconic stadia in the country, hasn't even got one.

Their animated manager from that night has now moved on. Steve Pickup is now baiting the ref and complaining to the fans behind the dugout at Barnoldswick Town, a place with a severe identity crisis stemming from the fact that it used to be in Yorkshire but was dumped in Lancashire following the great county boundary upheavals of 1974. Clinging on to their Yorky heritage by any means possible, they still compete in the West Riding Senior Cup.

Witton exceed even their high standards with the programme they've produced for the occasion. For two quid, you get the usual densely packed information, along with a range of features plus a detailed history of the Mid-Cheshire Cup and, anticipating the possibility of a penalty shoot-out, a profile of every Witton goalkeeper who has ever saved a penalty in one.

The game itself is open and competitive. As with the semi-final against 74, there is no hint of Vics' lowly position in the Midland League in their performance and they show a willingness to attack Witton from the start. There's a good flow to the game, both sides launching counter attacks in the kind of to and fro you want from a derby but don't always get. It's a frenzied context, against a backdrop of Witton fans going through a long-rehearsed repertoire of songs about how shit their opponents are, punctuated by the sad moan of a Northwich fan to the left of us who keeps yelling 'How many times, ref?' into the night, his howling tone unmistakeably that of a long-suffering fan who has had about all he can take but carries on taking it.

It's goalless at half-time and it's clearly going to take something special to break the deadlock. It comes ten minutes into the second half when Duckworth powers into the Northwich area to unleash a shot into the far corner and give the home side the lead. Northwich strike back quickly with Lloyd dispatching a lethal shot from outside the box. The atmosphere is cranked up further. This is a great game to be a neutral at.

At this point we're actively considering the prospect of penalties. Tim believes Witton's quality will see them through a shoot-out, but I reckon the Vics keeper has got a few penalty saves in him. Barely have I expressed this confidence in his abilities when he produces the game's only real error to give Witton victory, failing to deal with a high ball in the area and allowing Brazel to pounce to bring Witton what will be their only silverware of the season: indeed, the only silverware that's heading to anyone in this part of the world.

As at St Helens and Prescot, there are bouncing kids behind the goal but this time it's the ball-boys, who are all concentrated in the area and who I don't see doing any actual ball-boying during the game. We leave before the trophy presentation – such things have no real meaning for neutrals – the chanting of 'green and white shite' giving way to a drum-accompanied 'championes'. Championes indeed: the success of being the only team in the Northwich area not to have had a truly miserable season.

Attendance: 692

Wednesday 10 April 2024

More rain.

I consider the possibility of going to watch Winsford United in their scramble to remain in North West Counties League Division One South, but their game has been moved north – to Burscough – and I decide to pass. Meanwhile, more games are being called off and there's further rain forecast for the rest of the week. As a child, I often wished for a never-ending football season...

Friday 12 April

DCBL Stadium, Widnes

Northern Premier League West Division

Widnes 4 Prescot Cables 2

Both Prescot and Widnes must be pinching themselves they're even involved in this battle for the play-offs, especially the latter who, if it weren't for Skelmersdale's stadium deficiencies, wouldn't even be in this league. As a side note, Skelmersdale have just been relegated after one season in the North West Counties League Premier Division. It's worth remembering sometimes just how shitty things can quickly become for clubs and fans at this level: this time last season Skem were in a healthy mid-table position in our league, assured of being there this season, or so they thought. Also, today it was announced that Premier League clubs have spent over £400 million in the last two transfer windows on agents' fees alone. Join the dots.

Although I don't really want Widnes to make the play-offs, because it just seems wrong, my priority is for Runcorn to grab that second place which will mean home games in the play-offs and dropped points for Prescot would be a huge help. Although the topsy turvy nature of this league means it's hard to make such a statement with any certainty, this should be the trickiest game of what's left of their run-in: not only have Widnes proved unexpectedly formidable opponents for many teams this season, but they also play on this artificial pitch from hell...a skiddy nightmare of a playing surface where I saw Runcorn succumb meekly last season; I couldn't make it to the game here this season but Tim tells me we were even worse. I listened to the radio coverage where Sam and Jack declared the performance so bad they couldn't think of a single candidate for man of the match.

Widnes prove difficult opponents for Prescot too. Again, there's a contrast of styles: Prescot playing the ball around through the midfield and the home side going more direct. The latter approach pays off when a long ball finds James Steele in space and his finish is clinical. Widnes then go two up after Sean Miller converts a penalty following a handball in the area that only the ref seems to spot.

Then something bizarre happens. The usual Widnes crowd has been massively bolstered by travelling Prescot fans: there are clearly more of them here than Widnes supporters. At least until the second goal goes in, when literally dozens just up and leave. I regularly see football fans leave before the end of games, but this mass exodus well before half-time is a completely new experience. To me, you support your side and stay even if you're six down, but to leave when you're two goals behind this early in the game?

Prescot's players clearly possess a belief those fans lack. James Foley gets a goal back soon after the restart from the penalty spot, this time after a handball that everyone sees except, apparently, a small group of Widnes fans, who are howling at some fictional injustice. Just after half time they're level following a huge error from the Widnes keeper who seems to take the ball above his head with some comfort only to lose control, scramble around on the ground after it for a bit, then leave it to Kyle Sambor, who taps in,

The remaining Prescot fans are jubilant. 'Two nil up and you fucked it up,' they taunt. Well, not quite yet, as it turns out. They sing throughout the game, a predictable repertoire including the now tiresome 'football in a library' chants. One lone Prescot fan does attempt to be more original, improvising songs that no one joins in with, unsurprisingly because they just don't work: one is a stream of consciousness ramble about a Widnes move that breaks down while another to the tune of *Anarchy in the UK* ends with the somewhat anti-climactic 'Steve Daley, he wears yellow well'.

That's the boss, of course. Prescot's players are in that rank pale blue and grey kit again. Despite their lack of aesthetic appeal, for a while in the second half they look likely to win what has become an absorbing contest, cutting off the Widnes supply route and forcing them to play through them, which they can't do. 'We are the Bulls,' the Cables fans chant and 'We are the Wools,' sing the Widnes kids: it comes out sounding like one big, confused bundle of words. The visitors spurn chances to go ahead before they visibly begin to tire and Widnes strike after a move that appears to have run its course, only for Steele to arrive unmarked and fire in at the far post.

Prescot look beaten and they are. Their defence is all over the place as substitute Sharif Deans weaves through them to make it four for Widnes with two minutes remaining. You'd have thought any fans with a player called 'Sharif' would have created something around *Rock the Casbah* but the Widnes fans' repertoire lies somewhere between limited and non-existent.

Things have turned sour for the Prescot fans and a group of their kids start chanting invitations to meetings in the car park for some manly tussling after the game. Listen lads, I know some of the guys who live in the estate surrounding this ground and if they get wind of anything kicking off you won't be going beyond Whiston Hospital on your route home, put it that way.

The result keeps Widnes' play-off hopes alive but, more importantly, it's a huge boost to Runcorn's chances of grabbing that position at the head of the play-off pack. We see Billy Paynter, who's been in the crowd, on the way out and I voice my optimistic thoughts to him. He looks pleased but slightly bewildered: somewhere between 'wow, aren't our fans great?' and 'fuck, these people don't seem to have lives outside of football.'

Attendance: 601

Saturday 13 April

Potteries Park, Stoke-on-Trent

Northern Premier League West Division

Hanley Town 0 Runcorn Linnets 0

Driving down to Staffordshire, I ask Tim what he thinks is the worst game we've seen this season. I think eventually we agree it's the Runcorn-Nantwich stalemate on Good Friday.

Getting back into the car after the match, we agree we have a new winner.

This is dire. Runcorn fail to produce a decent chance in 90 minutes against a Hanley side who also have little to offer. It's hard to remember a proper shot on goal, even after James Askey's sending off for the home team with eight minutes left.

Hanley are far enough above the relegation zone to have essentially nothing to play for. They beat us at the APEC early this season, getting a second half winner in a forgettable contest. It's a familiar story today, only worse, and, although we come away with a point, we leave the ground with the sense of an opportunity missed weighing far more heavily.

Results elsewhere mean the play-off situation is tighter than ever. Witton and City of Liverpool both enjoy good wins and Bootle get a point at Leek. Should CoL win their rearranged game with Bootle on Wednesday night, there'll be just three places separating second and sixth and a win for Widnes at Runcorn next Saturday could bring them into the fight as well.

Elsewhere, both Wythenshawe clubs fail to win in the battle for promotion from the NWCL Premier. Bury's match is postponed but they've suddenly found themselves in pole position and will go up automatically if they win their two remaining games. Meanwhile, there are dramatic scenes on the last weekend of North West Counties League First Division North where South Liverpool need a win to leapfrog Ilkley Town into the final play-off berth. Ilkley are walloped 5-0 by Holker Old Boys and South Liverpool, three-up at half-time are coasting at AFC Blackpool. But Blackpool fight back and it's 3-3 going into injury time only for South to grab a late winner and book a play-off semi-final at Atherton LR.

After the shite-fest we've just been watching, it feels like this is all happening in another world.

Attendance: 242

Wednesday 17 April

Cowley International College, St Helens

North West Women's Regional League D1 South

FC St Helens Women 3 Runcorn Linnets Ladies 2

Cowley International College itself is easy enough to find but that doesn't mean we have an easy time locating where the game's taking place.

We're parked down the side-street the satnav led us to and walk in a large rectangle, pausing at the school gates to ask a teacher carrying a pile of books and papers to his car where the match is. He points across to a load of deserted rugby fields, which is the only place he can think of where they might be any kind of sports game, but there isn't a set of football goalposts in sight, let alone any players.

Eventually we give up and decide to walk back to the car. It's only when we reach it that we see the floodlights towering over us. The pitch is on the other side of the fence.

When we arrive, the Runcorn coaching staff are pleased to see our yellow and green hats and scarves – the only ones in evidence – and one of them asks us to come and join them. There's no dugout. FC St Helens Women usually share the Windleshaw Sports ground with the men's team but they're struggling to catch up on a fixture list decimated by the winter's bad weather. As a result, they're trying to fit in fixtures whenever and wherever they can, which is what brings us here.

Wythenshawe Women have dominated the league this season. They're unbeaten with a goal difference of more than +100 and have had the title in the bag for ages, frequently running up huge winning margins. They decided to go semi-professional this season, which has pretty much put them in a league of their own. Runcorn Linnets and FC St Helens occupy the pack of teams trailing forlornly in their wake, effectively competing for who finishes fourth and fifth.

It's a competitive encounter. While the home side constantly threaten a vulnerable-looking Runcorn defence, it's Runcorn who score twice in the first half to take a two-goal lead. It looks anything but secure, however, and the home side come out with greater intensity in the second half, taking the game to Runcorn and replying with three goals. There's a late call for a penalty from the Runcorn fans – basically us and a few players' parents in a crowd that a headcount reveals to total 28 – and the coaching staff are going mad over it, but the ref waves play on and the chance of a late equaliser is gone.

Those who don't pay much attention to the women's game often seem to believe that essentially teams at this level are just playing for fun and beyond that it doesn't mean very much. Yet at the top level of men's football, I've seen end of season games that resemble pre-season friendlies. Tonight, winning to secure fourth place rather than fifth meant everything to two groups of unpaid players, many of whom had come here straight from a full-time job to give everything in front of 28 supporters on an all-weather school pitch.

Saturday 20 April

APEC Taxis Stadium, Runcorn

Northern Premier League West Division

Runcorn Linnets 3 Widnes 2

We call it El Clasitol.

Not one but two toll bridges now divide the towns of Runcorn and Widnes; and much else does too. I've never had time for the local rivalries that persist between the two communities: I grew up in Widnes and my dad worked in Runcorn; I've worked, drunk, sung and done many other things on both sides of the Mersey too. The two towns have endured decades of deprivation and in my view any anger should be directed at those responsible for creating it. C'est la vie, as nobody ever says on either side of the river.

Though rivalry on the pitch is a crucial element in football, there are times when clubs need to stand together. Earlier in the week the FA announced it was scrapping replays in the FA Cup from Round One onwards. Whether Runcorn will ever progress to Round one of the Cup is debatable but not really the point. For clubs outside the top two divisions, a cup replay against bigger opposition can provide a massive financial boost. The decision was taken without any wider consultation and rides roughshod over the interests of the hundreds of clubs for whom participation in the competition can provide a lifeline. Clubs at this level, whatever rivalries they have on the field, have a common interest in coming together to fight the game's authorities who clearly have little interest in their fortunes, whatever platitudes are dished out about 'underdogs' 'giant-killing' and the 'magic' of the cup.

Among the many statements opposing the proposal, the one from those famous giant-killers Altrincham, recalling the club's third round replays against Everton and Spurs in the seventies, perhaps puts it best: 'Those games weren't just transformational from a financial basis for a club like Alty but were historic for us. Our kids hear about them. The pictures from those games adorn our halls. The recollections of those memories bounce loudly off the walls of every pub in town. The participants in those games will forever be local legends.'

The reasons the FA trot out for the decision are tiresomely familiar: that looking after those at the very top – in football's case the small number of clubs who play in Europe – will lead to benefits for everyone. It's a lie we've been hearing since the 1980s and it stands even more exposed now. The borough of Halton had the highest unemployment rate in the north-west in the early eighties and survived through the strength of its communities, not through anything central government or big business did. The same is true of football: clubs at this level have survived despite, not because of, the actions of those at the top of the footballing food chain. The disparity is all too evident in Pep Guardiola's rant after the FA Cup semi-final today when he bemoans Manchester City having to play their game three days after their Champions League Quarter-Final. Some teams outside the football league have had to play three or four games this week, their players usually working full-time in addition to that. It feels like a week in which the gulf between the game's elite clubs and the rest has never been more evident.

It's a good thing Pep Guardiola doesn't manage Charnock Richard. Aside from salary considerations and the lack of bankrolling from an oil-rich state, he'd be responsible for a squad who are currently having to play six games in nine days, leading up to the play-offs which have now been put back to Saturday 27 April: should they successfully negotiate that gruelling schedule, they'll still have a chance of playing in them. When they successfully negotiate five of them, the scheduled play-off date is further delayed while Charnock sort out their remaining business at 'home' to Pilkington (home, in this case, meaning, out of necessity, the neutral ground of Burscough).

They beat Pilkington, which means Kendal Town, who all this time have been biting their nails and delaying whatever plans semi-professional players have at this stage of the year, are denied a play-off berth and it's Charnock who will visit Wythenshawe Town in the semi-final the following Tuesday, the latter's neighbours Wythenshawe having edged out Bury to win the league. Unlike Guardiola's outburst, little media attention is given to Charnock manager Ryan Donnellan's headaches, nor to Kendal's Jimmy Marshall, who will presumably now be phoning his lads to tell them that the end of the season they didn't celebrate because they thought it wasn't yet the end of the season was, it turns out, the end of the season.

Other events during the week – which see Bootle docked a point for fielding an ineligible player and then lose their rescheduled grudge match to City of Liverpool – leave Runcorn, despite that abject performance at Hanley, in second place going into the last two games. A win here will confirm a place in the play-offs; two wins will ensure we play at home, something which could mean a huge financial boost for the club as well as a decent stab at promotion.

Widnes, meanwhile, still have three games to play and, the way results have been going, probably need to win all of them to secure a play-off spot. They seem to have brought about half their normal home crowd with them today and a good turnout for Runcorn brings the attendance close to the 1000 mark.

Billy Paynter's presence at the Widnes v Prescot Cables game will have told him a lot about the importance of winning the midfield battle against them. Fortunately, the Runcorn midfield three of Thompson-Doyle-Welsh are in dominant mood today and, after Anthony Kay's header gives Runcorn the lead in the second minute, they supply the bedrock for an efficient and dominant first half performance. We should have the game wrapped up by half-time but Thompson, Saxon and O'Neill all spurn good chances and it seems our wastefulness in front of goal could, not for the first time this season, be our undoing when Widnes draw level with a superb strike from Miller early in the second half.

Runcorn respond well and Thompson, through on goal again, makes no mistake this time when he just gets enough on the ball to prod it past the advancing Widnes keeper. Soon it's 3-1, substitute Adam Moseley latching on to a long ball in the area to finish decisively.

A second excellent strike from Miller deep in injury time gives Widnes a further consolation goal. Ello rues their defensive frailty after the game but, in truth, the scoreline flatters the visitors: a couple of brilliant goals have made it look respectable, but this was one of Runcorn's most convincing displays of the season. The play-off place finally secured, we travel to the final game of the regular season knowing a win will give us second-place and home advantage in the semi-final.

Attendance: 981

Saturday 27 April

Townfield Lane, Barnton

Northern Premier League West Division

1874 Northwich 0 Runcorn Linnets 5

The regular season ends here, on the slope of Barnton in the late April sunshine. It's 74's last game in the Northern Premier League, for now, of course, but they're likely to be playing at Barnton for some time to come. 'We have a great relationship with Barnton,' said Vicki England, who talks about how the two clubs are looking to the future, working together on ground improvements. There are limits to how much this can help 74 though. 'Ultimately, there's only so much you can do in terms of match day fundraising. We work brilliantly with Barnton but there are certain things where you think if we had our own social club, or had our own events and functions and fundraising, instead of having to hire somewhere...I know at Runcorn, that's a big part of it. Years ago, with the old Runcorn FC, the Linnets Club burnt down and that was a big source of the income and that was really the start of the end of the club.'

She's right, of course, and, although Runcorn Linnets now have a social club and bar, it isn't ever going to provide the support the old Linnets Club did. Consider, then, the impact of a club having no such resource and you get some idea of the additional difficulties faced by clubs without their own ground. Despite that, Vicki retains an optimism familiar to football fans who've been through bad times, together with a refreshing sense of pride in how the club has conducted itself during this nightmare season.

'We've known for a while what our fate would be. We don't moan about things. We've got a plan and we're just looking at next year. Ultimately, we've not been good enough but one of the things I'm most proud about is how we've just got on with it.'

Vicki's attitude encapsulates the optimism you need to keep going at this level. Even during the worst of seasons there is a germ of satisfaction to be found in battling displays, obdurate defending, sparks of quality that provide reasons to hope that things might be about to improve. Without that, English footballing culture wouldn't run as deeply as it does and clubs like 1874 Northwich, or indeed Runcorn Linnets, wouldn't survive. Bad times are part of the experience. Defiant optimism, sometimes based on the most meagre evidence, is what keeps us going.

Although Runcorn need a win here to make sure of second place, a draw could suffice if Prescot fail to win. Linnets fans, who have as expected turned out in large numbers, are expecting nothing less than a comfortable win. 74 haven't won a league game since October so many assume this will be a routine march to the runners-up spot for Runcorn, and it is. Many Runcorn fans are in fancy dress so, when Doyle opens the scoring, it's the cue to set off on a conga around the stadium, led by mascot Ron Corn and a trail of assorted jockeys, dinosaurs, aliens, blokes in lederhosen and a green and yellow pope, among others.

Their jubilation increases when Molloy adds two more before half time. Early in the second half, Moseley makes it four and Runcorn begin to make substitutions presumably with one eye on Tuesday night's play-off semi-final which, we now know, will be at the APEC. Gumbs adds a fifth before the end.

It would be churlish not to extend some admiration to 1874 Northwich as they continue to try to make a game of it even when the game is out of reach. Their heads have never dropped, Vicki tells me, despite many players leaving the club during the season. 'We've ended up with wonderful lads that give so much effort and I'm so proud of them. It's easy to walk away and the lads that we've got haven't.'

That's certainly in evidence today. Despite the scoreline, the home side continue to go forward and try to create chances even though, as is often the case with a side in their position, nothing comes off. We applaud them off at the end but understandably they look like a group of players desperate to get into the changing rooms and out of this season.

City of Liverpool draw with Witton, which is enough to see them grab the final play-off place on goal difference. For the second year running Witton finish just one place outside the play-offs and it's City of Liverpool we'll face in the semi-final. A lot of the fancy dress contingent stay behind celebrating but we head for the exit – there's still a lot of work to be done if we're to finish the season without the play-off disappointments of the last two years. There's optimism that home advantage will make a difference this time but, having won play-off semi-finals away from home in the last two seasons, we know that this is far from guaranteed.

Driving home, we pass Nantwich fans heading out of Leggies, the pub on the corner near Widnes' ground, in the direction of their coach. They've fallen short of the play-offs but finished their campaign with a win and look happy. A part of me almost envies them their uncomplicated end to the season and the simple pleasure of looking ahead to the next one.

Attendance: 560

Tuesday 30 April

APEC Stadium, Runcorn

Northern Premier League West Division Play-Off Semi-Final

Runcorn Linnets 0 City of Liverpool 2

The aim, of course, was to secure home advantage in the play-offs this year and we've secured it against a side for whom the whole concept of home advantage is something beyond their experience.

Expectations are high but tempered with caution. Defeat in the play-off finals in the last two seasons – first to Marine, then to Workington – occurred after we'd taken the lead to raise hopes in both games. City of Liverpool, meanwhile, have defied the odds to be in this position. Last season, they narrowly avoided relegation and this season's better form has, of course, been achieved despite the eviction by Bootle. To their players, every game has been an away game: why should this one be anything to fear? Especially as they've beaten us at the APEC twice already this season.

The game is all-ticket and, with hours to go to kick off, the club reports it's a sellout. At the very least, it will bring in much-needed revenue, but we want and expect more.

I've volunteered to oversee the car parking operation, which basically means getting everyone to park close enough together to allow for as many vehicles as possible to get into space that is normally ample but today will be limited. With an hour to go until kick off, we've already started filling up the overfill car park at the back and, shortly after that, I phone Tim, who's at the gates, to ask him to close them.

I enter the ground to find my normal spec has, predictably, been taken up but I manage to squeeze in anyway. Tim emerges just before kick-off: he'd been standing in front of the closed car park gates repeatedly fielding questions like 'Where the hell can I park then?' and 'Do Aldi clamp?'. The hum of conversation means there's a literal buzz in the atmosphere. Of anticipation? Fear? Exhilaration? All this and more.

Football doesn't need light shows or pyrotechnic cliches to generate atmosphere. Even a ground with a 1600 capacity can become an arena crackling with energy and the APEC is doing that tonight.

Maybe the tension transmits itself to those on the pitch, or maybe it's just time for another of those underwhelming displays, because the team basically don't turn up. After the Leek defeat, it's been all about securing second place and the home tie which, we hoped, would give us the advantage that would make a difference this season. I think many of us – including me – allowed ourselves to believe that would be enough. If such a script exists, the players haven't read it and neither have City of Liverpool.

As in the Liverpool Senior Cup game, CoL look in control from the first minute. Thompson and Doyle –both immense in recent games – are overrun in midfield and the pace of the Purps' forwards is forcing the Runcorn defence deeper until the inevitable happens and Morris gives them the lead before the break. Soon after half-time, Ryan Brooke hits the post but it's a rare goalscoring opportunity: there's none of the sustained pressure that encourages the belief that we'll get many more.

Substitutions are made in the second half, Thompson's withdrawal perhaps an admission that the player who has steadied us so effectively in recent games hasn't managed to bring that composure tonight. Molloy comes close for Runcorn: it's a rare chance and, once missed, you feel that might be fatal. It is. CoL immediately go up the other end and Morris scores his second of the game.

So many football seasons end in disappointment. There's not even the temporary adrenaline rush, this year, of getting to the final and taking the lead before it all falls apart, just a huge sense of anti-climax. I know I'll wake tomorrow morning and there'll be a few brief moments of relaxation before I remember what happened and I'll face a day of endlessly replaying the events of tonight in my head.

I expect many of the players will be doing that too.

'This year was a real good chance,' says Sam Phillips ruefully, echoing the thoughts of so many Runcorn fans. 'The plan was to play Ryan Brooke as a left-winger against Michael Simpson,' he tells me. Simpson was part of the Runcorn team that won the North West Counties League so many around the club know his strengths and weaknesses well. 'The game plan was to get the ball to James Hooper to cross to the far post and for Brooke to knock it down. But the game plan wasn't executed until the 51st minute.' Presumably that followed a not unexpected rollocking from Billy at half time. 'In the 51st minute Brooke beat Simpson in the air and hit the post.'

This rare attempt to apply the agreed tactics brought one of only a couple of good chances in the game, vindicating Paynter's approach, Sam believes. 'The players didn't execute the tactics that were put in place.'

Alan Pardew once said something interesting – I think it was just the once – about taking West Ham and Crystal Palace to FA Cup Finals, losing and then finding the next season that many of the players seemed unable to recapture the form that had taken them there. Some, he felt, were dwelling on things they might have done differently in the biggest game of their careers; others, who hadn't started, perhaps harboured a feeling that, had they made the starting eleven, they might have had a chance to influence proceedings rather than sitting frustrated on the sidelines.

Will Ryan Brooke be running that second half chance over and over in his head? Are Will Saxon and Eden Gumbs wondering whether an earlier introduction from the bench might have allowed them to get Runcorn on the front foot to prevent us from going behind? Part of the problem, Pardew said, is it's suddenly the end of the season: there's no chance to work through those the issues on the training ground or have a proper debriefing, just a shower and a shake of the hands and 'see you in July'.

That's how it feels now. 'See you next season,' I say to the guy who's been suffering next to me for the last two hours. We stay to applaud City of Liverpool off at the end. Some of them applaud back. Any disappointment within the ground is directed squarely at our own team. CoL deserve their win.

This is what I don't get about football. You seem to think you have better players than them...

This is not a good time.

I was just saying, surely in three games with better players you would at least...

Really not the time.

OK, so suppose you could press a button that means you finished outside the play-offs this season and didn't get a chance to play that match...

Give me the fucking button.

'I hope they win the final,' says a Runcorn supporter behind me as we leave the ground.

'So do I,' says his mate, 'because I'm sick of the sight of them.'

Attendance: 1600

May 2024

'We're seeing it as an adventure.'

Wednesday 1 May

The Swansway Stadium, Nantwich

Cheshire FA Women's Cup Final

Runcorn Linnets Ladies 0 Stockport Co. Ladies 9

I'm sitting in the main stand, transfixed by the sign opposite me: an advertisement for 'Ice Cream Vans'. Thinking about it, I suppose there must be a company that responds to the market's need for ice cream vans. I just can't imagine that very few people who come to this ground, either today or more regularly to watch Nantwich Town, will have need of one.

I'm not going to dwell on that. It was just one of the things that flashed through my mind while trying to avoid what was happening on the pitch.

It wasn't unexpected. Stockport are in the National League Division One North, rubbing shoulders with clubs like Leeds, Hull and Barnsley. One of the driving forces behind them is Lesley Wright, currently their membership secretary but a woman with a long history in the game, first with the pioneering Manchester Corinthians and later Manchester City Ladies, when they were still called that. Now, all teams in the WSL prefer the suffix 'women', neither of which has yet been adopted by the two sides we're watching today.

There are a few hundred fans here. Those in yellow and green who have followed Runcorn down to Nantwich are outnumbered by the Stockport contingent, who have come here to win and win well against Northwest Women's Regional League Division One South opposition. There's little doubt that they will.

It's weird watching a match like this when you're a supporter of the side getting heavily beaten. You find solace in any time your team spend in their opponents' half, long for breaks in play and hope the ref doesn't add much on at the end (she does). When Stockport make substitutions, you hope they'll be reserve players or aspiring youngsters who won't be able to take full advantage of the tiring legs of the Runcorn players. No such luck: many of those who come off the bench look even better than the players they replace.

In such circumstances, there's something to admire about the way the Runcorn players' heads don't drop. They keep competing for every ball, attempt to move the ball forward on the rare occasions they have it and you hope they get something constructive out of defeat against a much better side. It's going to be months before their next game so there's plenty of time to dwell on such a defeat.

The sun has long gone down behind the 'Ice Cream Vans' sign and, metaphorically, it's finally gone down on Runcorn's season with no silverware to show for it for either of the senior sides.

Saturday 4 May

We hoped this would be the day when we celebrated promotion. Instead, we have the news that manager Billy Paynter has quit. 'After Calum, the best manager Runcorn Linnets have had,' says Sam Phillips. I wouldn't argue with that.

'I think a lot of people turned on him after that semi-final because he tried something that's never been tried before,' continues Sam. 'and ultimately it didn't pay off.' Perhaps so, but it seemed to me some elements of the Runcorn support, for whatever reason, were unwilling to give Billy the credit he deserved. 'If Dave Wild was still here, we'd already be up,' I heard one supporter mumble in the disappoint aftermath of defeat at Leek. A lone voice, perhaps, but many others nodded their agreement and, looking at the social media comments at the end of the season, many were eager to climb on that bandwagon and drive Billy towards the exit. A sad end for a decent man who took Runcorn Linnets to their highest ever league position.

I never really shared the mass outpouring of anguish over Ello's departure: although I appreciated his achievement in taking us into the NPL, I felt his tenure had run its course by that point. And Dave Wild never seemed someone who you could take to in any meaningful way. But I'll miss the sight of that tall, slightly stooped figure scowling on the fringes of his technical area, baseball cap on head.

I thought about going to the play-off final between Prescot Cables and City of Liverpool. There was an opportunity of a ticket but I decided against it. It would hurt to be there, like attending a wedding ceremony you expected to be the groom at, watching from the sidelines while someone else waltzes off with what you feel should have been yours. I think about the Half Man Half Biscuit song *RSVP*, consider what the footballing equivalent of poisoning the fondue and spiking the punch with anti-freeze might be. There isn't one, I suppose. And anyway, this is a day to stay away and let others celebrate or drown their sorrows, whichever turns out to be most appropriate.

In the other play-off final today Wythenshawe Town face Bury for a place in what we now know will be Runcorn's league again next season. There has been a lot of pre-game animosity from Bury stemming from Town's decision to allocate only 200 tickets to them. You can understand why many Bury fans are aggrieved - their average attendance is more than 15 times that figure - but the bile and threats to turn up anyway kind of vindicate Town's decision. Having visited Town's ground, I can also understand that the operation today will be a difficult one to manage.

I stay home and follow updates online. The first half of the Wythenshawe Town game yields little online activity but at Prescot, where the kick-off is delayed by 15 minutes to get everybody in, things are not going well for City of Liverpool. Danny Mitchley is withdrawn with an injury on 10 minutes and is replaced by Josh Quarless, an experienced player but one who lacks

Mitchley's mobility. My immediate thought is that it may mean Prescot have to deal with fewer problems than we did on Tuesday and, close to half-time, that becomes even more likely when a red card for Max Allen reduces the visitors to ten men. In first half injury time, Alex McNally heads Prescot into the lead.

It seems to be plain sailing from then on and, when another header – from John Murphy – makes it two, the celebrations begin for the victorious Bulls. I think back to our visit there on Easter Monday. Had we lost we might have ended up playing Bootle instead of CoL in the semi-final and then...it's pointless speculation, of course.

Meanwhile, at the Ericstan, Wythenshawe Town have taken the lead with what an online video reveals to be a stunning volley from Sam Sheridan. Bury equalise with just seven minutes left, the cue for many of their fans to invade the pitch and begin chucking flares, vindicating further the security arrangements Town had implemented.

It goes to penalties and, following from a distance, I can only speculate that nerves are playing a part because each side manages to miss three, leaving the score at 2-2 going into sudden death. Town score the next one and Bury balloon theirs over the bar. A club that had no manager, players or even kit before the start of the season has beaten a former league side whose coronation as champions, let alone play-off winners, had been thought by many to be a formality when the season started. Bury will play in the North West Counties League again next season.

There's further embarrassment for Bury when video footage emerges of their fans fighting among themselves. Not a good basis from which to argue for a bigger allocation should they be in a similar situation next season.

Bury apologise for the mayhem and Town, for their part, are keen to stress the good behaviour of most visiting fans and publicly thank the Bury fan who stayed behind after the game to help them clear rubbish from the ground. Even so, it's not a good look for a club who, in football league circles, have received a lot of sympathy following the events that led to them being in this position.

As for Wythenshawe Town, for me they're the team of the season.

Elsewhere:

I've yet to visit **Sandbach United** yet. When I do they will still be in North West Counties League Division One South as they lose their play-off semi-final to Abbey Hey.

In North West Counties League Division One North, **South Liverpool**'s reward for squeezing into the play-off places is a semi-final at **Atherton LR**. After a good run of form, LR are the clear favourites but South edge it, Elliot Owen's 78th minute penalty giving them the win that sets up a play-off final at **Ashton Town**. Understandably, South head to Ashton in optimistic mood and again keep a clean sheet. It goes to penalties, with South emerging triumphant and heading into the NWCL Premier in August. It's an amazing end to the season – a late winner to secure a play-off place, a late(ish) winner to get to the final and a victory on penalties to secure promotion. In the perverse world of football this kind of thing always feels better than winning the league by a double-figure margin.

In the Northern Premier League, there's a dramatic end of a different kind to **Warrington Rylands**' season as they confirm their interim manager as the new permanent boss only to sack him two days later after uncovering details about his criminal past. To say the least, it takes the shine off their achievement of getting into the play-offs. Whatever shine is left is removed when they lose their semi-final to Marine.

Controversy in the National League play-offs benefits **Altrincham** as Gateshead are thrown out due to uncertainty about the lease on their ground. Rules state that any club in the play-offs must meet the criteria of the football league. In Gateshead's case, a letter from the council confirming the lease also unhelpfully highlights uncertainty about it in the future. As usual, it's the club and its fans who suffer but because of it Alty get a bye in the first play-off round, setting up a semi-final at Bromley. Having sold out the away end, a fleet of coaches heads down from Altrincham to see their side take a first half lead. It doesn't last, though, and Bromley hit back with three goals in ten minutes to set up a final with Solihull Moors. Alty will be in the National League again next season.

Feeling sympathy with Gateshead fans for their ordeal, Tim and I go down to Wembley to watch them in the FA Trophy final against Solihull Moors. It's a great game which Gateshead win on penalties, unleashing pandemonium in the Gateshead end where we're sitting. I've often seen those bare-chested Geordie five-belly types on such occasions but never thought I'd be grabbed by a bunch of them, my head forced into several of those bellies in a moment of abandonment and exhilaration. I can confirm they're every bit as blubbery and sweaty as they look.

Monday 13 May

Runcorn Linnets formally advertise the new manager position so any hopes that Billy may change his mind appear to have gone. Last summer at this time we were already busy signing players for the next season, so a quick transition unquestionably has its benefits. Or is it best to take some time and wait for the right man to be available? Rumours that we're waiting for Thomas Tuchel finally to clear his desk at Bayern Munich aren't convincing the bookies. Jurgen Klopp, I believe, just laughed.

Friday 17 May

Tuchel closes the door on any possibility of a reconciliation with the Bayern board but he's procrastinated too long and misses out on the biggest managerial vacancy of the summer: veteran defender Anthony Kay is confirmed as the new Runcorn boss, a move which seems popular with much of the fanbase. On the same day, Jamie Rainford announces his departure as player-coach having failed to get on the pitch due to injury last season. His farewell message suggests he hasn't hung up his boots just yet.

In other news, next season's make-up of Northern Premier League West Division is confirmed. As expected, the two Wythenshawe clubs are promoted to it and Congleton come up from the Midland League. Stafford Rangers and Atherton Collieries also join us following relegation from the Premier Division. The league has been expanded to 22 teams, meaning four more games next season, the prospect of which excites me more than it probably should. The big surprise is a reprieve for Hednesford Town, who 'do a Widnes' and remain in the league despite occupying one of the two relegation positions.

Membership of other leagues is also confirmed. Winsford United, like Hednesford, remain in North West Counties League Division One South despite feeling the cold breath of relegation down the backs of their necks. This was more expected, as promotion/relegation from and to the county leagues involves a hell of a lot of faffing about and, for a distance, seems more like the piecing of together of a giant jigsaw with the pieces left offer shuffled into the county leagues and games against teams who have mates rather than fans following them and where the presence of an intruding dog is just as likely to hold up a game as a head injury. Runcorn Town, who survived in a similar fashion last year, move across from Division One North to join them there.

Understandably, FC St Helens are cock-a-hoop after confirmation they'll take their place in the NWCL Premier Division next season. Their delight is understandable. They'll be in the same league as Bury who, they point out, were being promoted to League One in 2014, the year FC St Helens were formed.

The division has been expanded to 24 teams, meaning a dangerously long fixture list when you consider what happened last season. Charnock Richard fans should probably put on hold any holiday plans for next summer.

Thursday 23 May

Last season's top scorer Olly Molloy won't be returning next season. It's unclear where he's heading yet but hopefully it's to play at a higher level and no one will begrudge him that. He's guaranteed a good reception back at the APEC should he return, whoever it's with. Even more of a blow, perhaps, is that Sean O'Mahoney is heading to Australia.

'After Aaron Morris, Sean O'Mahoney is the best central defender I've seen playing for Runcorn,' says Sam Phillips. Morris was one hell of a player, playing a huge role in securing promotion from the North West Counties league before his transfer to FC United. We were fortunate to get Sean to replace him but now he's gone we're left with more massive boots to fill, especially with his central defensive partner now occupying the manager's office.

Friday 24 May

Runcorn are seeking help from a construction company to refurbish the manager's office so Tony Kay can move in. It needs new flooring and a desk, apparently. Was Billy Paynter's tantrum after defeat in the play-offs that bad?

Winsford United, no doubt keen to put last season behind them as quickly as possible, have already announced their full programme of pre-season games, including a match against FC United and another against tenants Northwich Vics, with whom they continue to share a ground but not a league.

Vics will, however, line up against 1874 Northwich next season as it's been confirmed that both will complete in the Midland League Premier Division. For Vicki England, it's expected, if not entirely welcome, news.

'We're seeing it as an adventure,' she says. 'There were too many northern clubs. They need to have another northern step five, and hopefully they'll look into it. If we were to appeal, we wouldn't win so let's get on with it.'

The biggest issues, she believes, will be around attendance and player recruitment. 'Whereas players have been recruited traditionally from Liverpool, Mid-Cheshire and Manchester we're having to think we need someone with links more into the midlands because that's where some of our players are going to have to come from.'

And the lack of away support from neighbouring clubs like Witton, Nantwich and indeed Runcorn won't help to maintain attendances, as Vics have found this season.

Sunday 26 May

While the mainstream media rub their hands over the transfer window's imminent reopening and the likes of Pochettino and Tuchel take another spin on the managerial merry-go-round, Runcorn fans are more concerned about which players could be following Olly Molloy and Sean O'Mahoney out of the club this summer. While fans of bigger clubs might sweat on the possible transfers of a couple of players, at this level you can see a large proportion of the first team disappear almost overnight, as happened in the close seasons after Ello and Calum departed.

So it's a good day, relatively speaking, when it's announced that McKenzie O'Neill and Keiran Knapper – neither of whom exactly set the APEC alight last season – are the only other confirmed departures. Eleven players commit to remaining at Runcorn next season. Of those still unconfirmed, the silence around Jacques Welsh – my player of the season – remains a concern. Later in the day, we announce the signing of Luke Wall from Bala Town as Tony Kay's squad for 2024/25 begins to take shape.

Tuesday 29 May

Chester tell their social media followers to brace themselves for a major announcement, which turns out to be that their new branded bucket hats have gone on sale. Only joking, they inform their fuming fans, following it up with the news that they've signed Jack Bainbridge from Marine. Some fans suspect the bucket hat ruse was simply an attempt to inflate the news about Jack, who played all of nine times last season for a club a level below them. He is, stress Chester, 'a hard-working midfielder'. The promotion champagne's already on ice, then. Although many were placated, or at least willing to give Jack a chance, several respondents weren't impressed: 'underwhelming' was a word used in some social media comments; 'released from Southport in our division a year ago,' was the wry follow-up from Warrington Town fan Sam Shawcross on Twitter.

There's a feeling in some quarters that the bucket hat had been a more enticing prospect. Perhaps that's why Chester rushed out a picture of Jack...in the new bucket hat.

Chelsea, no doubt wondering how, or how not, to announce their new manager, may well be taking notes.

June 2024

Get the yellow and green ribbons on it…

Thursday 6 June

With Sean O'Mahoney leaving the club and Tony Kay treading the newly replaced floorboards in the manager's office, Runcorn need central defenders and their search has brought Jack Grundy to the club. Jack was in the Mossley defence when Runcorn crushed them at their place last season. Hopefully there's more to his CV than that.

Friday 7 June

Jacques Welsh commits to Runcorn for next season. Get the yellow and green ribbons on it.

Sunday 9 June

Olly Molloy's destination is confirmed. He's signed for Bamber Bridge, who struggled in the Premier Division of the NPL last season and no doubt hope big Olly can terrorise defences at he did ours. The 82 goals they conceded in 2023/24 – third worst in the league – may suggest their real problems lay elsewhere.

Friday 14 June

All you can rely on at this level of the game are verbal commitments from players that they'll be back and sometimes they change their mind. Joe Thompson, who joined Runcorn in the spring, has decided to reverse his decision to stay, which is a disappointment. Will there be more?

Saturday 15 June

It's the middle of June, the Euros kicked off yesterday and today we have the first of the pre-season fixtures, with 1874 Northwich visiting The New Saints, who win the Welsh League every year even though they don't play in Wales. TNS win 10-2. If the idea was to start early to put the bad memories of last season behind them as quickly as possible, I'm not sure it's worked out.

Runcorn have revealed that they'll be off to clubs who really do play in Wales in their pre-season. The 'European tour' they announced yesterday, which quite rightly doesn't begin until July, will involve trips to Flint Town and Colwyn Bay.

Saturday 22 June

There's a Murdishaw Massive presence in the Poland end at their Euros game in Berlin. The Poles lose to Austria and are the first team to be eliminated but they take back with them the MM's stickers and, presumably, an expanded footballing vocabulary that includes words like Kay, Saxon, Brooke and, perhaps, 'get on the shoulder of that number four, Krzysztof. I've seen fucking milk turn faster'.

Monday 24 June

The sad news comes through that former Runcorn midfielder and captain Ossie Smith has died at the age of 67. Ossie was captain of Runcorn when I attended my first game and later that season became both the first Runcorn captain and the first black player to lead a side out at Wembley. A former Manchester United youth player, Ossie joined the exodus to Altrincham a season after John Williams' exit but always remained a much-loved player at Canal Street.

He played during a time when racial abuse of black players still had a significant presence on the football terraces. Brian Howman recalls a Runcorn fan shouting 'Got a fucking burning cross for you, Ossie' when he was playing against us for Altrincham. Sadly, Ossie and other black Runcorn players of the era like Don Page and Steve Skeete had to put up with that kind of thing regularly in those days. It's one feature of the match-going experience that's thankfully improved.

Wednesday 26 June

Runcorn continue to rebuild the defence following the loss of the O'Mahoney-Kay bridgehead, signing young prospect Harvey Washington from Kidsgrove Athletic.

July 2024

'We're all going on a European tour…'

Saturday 13 July

Barton Stadium, Winsford

Pre-Season Friendly

Winsford United 1 Northwich Victoria 0

I've not done two games in one day for a while and frankly I'm not sure I'm up to it anymore, but here goes. Winsford have conveniently arranged a noon kick-off so we can get to it and then make it to Cheadle in time for Runcorn Linnets' first pre-season game.

It's a game between landlords and tenants and, both of whom have just come off seasons they'd probably rather forget. In the end, Vics comfortably avoided relegation from the Midland League Premier Division with a late-season surge of form. Winsford won't want to rely on a convoluted and largely impenetrable mathematical process to save them this time round.

Barton Stadium was originally a greyhound stadium and that's why the floodlights here are more powerful than at most other grounds: they were made to cover the outer rim of the pitch where the dogs once ran.

Behind one of the goals is a pile of wood collected for an unlit bonfire. Perhaps things were so bad last season the Winsford board were preparing to torch the place. Ominously, there's a set of medieval stocks at the other end. A visual warning to this year's playing staff? Or manager?

Both the management team and most of the players at Winsford are new this season. Last season's nightmare campaign hadn't even ended when Dom Johnson and Dean Jones were brought in from Alsager Town, bringing most of the Alsager squad with them. Alsager didn't exactly set the league alight themselves last year, finishing in 12th place, but from where Winsford were sitting in the table practically anything looked like success. It remains to be seen whether such a radical move pays off but the evidence on the pitch today looks promising.

We stand close to the away team dugout. The Northwich Vics assistant looks like the kind of guy you wouldn't want a half-time dressing down from and before long he's laying into the officials with some force. He firmly believes the goal that gives Winsford a first half lead is offside, even though it certainly isn't, and from there his frustration continues throughout a match that is littered with the kind of niggling fouls I swear you never used to get in friendly matches.

Although Vics mount a more convincing threat in the second half, Winsford run out deserved winners. You should never read too much into pre-season friendlies, which are basically glorified training sessions, but Winsford acquit themselves well. On this evidence, they might not need the mathematics this season, or the stocks.

Park Road, Cheadle

Pre-Season Friendly

Cheadle Town 1 Runcorn Linnets 0

We should be able to get from Winsford to Cheadle in plenty of time and we do, only to find both the small car park and the road leading up to it already full of cars. The website had advised there would be plenty of space, but they clearly reckoned without the Runcorn travelling support, starved of real football for two months, descending in large numbers.

We end up finding a narrow street with a small car park at the end of it and get to the ground just minutes before kick-off, though not after attempting the kind of three-point turn I've never been particularly good at and in the process steering the car into some kiddies' toys that have been left outside a nearby house. A big shirtless guy comes out and I fear I'm in for the kind of pasting my ageing joints don't hold up well to these days, but the bloke just looks at the scene with the dismayed look of somebody who this kind of thing keeps happening to. I get out and apologise but there's no real damage done, either to me or the kiddies' toys.

Despite being in the North-West Counties League, Cheadle look fitter than a Runcorn team for whom pre-season is only just beginning and should be ahead by half-time. We keep the scores level and improve after the break. Ryan Brooke heads wide to squander our only real chance of the game.

Then tiredness kicks in. We look like we're going to hang on for a goalless draw, only for Morton to pounce and seal a deserved victory for the home side. There is some grumbling at the end from the Runcorn supporters. Someone mentions a 'shambles', which it clearly isn't: it's a practice game that's done its job in getting some minutes into legs, allowing Anthony Kay to start the process of building a team equipped to compete in the important games to come.

The boss comes on as a late substitute so it seems he intends to make himself available as a player next season. He's said he would have continued playing had the management opportunity not come up so clearly feels he 41-year-old legs still have something to offer. By that point in my life, my arthritic knee was already beginning to cause me problems. Tony has clearly looked after himself a lot better than me but that's a pretty low bar.

Tuesday 16 July

Runcorn play the first game of their 'European Tour', coming from behind to win 2-1 in Colwyn Bay. Adam Moseley equalises in the second half and a trialist secures the win with what was apparently one heck of a free kick. I can't be there and am constantly thwarted in my efforts to listen to Sam and Jack's commentary through some technological sorcery I don't understand. Another glorified training session, of course, but it's always better to win.

The Murdishaw Massive tweet a prediction that Moseley will bag 15 goals next season and I don't think they'll be far out.

Elsewhere, there's turmoil at Prescot Cables where the celebrations that followed promotion have soured 'following an evaluation of the club's financial obligations', as they put it. They aren't the first team to celebrate going up only to then realise they can't afford it. Manager Steve Daley and his assistant Pete Cuminskey, the management team who saved Cables from relegation in 2023 before taking them up this year, have been released from their contracts. Club captain Lee Hollett and five other players have followed them out of the club.

Saturday 20 July

Cae Y Castell, Flint

Pre-Season Friendly

Flint Town United 2 Runcorn Linnets 2

'We're all going on a European tour'. Kind of. We're just over the Welsh border on the banks of the Dee, in the shadow of the ruins of Flint Castle. Richard II was captured there by Henry Bolingbroke on his way to losing the English throne and starving to death in prison.

Our hosts' rather cumbersome name was a result of a more harmonious meeting of rivals, the merger between Flint Town and Flint Athletic just after the second world war. They moved to their current ground in 1993, a neat stadium which is now home both to Flint and local rivals

Connah's Quay Nomads. The club's women's team and Flint Mountain FC also use what is, predictably, a synthetic pitch.

I realise this is my first visit to a Welsh football ground since Runcorn's famous FA Cup win at Wrexham in 1989. Flint Town United are back in the Welsh Premier this season having spent a season in the Cymru North League, which they won. They extend a greatly appreciated welcome to Runcorn, even arranging a minute's applause as a tribute to Ossie Smith before the game.

The game commences and Anthony Kay is more vocal on the sidelines than he was at Cheadle. 'Head the fuckin' thing,' he shouts as the ball bounces around the Flint area and Jacques Welsh does just that, nodding the fuckin' thing over the line to give Runcorn the lead. It always feels like a lead we'll struggle to hold onto though, with Flint's repeated diagonal balls frequently allowing them to find space down the left. It's one such ball that leads to their equaliser and we go into half-time level.

The introduction of Adam Moseley after the interval significantly strengthens Runcorn's attacking armoury. His presence on the left immediately forces the Flint defence to back off and he's the source of several promising attacks before his run in the area presents the chance from which James Hooper scores from close range. Sadly, Flint have already scored a second by that point and the game finishes as an enjoyable and hard-fought draw, at the end of which there remain concerns about Runcorn's defence, to say the least.

Elsewhere, the Prescot Cables managerial merry-go-round has finally gone full circle. Dave Dempsey was recruited, declared himself 'immensely proud' to be boss and then immediately quit. The result? Steve Daley, whose departure triggered this mad dance, is now back in the manager's seat.

Tuesday 24 July

APEC Stadium, Runcorn

Pre-Season Friendly

Runcorn Linnets 3 Bolton Wanderers U23s 2

Against a good team of Bolton youngsters, Runcorn put on a promising display of attacking football and secure the win courtesy of an Adam Moseley winner. Coming away from the ground, my only worry is that Bolton will have seen how good Adam is and take him back on the coach with them.

Runcorn open the scoring through a bullet header from Jacques Welsh but Bolton respond well and have most of the possession for the rest of the first half, an unfortunate own goal from Welsh bringing them an equaliser.

In the second half, Bolton take the lead. From a free kick on the right, Runcorn are slow to organise on the edge of their area and Eze finds the space to drill in a shot that squirms out of Passant's arms and over the line.

But Runcorn refuse to lie down and draw level when a corner isn't dealt with by the Bolton keeper and somehow ends up in the back of the net. Our one trialist in this game is receiving congratulations but it's not clear who got the final touch.

There's nothing messy about Moseley's winner though. Welsh, who has a busy and eventful game, does brilliantly on the right to find a way into the Bolton area and his cross is met with a thundering drive that goes in off the bar.

It leaves me in that state of pre-season optimism, replacing all doubts from the weekend, that experience tells me is unlikely to last until September.

Attendance: 382

Thursday 26 July

The identify of the trialist involved in that equaliser at Bolton is revealed: his name is Sam Carr and he's signed on for the coming season. This is good news: he looks a decent option in central defence. The bad news is he'll be on holiday for two weeks at the start of the season.

Friday 27 July

Ruskin Sports Village, St Helens

North West Counties League Premier Division

Pilkington 2 Ramsbottom United 2

FC St Helens' promotion means there'll be two teams from the town in this division for the first time ever and there's already a buzz about the return of the 'El Glassico' derby on Boxing Day. The last one was between Pilks and St Helens Town in February 2022, prior to the latter's relegation.

Pilks have been travelling in the other direction and, last season, played in the FA Cup for the first time while suddenly enjoying their status as the town's foremost football club. As their name suggests, they originated as the works team for the Pilkington glass manufacturing company, who've long since moved out of the town, leaving only the football and rugby clubs to maintain their historic link with the area.

The recent rise and expansion of Pilkington FC hasn't come without its problems. Their women's team and numerous youth teams from various age groups also share this facility and there are rugby union, rugby league and cricket teams using the sports village: in total 29 different teams now call the site home or try to. The recent closure of eight changing rooms for renovation has generated such an organisational headache that the rugby union team have had to move their games to nearby Parr Stocks despite having been residents at Ruskin for over 70 years. They aren't happy about it.

Successful expansion of participation in sport has a downside, or more specifically a headache for those who provide the facilities for it. The popularity of those facilities brings its own problems in terms of wear and tear, leading to the current scenario. The early start to the North West Counties League season can't be helping either, though it may help prevent a repeat of the fixture congestion that brought such a messy end to last season.

Ramsbottom United were relegated from Runcorn's league the season before last and their 'Rammy Ultras' flag hangs at one end of a ground, which is adjacent to a cricket pitch where a game is also taking place. In this one, Ramsbottom take the lead before Ellis fires home following an excellent solo run to equalise for the home side. It's an even contest, with both sides enjoying periods of possession before Bott looks to have won it for Pilks with a goal four minutes from time, a superb shot from the edge of the area crashing in off the bar.

But Ramsbottom aren't beaten and, deep in injury time, a corner is only cleared to the edge of Pilks' penalty area and the visitors fire home an equaliser to share the opening day spoils.

Attendance: 80

Sunday 29 July

'We're all going on a European tour...' Well, me and my wife are – to Hungary, Slovakia and Austria - which means I miss Runcorn's last two pre-season games, a 4-1 defeat to Crewe Alexandra and, more concerningly, a 1-1 draw at home to Liverpool League side MSB Woolton. Tim goes to the Woolton game and reports a hugely underwhelming performance while I placate myself by guzzling the Reketye microbrewery's Dr Banghard Porter at Beer Brothers in Budapest.

August 2024

'If I could do what those c** want me to do, I wouldn't be playing for Runcorn.'**

Tuesday 7 August

Jericho Lane, Liverpool

FA Cup Extra Preliminary Round Replay

South Liverpool 2 Handsworth 0

I drive to the ground with *Handsworth Revolution* by Steel Pulse going through my head. This is a different Handsworth – hailing from Sheffield rather than Birmingham – but once that song's in there it's not easy to get it back out.

The early rounds of the FA Cup receive close to zero media coverage but the difference between going out in the preliminary rounds and making to the First Qualifying Round can be huge for the clubs involved. Winning in the extra preliminary round guarantees £1125 in prize money: small beer, perhaps, in a world where Neymar reportedly receives a quarter of a million a season just for agreeing to wave to fans, but enough to provide some much-needed financial breathing-space for clubs like these, in the North West Counties and Northern Counties East leagues.

Not to mention the additional gate revenue, particularly when a game goes to a replay as this one has, secured by South Liverpool with a penalty in the seventh minute of injury time. And there's quite a bit of gate revenue: the attendance is more than double South's average from last season. People who say the FA Cup has lost its magic are just looking in the wrong places.

It may be overstating it a bit to say that South have a rich cup history, though that might depend on what you mean by 'cup'. They won the Welsh Cup in 1939, back when clubs within sheep-shearing distance of the Welsh border entered the competition and have bagged the NPL Challenge Cup and Presidents' Cup, the Liverpool FA Challenge Cup, Pyke Cup, the George Mahon Cup and Lancashire Challenge Trophy at various points in their history. However, the best they ever managed in the FA Cup, even in better times, was the second round, the most recent of their appearances ending in defeat to Workington back in 1964.

It's unlikely Jericho Park will witness such adventures any time soon, but those present tonight are treated to an impressive performance from the home side, who establish a two-goal lead in the first half and never look likely to relinquish it, though Handsworth more than play their part in an entertaining contest. The first goal comes from Chris Happi-Fankam, a young forward recruited from City of Liverpool in the summer whose performance leading the line is exceptional. Glendon adds a second just before half-time, finishing at the far post after an excellent counter-attacking move.

South set up an interesting encounter with Witton Albion in the next round. They'll be underdogs in that one but Witton have had had a difficult pre-season and have recently parted with their manager, so what the media like to call 'the ingredients for a cup upset' are in place, or at least some of them. Just as importantly, Witton have a decent travelling support so the ingredients for another good pay day are there too.

Attendance: 287

Saturday 11 August

I should be at Wythenshawe watching Runcorn's opening game of the league season but I'm a lazy bastard and decide to stay at home and watch the Community Shield with Sam and Jack's commentary in my ears.

Kismet has other ideas. Technical problems prevent a Bucket FM broadcast so I'm instead reliant on updates from my son, who has done what any real fan would do and gone to the game. Not that there are many updates. It's evidently a very dull encounter in which Runcorn look the better side but fail to register a shot on target as the match settles into a scrappy and disjointed goalless draw. A 0-0 result against a promoted side who lost to Pilkington in the FA Cup in midweek doesn't feel like a precursor to an assault on the championship this season, but it's early days and all that. At least the new central defensive partnership of Washington and Carr have a clean sheet under their belts.

Tuesday 14 August

APEC Stadium, Runcorn

Northern Premier League West Division

Runcorn Linnets 2 Widnes 2

First chance to work the new season ticket is also the first El Clasitol of the season. There's a tribute to Ossie Smith before kick-off. A wreath is laid in the centre circle and the minute's applause is impeccably observed. The PA system isn't working so there's no announcement about what's going on within the ground, but somehow that adds to the poignancy of the occasion: Ossie was well-known and well-loved enough for the event not to need any framing. Even younger fans who never saw him play are clearly aware of his legendary status.

The dark clouds pay a silent tribute too, and much of the game is played in heavy rain. Though Runcorn are good for their early lead – from a Brooke header – the departure of Doyle in the first half through injury means a reshuffle, with Jacques Welsh operating essentially as a lone central midfielder.

The solution seems obvious: Tony Kay needs to bring himself on in a deep-lying midfield position. It's the kind of thing that seems a no-brainer from the sidelines but presumably Tony knows how much, or more to the point how little, he's got in his legs. By the time he does come on we're well into the second half and Widnes have moved into a 2-1 lead. 'We are the Wools' chant their fans.

'Do you think they're singing it ironically?' I wonder aloud.

'Look at them,' says Tim. I see a bunch of kids mainly between 9 and 12. Point taken.

But Kay's introduction changes things and late in the game Runcorn begin to threaten the Widnes goal. It's enough for Ello, unusually quiet for much of the game, to get in trouble with the ref for mouthing off and his feigned protestations of surprised innocence – hands pointing to his chest in a 'me?' gesture – offer familiar comic relief while the introduction of Luke Wall on the right creates problems for one of his many former teams (he played for Widnes in 2021-22). But it's Moseley who secures the equaliser, his shot from the left angle of the box finding the far corner.

'The lads are disappointed,' says Ello after the game, and understandably so: Widnes were the better side and Runcorn's relief at securing a point can't mask some concerns about squad depth, especially as Doyle mutters the dreaded word 'hamstring' in answer to a supporter's query as he makes his way towards the dressing room.

Attendance: 610

Tuesday 20 August 2024

Ericstan Park, Wythenshawe

FA Cup Preliminary Round Replay

Wythenshawe Town 3 Runcorn Linnets 1

I was away at the weekend so I missed Runcorn's 2-2 draw with Wythenshawe Town in the FA Cup. The draw means the scheduled league trip to Avro is off and we have this replay instead. FA Cup replays have now been eliminated from First Round Proper, as it's called, but in the qualifying rounds we still have them, which is how it should be. The Town ground has seen some improvements since we were here last season and there's now a sturdy fence behind the goal where previously there was little more than a building site. Still no turnstiles, though, and Ericstan Park is clearly still a work in very slow progress, partly because a nearby resident has raised objections to plans to put in a new stand and toilet block, allegedly fearing any expansion will turn nearby streets into car parks. Personally, I'm not seeing the link between better toilets and more traffic, unless the resident thinks they'll be so good drivers will be queueing round the block to use them.

Runcorn recruited two loan signings – Taylor Bowen and Jaden Jones - from Blackpool just before the weekend. They both start here. Jones looks technically good but a player who may need time to become acquainted with the physicality of the game at this level, while Bowen looks reassuringly close to the finished article. He opens the scoring for Runcorn with a deft flick over the head of the advancing keeper.

Sadly, that's as good as it gets. The goal comes against the run of play and turns out to be a rare highlight in an otherwise abysmal performance. Boyd equalises for the home team before half-time and the only surprise is it takes them until four minutes from time to take the lead, Wilshaw providing the finishing touch after a mad, self-destructive melee in the penalty area. He adds another in injury time and Town deservedly go into the next round and a trip to Whitchurch Alport.

My hunch is Runcorn make them look better than they probably are. When we aren't being muscled out of possession, we're invariably giving the ball away anyway. The body language is that of players who aren't enjoying their football and the travelling Runcorn fans make it clear we aren't enjoying it either.

Predictably, alarm among supporters spills online where outraged fingers are pointed in multiple directions – players, managers and board: there isn't any real consensus as to where blame for this mess lies. The Murdishaw Massive are encouraging fans to become trust members if they want to see change – whatever form that change might take – and there is enigmatic talk of people 'who you may believe are furnishing their own egos.'

It's right they aren't naming names online but the buzz around many of those at the ground alleges confusion and disagreement at board level about the way forward for the club, of Billy

Paynter's disillusionment fuelling his departure – one guy even gets on the phone to Billy at the ground (or pretends to – I'm not entirely sure) to tell him what a 'fucking mess' we're seeing tonight. There's disaffected mumbling about Anthony Kay being an appointment 'on the cheap'.

I've no idea how much, if any, of this is true. What is certain is that the potential gravy train of a cup run has already come to a grinding halt and we can only hope there are some hard truths being delivered in those Runcorn changing rooms. This was not one of those languid, spiritless performances we saw too often last season: this was something else, an uncoordinated, fractious mess that points squarely to a hard season ahead if not addressed immediately.

Attendance: 355

Saturday 24 August

APEC Taxis Stadium, Runcorn

Northern Premier League West Division

Runcorn Linnets 2 Hednesford Town 6

Before the game comes the announcement that Billy Paynter has been appointed as new manager of Connah's Quay Nomads in the Welsh League. Interesting how many are now vocally giving him retrospective support following this bad start to the season. For those who were hoping he'd come back – which, let's face it, was never going to happen – it's yet more bad news and certainly not the end of it today.

Runcorn are expecting a big crowd for this one, augmented by the large travelling Hednesford support, so it's surprising when I arrive at the ground reasonably late and find the car park half full. Inside the ground, the Shed is similarly depleted with more away fans in it than Runcorn supporters. Take the visiting fans out of the crowd and it's a hugely disappointing attendance. Following our difficult start, are people already voting with their feet? Or have unusually large numbers chosen to go away for the bank holiday weekend?

Whatever the reason, they miss a first half that is Runcorn's best of the season so far, despite us suffering another injury when Pete Wylie is forced off. After dominating the half, we finally get a reward before half-time when Eden Gumbs heads home from a corner. The second half begins in similar mode, with Moseley drawing a fine save from the keeper in what seems set to be the response to the Wythenshawe Town game we were looking for.

Then the wheels fall off. Some good play down the left side gives Hednesford an equaliser through Rob Stevenson, last year's player of the season in this league. Hednesford, having avoided relegation by the back door, have received a significant cash injection and are apparently awash with the stuff, enabling them to lure Stevenson from Leek Town even though it means him stepping back down to a lower league.

It's a goal from which Runcorn never recover: our defence is all over the place and every time Hednesford enter the box they look like scoring. We get to 5-1 down before Sam Barratt pulls a goal back but even then Hednesford have the last word, scoring another in injury time to administer the worst defeat I have ever witnessed for this or any Runcorn side, home or away.

Broadly, there are two kinds of football fans and a second half performance like this picks them out. Some are determined to support the team long after any hope has gone of rescuing anything from the game, and I like to think I'm among that contingent. And there are others who prefer yelling to each player how 'shite' he is, howling in frenzied exasperation even before a player has received the ball to do anything wrong with it. It's a horrible, miserable afternoon and the sound of many such voices in the smaller than expected crowd certainly doesn't make it any more enjoyable.

I understand the need for football fans to vent their frustration but wonder whether those who do it in this manner are under the impression they're doing something productive. Does the man close to me who's been at it for most of the second half go home to a post-match conversation with his wife that goes something like:

'Did they win, Harold?'

'No, Doris. They're a bunch of useless bastards, as I keep telling them.'

'Never mind, dear. Maybe if you keep telling them, they'll do better.

'It's my mission in life, Doris. Until I see players in that Runcorn shirt performing at the level of Lionel Messi, I'll keep telling them what useless bastards they are.'

'I'm sure the penny will drop one day, Harold.'

In the late eighties, Brian Howman tells me, he sometimes went for a pint after the game with Runcorn defender Paul Rowlands.

'He scored an absolute worldie one day from a long way out, an absolute belter. There were these guys who used to stand in front of us, used to give him down the banks and he ran over to these guys and hugged them.' In the bar after the game, Rowlands revealed to Brian that he'd been intending to hit them but thought better of it. 'Thing is,' he told Brian, 'if I could do what those cunts want me to do, I wouldn't be playing for Runcorn, would I?'

I join around twenty Runcorn fans in the barren Shed to applaud the sons of Rowlo, or today's recipients of terrace abuse, off at the end, willing them to keep their heads up, looking ahead to Monday and the promise, surely, of better to come.

'One word for that: fucking shite,' says a supporter behind us as we file out.

'That's two words,' observes his mate.

With so many leaving before the end, at least it's easy to get out of the car park and away from the horrors we've witnessed. But I should know better, because they linger in the mind long after that. We do this to ourselves, football fans: sacrifice entire weekends on the altar of a couple of dismal hours on a Saturday afternoon.

Tony Kay describes himself as 'embarrassed' and 'soul-destroyed' after the game. His body language leaving the pitch tells us as much.

Attendance: 579

Monday 26 August

Wincham Park Stadium, Wincham

Northern Premier League West Division

Witton Albion 4 Runcorn Linnets 0

In his interview after Saturday's game, Anthony Kay said he welcomed a quick opportunity to bounce back today but in truth Runcorn fans arrive at Wincham Park with a rather different set of expectations. Even at this stage of the season pre-season talk of another tilt at promotion have given way to a more sober assessment of our prospects. We couldn't be heading for a relegation fight, could we?

By five o'clock the prospect seems all too real. Witton are gifted a goal after four minutes when Bayleigh Passant doesn't so much fail to deal with a free kick as help it into the net. He redeems himself later in the half, saving a penalty after a clumsy, mistimed challenge in the area brings back all too vivid memories of Saturday's calamity. Could we capitalise on this reprieve? We begin to offer some promise going forward but look wide open every time Witton attack.

Tony Kay takes himself off at half-time, three games in six days clearly too much for the 41-year-old boss who can't have envisaged any more than occasional appearances this season. The absence of any defensive options on the bench means Jacques Welsh drops into the back four and his absence in midfield leaves us even more exposed to Witton's attacks. A home fan near me observes, with what appears to be genuine sympathy: 'This is the worst Runcorn side I've ever seen. It's normally a battle when we play you.' He seems embarrassed for us. Pity is horrible. Give me an opposing fan rubbing my face in it any day.

Witton can hardly fail to take advantage, scoring a second before a wild challenge from Welsh on the edge of the area brings another penalty and a second yellow card. This time Witton make no mistake from the spot and the 10 men look to see out a game that has effectively become about damage limitation. We watch us concede a fourth before trooping dejectedly back towards the car, relieved that the final whistle has blown on what could be my worst Bank Holiday weekend since the great Ainsdale wasp attack of '84.

Injuries are part of the problem. We don't have enough fit defenders and the absence of Doyle has left a massive gap in midfield. Jaden Jones is a good footballer but he'll need games in his legs before he can fill it and that requires time that Tony Kay may, on this evidence, not have.

But injuries are not the only issue. Confidence, understandably, looks at rock bottom. Too many of the ten goals conceded in these two games have been due to concentration lapses or unforced errors. We're giving the ball away cheaply and, when we do, we lack the tenacity to win it back. I could go on. Perusing the scores in our league later that day, I envy those sides who've taken part in a normal game of football with a normal result at the end of it, which is most of them.

Atherton Collieries' failure to win means we're at least spared the prospect of seeing Runcorn at the bottom of the league. As comforts go, it's small bordering on non-existent.

Attendance: 672

Saturday 31 August

APEC Taxis Stadium, Runcorn

Northern Premier League West Division

Runcorn Linnets 1 Congleton Town 0

Alan's back for this one. I tell him I've never seen Congleton before, a claim he debunks in typical fashion by pointing out I was with him and Cousin Andy for Winsford United v Congleton in December 1990, a game I have absolutely no recollection of. This is entirely due to a failing memory which is also responsible, I later realise, for me forgetting that I saw Runcorn beat them in a Cheshire Senior Cup game here a few years ago.

Last season, it was Congleton who knocked Runcorn out of that competition, and since then they've secured promotion from the Midland League. They've made a good start to this season too and, our expectations reshaped by the last three performances, we're expecting another difficult afternoon today.

Whatever the outcome, Sam Phillips is among those calling for patience among supporters 'If we'd won on Monday, Saturday would have been forgotten. We can't judge the manager until we're ten games in. If, at that point, we're still second from bottom, I'm 100% behind getting rid of him, but he's just had a bad start, that's all.'

He also doesn't believe we should ignore the role injuries have played in that poor start. 'If you look at our squad, Anthony Kay is Runcorn's fifth choice centre back. Jack Grundy hasn't played since pre-season because he broke a bone in his leg. So we brought in Sam Carr, who played for a couple of games, and then he went on holiday, booked when he didn't have a club. Your fourth choice is Peter Wylie, who goes off injured after four minutes against Hednesford Town. Anthony Kay knows that we don't want him on the pitch, but he's having to play. I think it's really difficult to judge him until he's actually had a chance to be a manager.'

A fair enough assessment but that doesn't mean a rash early decision won't happen, of course. Atherton Collieries, the only side below us in the league going into this game, sacked their manager during the week. The media attention may be less intense at this level but the pressure for managers to succeed is just as real.

The news before kick-off is that Manchester United youth team keeper Tom Myles has joined on loan and will go straight into the side today. Is Bayleigh Passant carrying the can for those recent defeats? It feels a bit harsh on Bayleigh, who did well for us last season and certainly can't be blamed for most of the goals we've conceded, but I've seen Tom play for the United youth team and he's an excellent young keeper.

Another new signing in the side today is Karl Clair, an experienced midfielder recruited from Llandudno. James Carr's return from holiday now means Anthony Kay doesn't have to name himself in the side.

Clair immediately looks the part, a combative player who's also a talker and an organiser: straight away we look far more solid in the centre of the park than we did last weekend – not difficult, admittedly. Sadly, one thing we haven't put behind us is the problem of injuries during games: both full backs are forced to leave the field before half time, James Short limping off to be replaced by Eden Gumbs while Sam Barratt picks up a nasty looking shoulder injury. Fortunately, Peter Wylie is fit enough for the bench and can replace Sam at right back but, again, the boss is facing a position where he's only one injury away from having to play himself.

For now. it feels like a test of the remaining players' fortitude and mental strength and, even with those injuries, we look a lot more robust in defence and central midfield. It's a game of few chances, remaining goalless until deep into the second half. Then Luke Wall cuts in from the left: we're expecting a cross but he fires a magnificent angled shot across the keeper and into the net. It's a hard-fought victory, the kind of narrow win that can feel better than a 5-0 rout, especially in our current circumstances.

The players leave the field to loud applause from the Shed. Anthony Kay looks like a man who's just had a huge boulder lifted off his back, for now.

Attendance: 564

September 2024

'Things have got to change, starting tomorrow.'

Saturday 7 September

I'm in Florence. My wife doesn't like football and there are times when, in the interests of maintaining the *pax matrimonium* (well, we *are* in Italy) you've got to do things together. And besides, I love my wife and I love it here.

Tim is at the FA Trophy game between Runcorn and Pontefract Collieries and messages me that Runcorn have taken the lead through new signing Lewis Nolan. I'm walking round Florence with a smile on my face, taking in the magnificent cathedral and talking about coming back here for an extended stay next year. We meet some guys from Manchester in a bar. It's an ale place and I enjoy a couple of good pints, basking in the magnificence of the Florentine architecture and the knowledge that all's right in the world of football.

Then, as has been the way of things this season, it all falls apart. Pontefract are awarded a penalty. A small cloud floats over Florence. They miss it. I look up: a cloudless sky. But not for long. Jaden James is sent off after a second yellow and Runcorn concede an equaliser. Pontefract grab a winner late on.

We've gone out of both the Trophy and the Cup at the first hurdle this season. Florence, despite its piazzas, statues, museums and gelati, suddenly feels like New Brighton in the eighties.

Wednesday 11 September

Northern Premier League West Division

Whitebank Stadium, Oldham

Avro 3 Runcorn Linnets 1

Reasonably speaking, it's too early for the season to be in crisis. But supporting a football club has bugger all to do with reason and, on an emotional level, crisis is what it feels like.

Tim tells me we weren't that bad in the FA Trophy game so a win tonight would feel like we've at least retained the potential for upward momentum hinted at in the Congleton game. This match is the one cancelled earlier in the season to make way for our calamitous FA Cup replay at Wythenshawe Town. Surely we've moved on since then?

One player certainly has. James Hooper has signed for Witton Albion, one of the many clubs he's represented before in his long career. Deserting a sinking ship? Or just frustrated at not being a regular fixture in the side, even a failing one? Or are the rumours that some players are unhappy with Anthony Kay's management and Hoops, one of the more vocal members of the squad, has set forth an expletive-laden opinion? Right side of attack is one position where we're well off for options so a more sober assessment might be that he's being released so we can make improvements elsewhere.

Tonight, any thoughts that we're in the process of turning the corner receive a severe blow. Although recovery from injuries and squad acquisitions mean we're now able to field a team where players are in their preferred positions, it's the same problem we had at Witton: every time Avro go forward they look like scoring, And score they do, first from a cross from their right after Runcorn fanny around rather than putting the thing out of play and buying the time to regroup, then again when the Runcorn defence collapses, literally in some cases, to allow the home side an easy finish.

We bring on Taylor Bowen and Jacques Welsh at half time and both make a difference. Jacques adds solidity to the hitherto largely absent midfield and Taylor begins to give the Avro number 5 – whose lack of height hasn't been tested nearly enough – something to think about. I begin to sense there may still be a way back into the game, but that train of thought is rudely terminated when the Runcorn defence fail to deal with a standard ball over the top and Avro make it 3-0.

Brooke grabs a consolation and, to the players' credit, Runcorn attempt to make a fight of it in the later stages. We're chasing the game forlornly, though, and Tim and I troop off back to the pothole-ridden car park with the cheers of a handful of victorious Avro fans – a handful is pretty much all they've got – in our ears.

They say the league table, even this early in the season, doesn't lie but we're fourth from bottom and that feels like a frankly generous assessment of our true merits at this stage.

'Things have got to change here, Sam, starting tomorrow,' a defiant Anthony Kay tells Sam Phillips in his post-match interview.

Attendance: 190

Friday 13 September

North West Counties League Premier Division

Anfield Sports & Community Centre

Lower Breck 4 Abbey Hey 0

'Somehow the big blob in the middle (of Liverpool) had nothing other than Liverpool and Everton,' City of Liverpool owner Paul Manning told Simon Hughes, 'which is remarkable when you consider the appetite for football in the city.'

This must have been news to Lower Breck, already active while City of Liverpool were just a twinkle in Manning's eye. Lower Breck almost literally exist in the shadow of Liverpool's ground, which is why they often play home games on Friday nights and delay mid-week fixtures until Thursdays when Liverpool have a Champions League match. Any clash, you suspect, would bring the Breck attendance close to zero and even those present, including many of the players. might be more focused on the crowd noises emanating from the west. Nonetheless, Lower Breck have established a thriving set-up here and there's certainly evidence among the crowd tonight that they're filling the gap Manning's team, now playing in Widnes, talked about.

Breck have made a good start this season. They're fourth in the table going into this match and a win here would take them to the top of the league, at least until tomorrow. Abbey Hey are three points behind them but have played a game more.

'The Anny', as they call this ground, has an artificial pitch, which is regrettable but understandable. I've been talking to Bren Connolly about whether Runcorn will ever go in this direction. Thankfully, there's a desire not to, but he's certainly aware of the benefits. Recently the pitch at the APEC was used five times in eight days by the men's and women's teams: not so bad at this stage of the season but when that kind of schedule occurs during the winter months it can place huge demands on the ground staff.

'The pitch has been quite a challenge,' Bren admits. 'At the end of the season the pitch is ripped up, basically. That costs an awful lot of money. It's fantastic at the start of the season but when it starts to get wet it doesn't seem to take the wear that we anticipated it would.'

So it's understandable that surfaces like this are increasingly common at this level. Anfield Sports & Community Centre is, as the name suggests, a community facility, home to several clubs and available for hire so it sees a lot of activity. Breck began as a youth team before merging with local club The Famous Grapes, eventually joining the North West Counties League in 2016. The programme is great, with a classic Subbuteo cover design and, among other things, an article about the 'Sheffield Rules' football of the mid-nineteenth century.

The football's good too. A frenetic and competitive early contest swings firmly in the direction of the home side when Buckley heads them into the lead in the 19th minute. Collings grabs another before a superb move from left to right culminates in Millington making it three just before half-time. In pure footballing terms, it's the best goal I've seen so far this season.

The assessment at half-time from the Abbey Hey Twitter account is somewhat generous, claiming the only difference between the sides is that Breck have taken their chances. Certainly, listening to the Abbey players talking as they leave the pitch, they feel they're not doing enough and they're right. For me, there are echoes of Avro on Wednesday night: Abbey look wide open at the back at times, shouting for offsides that never are and looking in danger every time Breck attack down the right. If they coordinated their defence as well as they're coordinating their howls of protest at the ref, they may stand more of a chance.

When Breck score their fourth – a horrendously misjudged back pass allowing Dowling to race through and capitalise – the game fizzles out. On this evidence, Breck look more than capable of mounting a promotion challenge this season. There are several players out there who look good enough for the next level up.

I look in vain for the presence of Runcorn scouts.

Attendance: 288

Saturday 14 September

APEC Taxis Stadium, Runcorn

Northern Premier League West Division

Runcorn Linnets 0 Trafford 2

Sam Phillips called for Runcorn fans to wait ten games before making a judgement on Anthony Kay. Well, this is game ten and many of those present at Avro on Wednesday night were making it clear they were already running short on patience.

Right now it feels like we've switched places with Trafford, who occupied a position perilously close to the relegation zone for much of last season. Going into this game they're in second place while we are the ones in peril. Many observed last season that Trafford looked too good to go down, which proved correct. Does that apply to Runcorn now? Frankly, on the evidence of those games at Wythenshawe Town, Witton and Avro, no.

The Murdishaw Massive have been enquiring about bringing a sheep to the game. This is partly in response to a local newspaper story but it's funnier without the context so I won't go into that. They say the sheep will be on a lead and they'll bring a poop shovel with them. It's not much bigger than a dog, they point out, but a bit noisier.

In the event, the sheep doesn't turn up but Runcorn do, playing our best football of the season from the first minute. Another loan signing from Blackpool, Tyler Hill, makes his debut and slots in well at left back. Welsh has returned to the startling line-up to fortify the midfield and Bowen has earned his start up front following his efforts at Avro. Runcorn dominate in the way Avro dominated on Wednesday: the only difference is Trafford aren't giving away cheap goals and their number 4 is dealing with everything in the air. Just before half-time the visitors create their only chance of the half and score from it, Noble sliding the ball in from a narrow angle.

Heads don't drop and Runcorn press forward in the second half. Bowen finds himself through on goal and the Trafford keeper rushes out of his box. 'Take everything' is usually the advice to keepers in such situations and this one does exactly that, except when he sends Bowen into temporary orbit over Murdishaw he fails to take the ball too. A straight red.

With most of the second half to play, surely Runcorn can capitalise? We've been by far the better team even against eleven and now, not only do we have an extra man, one of Trafford's outfield players is donning the departing keeper's shirt, which is good news for the kids in the Shed who can continue their rendition of 'Number 1's a wanker' without any revisions.

Whatever number 1 may be, number 4 is still heading away practically everything that comes into the box and, when he doesn't, the ball still won't fall to a Runcorn foot or head. We're throwing everything at them when, with six minutes left, Nisbett collects the ball for Trafford and runs at a Runcorn defence that largely isn't there, finishing calmly in front of the small bunch of Trafford fans who surely can't believe they've won this.

For me, this feels even worse than the Avro game. Although there are a couple of boos at the end, most of the home crowd understand what's happened here, even if we can't quite believe it. It's clear the players can't either, as we collect in the Shed to cheer them off with shouts that are mostly supportive, defiant and, despite the outcome, guardedly optimistic. Anthony Kay has had his tenth game but there is nothing in this performance to sack anybody for. He walks off separately from the players, looking like a man who can't figure out what he did to deserve that. The league table now shows us third from bottom and the two teams below us both have two games in hand.

No sheep at the APEC today, but plenty of shit.

Attendance: 481

Saturday 21 September

Bucket Hat FM

Keen to see how you manage this one, Whitby. It's 2.15, you're in Manchester and Runcorn are playing way down the M56 at Vauxhall.

Any chance you can make some suggestions rather than pointing out the bloody obvious?

I've got nothing, mate. But you've still got to visit Vauxhall for this book.

I know.

You missed the Runcorn game there last season too.

I know.

And even if you...

I fucking know.

You could catch an hour of it.

Testing my patience now.

There are few fixed rules in life but one of mine is that I don't do partial football matches. If I can't see the full ninety minutes plus injury time, it doesn't count. It's a hill I'm prepared to die on. Well, maybe not die.

I reach home just in time to hear the Bucket Hat FM commentary starting. Last season this match was Sam and Jack's finest hour, the day of the Hooper 'mummy' and Allardyce anecdote. Is it just me or has the Linnets' disappointing form got to them a bit? Sam is as fluent as ever and Jack's humorous asides still hit the mark, but he never seems far away from a frustrated expletive and is that a nervous waver in Sam's voice?

There's an entertaining rant from Jack about how the Premier League is over-rated and not as good as it was 15 years ago. He also lays into the hype about the upcoming world heavyweight boxing match, saying he'd rather watch two guys going at it in Runcorn Old Town.

With the teams below us not playing today, it feels like we really need a win against a Vauxhall team who've made a good start to the season. It feels like even a draw, which would take us out of the relegation zone for now, would fail to relieve the pressure.

On the half hour mark the opportunity is presented to us. Ryan Brooke is brought down for a penalty and keeper Atkinson is sent off for the foul. Then, bizarrely, the ref changes his mind and gives him a yellow. Jack and Sam agree the red would have been harsh and, of course, VAR hasn't yet extended its tentacles as far as Ellesmere Port or the NPL. Continuing the pattern of the season, Brooke can't continue: he's broken his collar bone, we're told, and is replaced by Jorge Dwyer, a young player who's making his debut. Eventually, Taylor Bowen steps up to score the spot-kick and give Runcorn what sounds like a deserved lead.

On Twitter, the Murdishaw Massive are calling it the best first half performance of the season – admittedly, the competition for that accolade is not fierce. The nervous waver has disappeared from Sam's voice as he informs us that the tempo has dropped in the second half but Runcorn are still on top. Anthony Kay comes off the bench for us and Kevin Ellison for them – a combined age of 86 – and when the veteran Ellison challenges Tom Myles for a high ball Runcorn's Twitter notes there's a 27-year age gap between the two players.

Ellison can't help Vauxhall to pierce the Runcorn defence, though, and a dogged second half display secures the first away victory of the season. We're up to 16th in the table. Nosebleeds beckon.

Attendance: 269

Saturday 28 September

APEC Taxis Stadium, Runcorn

Northern Premier League West Division

Runcorn Linnets 4 Mossley 1

It coulda bin us. Before the game, I catch some of Wythenshawe Town's FA Cup match against Farsley Celtic on BBC. Had we seen them off earlier in the competition, we might have got our hands on some of that TV cash.

This has happened before. Marine's celebrated cup run in the 2020-21 season, which culminated in a televised home tie against Spurs, would have been a lot shorter had they not beaten us in a penalty shoot-out in the qualifying rounds. The money from such things can make a huge difference at this level and Marine duly rode on a wave of it to promotion via the play-offs, also at our expense.

I shrug off any residual dismay and watch open-mouthed as Runcorn blow Mossley away in a performance packed with energy, spirit and great goals. Where did this come from? Is the masterpiece Anthony Kay has been quietly fashioning now revealing itself?

I've volunteered for stewarding duties outside the turnstile. The club have done away with the paid security here, plus the dog employed to detect anyone trying to smuggle flares into the ground. 'I've been asked to sniff out any pyrotechnics,' I tell someone who asks. 'I'm a lot cheaper than the dog.' I'm not as cute though and nobody tries to pat me.

The paid security and the dog have been an unwanted expense for a while. 'Generally speaking in this league supporters are excellent,' says Bren Connolly, 'and there's very little need for any serious stewarding. Safety of our supporters is one of our top priorities, though, and that's why we brought in some paid security, which is an additional draw on funding.' It's very rare they're called upon to do anything, though, so it makes sense to dispense with them and just have me, as Tim puts it, 'basically standing around doing nothing'.

The attendance today is slightly up on the Trafford game. Mossley's loyal away following are here as always – I recognise many of them – and, to their credit, continue to make a noise even as their team are being demolished before their eyes.

It's a freak goal from a free kick that starts the demolition, Luke Wall's delivery into the box evading everybody to sneak in at the far post with barely a minute on the clock. Mossley equalise after a careless lunge in the area brings a penalty and we wonder if an all too familiar story this season will unfold.

Not a bit of it. Adam Moseley crowns his best performance of the season so far – he's not alone in that – with a magnificent curling effort from outside the area to restore the lead. Before half-time Jaden Jones makes it three, spearing a low shot beyond the reach of the keeper.

Jones is awarded man of the match at the end but for me it's Luke Wall who deserves the accolade, not for the first time this season. He was the one player to maintain a consistent level of performance during that terrible start to the season and he's the architect of the fourth goal, setting up Will Saxon, who's returning from injury, to finish through the keeper's legs.

It's back-to-back wins for the first time this season and many of us gather in the Shed to applaud both teams off, something which still yields puzzled faces among some of our opponents, especially on a day like today. 'Are they taking the piss?' you can see some of them thinking. We're not but it's nice to have secured the kind of result that makes them think it.

Attendance: 501

October 2024

They make Dave Bassett era Wimbledon look like early seventies Ajax...

Tuesday 1 October

I spend more of the day than is healthy for me counting the games that fall victim to the weather and hoping the Hanley Town v Runcorn game will join them, because I can't go. There's a pitch inspection at 2pm and just as I begin to speculate on when the rearranged game might take place, the announcement comes through that it's on.

So it's Sam and Jack again and the hope that, in my absence, Runcorn can do something they failed to do last season: win a third successive game. Optimism is high after Saturday but we know how fickle a thing form can be in this league, so no chickens are being counted, much less plucked.

Then comes the announcement that illness prevents a Bucket Hat FM broadcast going ahead so I must again rely on those online updates. Bad news not only for me but for the small but significant army of Runcorn Linnets fans around the globe.

Anyway, the experience proves a satisfactory one when, before half time, it's announced that Runcorn have taken the lead through a Taylor Bowen header. Bowen adds another in the second half and, though a Jacques Welsh own goal late on brings a few nervous moments, Runcorn see the game out to record a 2-1 win. Suddenly we're in eighth place, only four points behind the leaders. Not cause for lighting up the bridge in yellow and green just yet, but a welcome reason to be cheerful accompanied by a huge dollop of relief.

Saturday 5 October

Ericstan Park, Wythenshawe

Northern Premier League West Division

Wythenshawe Town 0 Runcorn Linnets 0

We return to one of the scenes of those early season atrocities with a new spring in our step. At least I do, and I hope the players have one too because belief has been restored among the Runcorn faithful that, despite early signs, the season could still be a successful one.

It's certainly a very different experience from that cup replay, when we were so wide open you could have driven a tractor through our defence. This time, there's barely any room for a bicycle, in either area. The only common feature is the loud Town keeper, who constantly harangues the ref, even over decisions made at the other end of the pitch.

It's the end of our winning run but feels like a point earned, certainly a measure of our improvement since that earlier game here, demonstrating that we're now equipped to handle tight games like this one and squeeze something out of them. Doyley makes his long-awaited return from the bench in the second half, while Luke Wall, last week deservedly crowned Runcorn Player of the Month for the second month running, once again looks the most likely player to unlock a resilient Town defence, which now includes former Runcorn player Aaron Morris, referred to by Sam Phillips as 'the non-league Virgil Van Dijk.'

His defensive capabilities contribute to the stalemate. Hardly a classic but, given some of our experiences this season, we'll take it.

Attendance: 318

Sunday 6 October

APEC Taxis Stadium, Runcorn

North West Women's Regional League D1 South

Runcorn Linnets Ladies 4 Wirral Phoenix 2

Runcorn Linnets Ladies have a new manager, Jack Slater, who previously worked with the grassroots club Runcorn Sports, which led to his involvement with the women's game. 'Runcorn Sports asked me if I'd manage their women's team,' he tells me. 'I did that for a year and a half and I really enjoyed it. Then I was approached by Runcorn Linnets.' They've made a good start to the season, including a convincing 6-2 win against Macclesfield here and a 10-0 victory over Skipton Town in their first ever game in the Women's FA Cup, a match in which Molly Bennett scored seven times.

Since then, things have got tougher. Despite a good showing against league leaders Poulton Vics, Runcorn lost 3-0 and were defeated 1-0 by FC St Helens here last Sunday. In between, they exited the FA Cup after defeat at Fleetwood. Early season optimism has been replaced with a more tempered view of their prospect. Promotion is and was always unlikely and Jack isn't even thinking about that.

'We want to do better than last year,' says Jack, a more modest aim, allowing him to develop and build a squad that can challenge for honours next season. Jack has the kind of infectious conviction that makes you believe him and, despite those recent disappointments, there's already evidence that this is being passed onto his players. He now combines managing the women's team with a full-time job and refereeing, often officiating in a Sunday League match before coming up to the APEC for the women's game.

In addition to improved playing levels, online coverage of Linnets Ladies has also improved this season, with photographs and squad numbers of all the players on the website and regular match updates on social media. It's part of an effort to raise the profile of the women's team and something Kelly Jones is keen to build on further. 'We've got the pictures on the website now, but if you look at the home page, it's still the men's team. I want to see us giving the women's team and the development teams an equal profile.'

'How do you raise the profile of the women so that somebody can say that they know maybe five of the players?' is how Jack puts it. He believes that by taking such small steps forward we'll be able to generate more interest among Runcorn supporters and across the town. 'There are some people who'll say they didn't even know the women's team were playing this weekend. Realistically, the men's team are always going to be number one so it's about how the women create their own identity, but for the club it's about how does it enhance everything? It's about us all together.'

Phoenix drew 3-3 here in a pre-season game. They were promoted last season and certainly look good enough to sustain a presence at this level, but they're a team Runcorn should and must beat to achieve Jack's aims.

We always look likely to do so, taking the lead through Chloe Fairclough, only to be pegged back by a breakaway Phoenix goal later in the first half. The advantage is restored through Emma McLarney just before half-time but a second half mix-up in the Linnets defence allows Phoenix an equaliser they scarcely deserve.

A few scares after that lead to some worries that Runcorn might throw all the points away but a superb move on the right ends with Molly Hewitt finishing at the far post to restore the lead and this time Runcorn aren't giving it up, Hewitt grabbing her second goal to put any lingering doubts to bed. Despite giving those goals away before half-time, there's evidence that this is a more well-drilled defensive unit than we saw at St Helens at the end of last season. Women's football is a rapidly improving game at this level, though: for this team to achieve the target Jack has set it'll need not just progress, but faster progress than everyone else.

Tuesday 8 October

APEC Taxis Stadium, Runcorn

Northern Premier League West Division

Runcorn Linnets 1 Newcastle Town 2

There's renewed optimism around the APEC, which is filled with pre-game talk of how a win tonight, followed by victory at Atherton on Friday, could see us begin to establish ourselves among the contenders this season. We've certainly had our fears of relegation quelled in recent weeks and football fans, let's face it, can be as fickle in their assessments of their teams' performances as those performances themselves.

And it all looks very promising. We start strongly and Doyley, making his first start since the injury, gives us the lead, pouncing on a loose ball after a parry from the keeper.

But Newcastle look more than capable of getting back into the game and they do, Tom Jones scoring with a superb swerving shot that evades Tom Myles and finds the top corner. From there, they always look the more likely winners and Myles is busy, forced to tip two shots onto the post during a second half in which Newcastle's front three are causing mayhem in the Runcorn defence.

I begin to think retrieving a draw from this wouldn't be a bad outcome when Jones pounces again to give the away side a deserved win. For Runcorn, it's not been quite as bad as those early season displays but there's a feeling that a gate to the play-off places had been left open and we've failed to go through it.

Fans who were filled with pre-game optimism shout 'rubbish' at the final whistle. I hear a man explain to his son that 'the players just aren't good enough.'

It can feel like this when a (brief) good run comes to a sudden and abrupt end. Football fans often react badly when suddenly reminded of our team's failings because they affect our mindsets, our well-being, everything. Put bluntly, they're our failings too.

Better to approach football games from the viewpoint that there are bound to be emotional ups and downs because that's just how football is.

And do you follow your own advice on that?

Probably not.

Attendance: 484

Friday 11 October

Alder House, Atherton

Northern Premier League West Division

Atherton Collieries 1 Runcorn Linnets 2

Without the Lancashire Coalfields, the various industries that gave birth to so many of the clubs in this area would never have taken off. No glass industry in St Helens means no Pilkington factory and no Pilkington FC. Why did Prescot become one of the first towns in the country with a functioning rail link? To transport coal. Runcorn's industrial importance was secured by its strategic position in linking mid-Cheshire salt production and the clay works of the Potteries with the coalfields to the north. Without that coal, there'd be no wire works at Warrington and no works team to form Warrington Rylands. Actually...no, I'll leave it there.

Atherton's industrial heritage arguably pre-dates what we think of as the industrial period: they were manufacturing nails here in the 1300s so, when industry took a firm hold on East Lancashire four centuries later, Atherton was well-placed to provide the nuts and bolts, not to mention the ironwork for industrial machinery. By then, coal mining had begun in the Lancashire Coalfield and the six pits that opened in Atherton meant this busy area of Lancashire became even busier.

Formed in 1916, Atherton Collieries are the older of the two Atherton clubs, established by miners from those six pits to raise funds during the First World War. This ground has been their home ever since. Like many clubs in former mining areas, they have retained the name to represent a community identity not easily erased, unlike the pits themselves.

There are still over 100 clubs active in England with roots in mining communities. Writing about Rainworth Miners' Welfare, Mike Bayly notes that the football clubs who've survived in these areas 'are the only constant and tangible reminder to the outside world of this proud and important heritage...the impact of a Miners' Welfare team reaching Wembley or making a televised FA Cup appearance could do wonders for the public profile of so many areas.'

While Rainworth, from Nottinghamshire, did indeed reach Wembley, playing in the FA Vase Final of 1981-82, the highpoint of Atherton Collieries' existence was promotion to the NPL Premier Division as West Division champions in 2018-19. Last season, they came crashing down again after finishing bottom. However, their continued participation at NPL level arguably represents and more significant achievement. Clubs like Sherwood Colliery, in Nottinghamshire, and Pontefract Collieries, in Yorkshire, are currently thriving in the NPL's East Division, while Easington Colliery are in the top division of the Northern League and clubs like Armthorpe Welfare and Club Thorne Colliery continue to carve out an existence in the North Counties East League. In the area covered by this book, however, Atherton Collieries are the only remaining standard bearers for the Lancashire Coalfield.

It's one of many reasons to want to see them remain at this level, but Colls have begun this season poorly. When Runcorn stood next to bottom in the league, they were the one team below us. They won their last game at Hanley though and, after the sobering experience of Tuesday night, no one's taking this Friday night trip to Atherton lightly.

On the one hand, it's an early chance to put Tuesday night behind us. On the other, it's a third game in six days and so many Runcorn players put in laboured performances on Tuesday that I wonder how much that tough battle at Wythenshawe Town took out of them. I'm driving up to Atherton but Runcorn have filled a coach for the game so, as usual, we arrive in large numbers, belief and expectation evidently restored that we can still make something of this season.

It's a great night, probably the noisiest Runcorn away end I've ever witnessed, maintaining a rough medley of songs and chants throughout the game. The APEC has been completely stripped of flags: they're all here. 'Runcorn must be empty tonight,' mumbles a Colls fan close to me. Thanks to us, the attendance is approximately double that of their last home game. When Mike Blackstone visited the ground in 2003, Colls were struggling in the North West Counties League and the attendance was just 68. Blackstone calls Alder House 'a ground with a bit of a rundown appearance consisting of a real mish mash of stands and buildings which seem to have seen better days.' To me, though, it has a mangled, earthy charm: you can feel ghostly echoes of the club's industrial past in every yard of terracing.

Colls are so Route One they make Dave Bassett-era Wimbledon look like early seventies Ajax. The ball is pumped up into the night sky so often that Grundy and Washington, reunited in central defence, spend so much time looking heavenwards they've secured Royal Astronomical Society membership by the end of the game. They deal with everything that arrives from space, helped, it must be said, by Atherton forwards who look ill-equipped to deliver on the tactic.

Runcorn go into half-time two goals up, courtesy of two free kicks from Luke Wall which find the heads of Jack Grundy and Tyler Bowen respectively. On both occasions the Colls keeper might have done better, stranded in no man's land for the first goal and rooted to his line for the second.

Colls have more possession in the second half but Runcorn are sharp on the break, now playing uphill on probably the most severe slope in the league. We pass up several chances to extend the lead and begin to wonder if we may come to regret this when Colls pull one back at the end of normal time. They've got it on the ground for once and it works in their favour, making me wonder whether they might have been better trying something like that earlier.

The ref finds six minutes of injury time from somewhere and we're beyond nine minutes when he finally blows his whistle. 'They were better than us,' mutters a Colls fan as we leave the ground. Her companion lets out an ironic grunt, like it's a statement of the bleeding obvious. Which it is. Unless Colls change their approach, I think we've just seen one of this season's relegated sides, and, much as I'd love to see our hosts turn it around, it's good to be able to say it isn't us.

Attendance: 543

Saturday 12 October

Barton Stadium, Winsford

Midland League Premier Division

Northwich Victoria 1 Studley 1

Earlier this year, Tony Fallows, one of the co-owners of 1874, resurrected the idea of reconciliation of the Northwich clubs in the Northwich Guardian, bringing together not only the two estranged Northwich sides but roping in Winsford United too, to form 'Northwich United'. As Fallows says, the three sides have all had dire recent experiences as separate entities and merging would, overnight, create a bigger club that could pool local support more effectively, providing the platform for a better future.

Several major problems stand in the way. Among them is that many Northwich Victoria fans still consider themselves the 'real' club in Northwich and are understandably very attached to their historic name: getting them to change to 'Northwich United' or anything else won't be easy. Winsford have a proud separate history and asking them to abandon the name of their town would be similarly fraught with difficulties. As the only team of the three with a ground, they would be well-positioned to drive a hard bargain. There's also the not insignificant issue that some fans of the two Northwich clubs really don't like each other.

Vicki England, as we know, isn't among them but she doubts there's any prospect of reconciliation any time soon. 'There is a mutual respect between the clubs' boards, but there's still an element within both fan-bases that just wouldn't entertain it. You've got people that have got an affinity to Vics in our ranks but there are also new supporters who've come along who never went to the Drill Field, don't have the history, don't have the affinity and they're saying, "Why would we?"'.

She is aware of the proposal from Tony Fallows but says there are other suggestions floating around. 'There are people in the town who say, you know, it's got to be a three-way with Witton,' she says, aware that this would add further complexity to a situation that's frankly complicated enough. Witton, after all, are the one club who seem to be doing OK out of the current arrangement and their rivalry with Vics massively outdates these more recent local tensions. 'Although the rivalry has mellowed,' says Vicki, 'it's still there. They would look and say, you know, what have we got to offer?'

The other very sizeable risk, whatever permutation is offered, is that some would simply refuse to accept the arrangement: the history of football in the Mid-Cheshire region carries a warning that fans of some (or all) of the existing clubs may ignore the outcome of any merger and just decide to carry on as they are. Northwich United could quickly become yet another club in an already crowded area.

Mark Harris, former chairman of Witton, gave a candid summary of the difficulties involved in any kind of permutation. 'You'll never get universal approval and football supporters are intelligent and difficult to win over. You are risking alienating lots of people.'

Clearly any such arrangements remain fraught with difficulties, but the current season has brought improved fortunes in this part of the world. Winsford United are currently third in North West Counties League Division One South. While Vics occupy a solid mid-table position in the Midland League, 1874 are in the top half and have games in hand on runaway leaders Lichfield following a cash-generating run in the FA Cup. 'It's massive,' Vicki England has told me. 'There's talk of big clubs disrespecting the FA Cup but at our level, it's huge. We were drawn away at Guiseley, who were top of the NPL and for around 60 minutes we held our own. But a great experience for the lads.'

Vics managed a draw at Barnoldswick Town in the Preliminary Round of the Cup but lost the replay. Once again, they face an uncertain future. The groundshare arrangement is due to remain in place until summer 2027 but there are rumours it may be terminated prematurely. Inevitably, such uncertainty doesn't help a club to move forward and, though Vics are more familiar with such pressures than most, that doesn't necessarily make them any easier to deal with and carries the added weight of the 'oh no, not again' factor.

Vics' opponents today are currently also hanging around mid-table so we're expecting a tight game and that's what we get, albeit with a twist.

The twist comes early when Vics keeper Kier Barry goes down injured and can't carry on. There's no reserve keeper on the bench so Callum Parker goes in goal. Understandably, Sudley wish to test him and pump high balls into the box, the Vics defenders forming a protective cordon and throwing everything in their way. Anything that gets through is, for now, being gathered by the keeper to huge cheers from the Vics fans. It's not exactly one for the purists, but it's an intriguing contest of sorts.

Vics are handling the pressure well and begin to establish some dominance, leading to Coop giving them the lead just after the half-hour mark. Like Atherton Collieries last night, Studley might be better advised to ease off the high balls which the Vics defence are comfortably dealing with and get it on the ground. They eventually do that and grab an equaliser.

Parker's performance in goal is warmly received by the Vics fans at the end. The Studley manager, who's been bouncing around his technical area shouting abuse at his players for much of the game, continues to look dissatisfied at the final whistle, but he's been wearing a deep frown since kick-off so that might just be how he looks all the time.

On our way out of the ground, we learn that 1874 have drawn away at Shifnal but that Lichfield have unexpectedly lost 4-0 at home to Brocton. There could be life in the title race yet and there's every chance one of the Northwich clubs will be involved in it. Sadly, for the long-suffering Vics fans, it's unlikely to be them.

Attendance: 159

Wednesday 15 October

Wincham Park, Wincham

Cheshire Senior Cup First Round

Witton Albion 0 Runcorn Linnets 3

The Bank Holiday Monday Massacre is still fresh in our minds as we begin our Cheshire Senior Cup campaign at Wincham Park. Following early exits in the FA Cup and FA Trophy and being so far off the pace in the league, the county cups, as usual, offer the best (only?) route to success this season. This is not the easiest draw we could have had, though.

Not that Witton are doing particularly well. They haven't won a game in the league since inflicting that thrashing on us. They've also recently lost their goalkeeper and captain Danny Roberts to Nantwich and come into this game off a 1-0 defeat to ten-man Mossley. Runcorn, as Andrew Simpson's column in the always well-informed programme notes, have only lost one in the last six. 'Boss Anthony Kay has options again and is reaping the benefits in terms of results,' Simpson sagely records. He anticipates Witton will be in for a much tougher game this time and he isn't wrong.

I love the Cheshire Senior Cup. Runcorn won it five years running in the eighties and I was there for the last four finals: victories against Northwich Vics, Altrincham and Macclesfield Town twice. We haven't won it since, though, having blown a huge opportunity to do so in 2018-19 when we got to the final, or thought we had, before being thrown out of the competition for fielding an ineligible player in the semi-final against Cammell Laird.

This game is like a mirror image of that August encounter with Runcorn on the front foot from the first minute, carving our way through the Witton midfield at will and going in two up at half-time courtesy of two Adam Moseley goals. The first is a superb solo effort, the second a fierce shot from the edge of the area after being set up by Will Saxon, who delivers a selfless, hard-working performance on the right side of the attack.

We spurn several chances to extend the lead in the second half, and there are some mystifying offside decisions by the liner to deprive us of a few more but we finally go three up when recent recruit Adam Morgan fires home from a Luke Wall cross. More or less straight from the restart Witton are reduced to ten men when Cushion is sent off for a two footed challenge and we enjoy the unusual luxury this season of getting the cigars out long before the final whistle.

For once, we trudge back through the asphalt of the Witton car park with smiles on our faces. Not only are we through to the next round, but we've put out a team with serious designs on the competition. With Vauxhall Motors causing a shock by eliminating Altrincham – who walloped us in the semi two years ago – the path to getting Runcorn's name back on the CSC trophy already looks a lot clearer than we might have expected.

Attendance: 347

Saturday 19 October

APEC Taxis Stadium, Runcorn

Northern Premier League West Division

Runcorn Linnets 0 Nantwich Town 1

Back at the APEC after two memorable victories on the road, Runcorn face another side with much to smile about following a good recent run of form. On Tuesday Nantwich beat high flying Vauxhall 2-1, that win coming off the back of a 6-0 thrashing of Trafford, whose early season optimism has recently been punctured. We're expecting something more memorable than the dour goalless draw these two played out towards the end of last season.

Ultimately, it becomes an experience we'd much rather forget. Nantwich are comfortably the better side, taking the lead through Mellor in a dominant first half performance. The one goal deficit flatters Runcorn at the break and we make two changes at half time, Karl Clair coming on to fortify a midfield that has too many shades of those early season games about it and new signing from Bala Town Naim Arsan making his debut on the left.

And we look better, though not good enough to carve out more than a couple of chances while Nantwich come close to adding to their lead, drawing one excellent save from the restored Bayleigh Passant and hitting the bar twice. There are shouts for a Runcorn penalty late on which leads to some booing of the officials from the Shed at the end but I'm not convinced and in truth we've been beaten by a better side.

We'll go into November with just two wins from seven home matches in the league. We're unquestionably better than we were in those early season games and Arsan looks a good signing, but this kind of home form is still the stuff of relegation candidates rather than play-off contenders.

Attendance: 581

Tuesday 22 October

Sandbach Community Stadium, Sandbach

Cheshire Senior Cup Round One

Sandbach United 5 Barnton 0

It's a 50-50 ball. Both men are moving towards it, a quick glance passing between them saying more than words can: if both of us continue this trajectory it'll mean a heavy collision and almost certain embarrassment as at least one and maybe two fat blokes squirm around on our backs like upturned tortoises. Better to pull out now, I think, but my legs are still carrying me forward. Thankfully, he's got better brakes and he applies them in time. I retrieve the ball from just behind the bin and push it back under the five-bar gate that forms part of the perimeter fence. The Sandbach player collects it and takes the throw-in.

Sandbach United have established themselves as a community club of some note. In last year's Cheshire FA Football Awards, they were named Inclusive Club of the Year, their grounds team won Grounds Team of the Year and Myles Hocknall received the award for New Volunteer of the Year. First impressions are of a lovingly crafted stadium with an welcoming atmosphere for the visiting fan. There's a good social area. the ambience of which reminds me of Morecambe's long-derelict wild west sea front bars – except, of course, there's no sea front in the middle of Cheshire – with small but neat covered stands on one side of the pitch and behind one goal. It's a grass pitch, a level surface that I unkindly suggest Barnton, who play much of their football on a muddy slope, may struggle to get used to.

Runcorn already having booked our place in the second round of the Cheshire Senior Cup. we're checking out a contest between two North West Counties sides, the kind of teams who, in normal circumstances, we'd expect to beat should we face them at a future stage.

Founded in 2004, Sandbach United are the most southerly team in our rectangle. They're mid-table in the NWCL South, three places above their visitors, so I'm expecting an even contest, which we don't get.

The teams do look well-matched early on so the way things progress leaves the small group of Barnton supporters to our left struggling to understand where it all goes wrong. It starts with Bevan finishing with the deftest of touches after he's turned a Barnton defender on the edge of the area. We almost get an even better goal just before half-time when ex-Runcorn player Keiran Nolan – now Sandbach's captain – sees his shot from distance saved by the Barnton keeper, who then watches in vain as it bounces down off the crossbar and into the path of the waiting Bevan, who bundles it over the line for his second.

Sandbach are purring now and make the game safe nine minutes into the second half when Bevan pounces on confusion in the Barnton defence, rounding the keeper for his hat-trick. You can see an increased assurance in every step: during the game they've gone from stumbling semi-pros to elite practitioners of the footballing art, something that only goals and the confidence they give can bring to sides at any level. Suddenly, against bewildered opponents who understandably feel they haven't done a lot wrong, almost everything they try is coming off. Falcao finds Socrates who picks our Zico...I rub my eyes. For a moment they almost had me fooled.

Barnton have gone in the opposite direction; every touch is uncertain and there's frustration when even their better balls are blocked by a well-placed Sandbach head or foot. The home team, and Bevan, get a fourth and Goodwin adds a fifth before the end. The Bach are through to the second round and an away game at Chester. 'It'll be nice, never been there,' says an understandably delighted Sandbach boss Declan Swan after the game. A glamour tie? That may depend on whether Chester field something close to their first team, rather than the academy players who squeezed through on penalties at Alsager last night.

Saturday 26 October

DCBL Stadium, Widnes

Northern Premier League West Division

City of Liverpool 0 Runcorn Linnets 1

City of Liverpool's forlorn search for a ground has landed them here, pretty much on my doorstep.

Which is convenient for me, though it's not where they want to be and the club are furious that their latest attempt to secure the site for a ground in Liverpool has been rejected by the local council. The targeted site is Rathbone Park off Edge Lane which the club want to restore and build a small stadium within. It sounds like something very much on the model of South Liverpool's Jericho Park home, so what's the problem?

'Concern that the proposals would take away recreational space from the community, as well as causing transport problems locally,' according to a Liverpool City Council spokesperson.

The club view this as nonsense. Their proposal includes plans for enhanced community use, reviving the park rather than bulldozing it out of existence, while the idea that a few hundred fans would add much to the regular Edge Lane gridlock also sounds unconvincing. Having driven to Lower Breck's ground and Everton Women's Walton Hall Park at around peak time recently, my experience is that only a small proportion of the traffic heading in that stops at the grounds. It's unlikely this one would be any different.

The club are seeking local support: their petition already has well over a thousand signatures, suggesting sympathy rather than resistance from the bulk of the community. Even so, I can't help thinking it's the kind of thing the founders of CoL ought to have thought through before devising plans to create a new club in a city already full of them.

Nor, you suspect, have co-owner Peter Furmedge's attempts to secure a voice on the city council done much to help their cause. His Beacon Liverpool website, at the time of writing this, doesn't mention anything about the club or the campaign to get a new ground: it's more a declaration of socialist values which, again, isn't exactly covering new ground in Liverpool. In addition to the ruling Labour group, council seats are contested by Community Independents (formed by dissident former Labour councillors), TUSC (an amalgamation of various socialist groups) and the Northern Independence Party, another group founded by former Labour activists. For new socialist parties, the electoral field is every bit as crowded as the footballing one so it's little surprise that Beacon Liverpool have failed to find any kind of foothold. While I have sympathy for the fans who have rallied around the club, the whole venture still strikes me as cack-handed and poorly thought through.

Anyway, for now they're in Widnes and, after last season's march to the play-offs and subsequent dismantling of our title hopes, back in the more familiar territory of the relegation zone.

Runcorn secure a narrow but deserved win with an early goal from Will Saxon – a delightful chip over the oncoming keeper – to further solidify our position in the top half of the league. It's an intense encounter in which Runcorn require something of a rearguard action after scoring but take control in the second, at least while Adam Moseley – who comes on as a half-time substitute – is on the pitch. Adam terrorises the CoL defence before being withdrawn under concussion protocols after he's poleaxed by a Schumacheresque challenge from the keeper.

As with Schumacher's infamous assault on Battiston in the 1982 World Cup, the ref doesn't even give a free kick and an element of the CoL faithful sadly descend to the level of giving a clearly disorientated Moseley abuse as he leaves the field. It's an extension of a repertoire that, in its mildest forms, ranges from the predictable 'Wools' to the more elegant 'six-fingered fuckers' throughout the game. There's a crackling atmosphere, certainly better than when we play Widnes here, though I can't help thinking that, since that challenge on Moseley, the repartee is beginning to call into question that treasured scouse reputation for wit. Adam later reports he can't remember anything between the keeper's challenge and finding himself in a hospital bed.

There's a second controversial incident at the end of the game when the ball appears to strike a Runcorn hand in the area. The ref waves away the Purps' howls for a penalty. A shirker of big decisions, maybe? If so, the ref has levelled up his shirking and Runcorn deserve the win for an excellent battling display. If only we'd competed like this against them in May.

'Prescot are in the top half of the league now,' Tim replies, looking at his phone. 'They've just beaten Ilkeston.'

It coulda bin us, part 2.

Attendance 473.

Tuesday 29 October

APEC Taxis Stadium, Runcorn

Liverpool Senior Cup Round One

Runcorn Linnets 1 Bootle 0

Can we begin to translate our improving away form into something that's at least respectable at home?

The first of three consecutive home fixtures, this first round tie in the Liverpool Senior Cup provides the first opportunity against a Bootle side that shipped four goals at home to Widnes on Saturday and earlier in the season squandered a three-goal lead to lose 6-3 to Vauxhall Motors. Like most sides in the NPL West Division, though, they've been up and down, so as usual it feels like anything could happen tonight.

What happens is we win, somehow. The visitors are the better team throughout, dominating possession and frequently testing the Runcorn back line. However, Bayleigh Passant only has a couple of worrying moments as Bootle fail to turn their good build-up play into clear-cut chances.

Or perhaps I should be congratulating the Runcorn defence who, after looking anything but secure in those early games, have now produced back-to-back clean sheets to secure 1-0 wins. Peter Wylie, captain for the night with no Short or Welsh in the starting line-up, is awarded Man of the Match by the Bucket Hat FM team but it could easily have gone to Harvey Washington alongside him.

Thankfully, Bootle produce more of a threat in front of their own goal, Courtney Duffus handing Runcorn the early goal that proves crucial by heading into his own net from an 11th minute corner. As with the Cheshire Senior Cup, a potentially difficult first round game has been negotiated and we'll form NWCL opposition in the form of Ashton Town in the next round. Optimism, at least in the senior cups, remains undimmed.

Attendance: 298

November 2024

'It feels like, in the two weeks we haven't played, they forgot each other.'

Saturday 2 November

APEC Taxis Stadium, Runcorn

North West Premier League West Division

Runcorn 2 Chasetown 3

Wythenshawe Town have been forced by the NPL to postpone their game against Stafford Rangers due to the club's failure to submit requested financial information. As a result, they've been suspended until they come up with the missing info. It sounds like something that'll blow over quickly. Town have enjoyed a sharp rise in recent years and maybe the various rules and regulations are taking a while to digest. I'm not going to join those joining the dots to come to a solution some Runcorn fans want to arrive at: to wit, that a team involved in some financial chicanery removed us from the FA Cup this season. That was down solely to our own inadequacies.

Some of those inadequacies are on display today. 'We're a more resilient side now,' I confidently declare at half-time to Alan and his wife Christine, who's begun to join him at recent matches, sitting in the APEC's small stand. At this point, Runcorn are 1-0 up and showing the kind of resolve which, I optimistically predict, will bring another clean sheet. The goal comes from a penalty, converted by Naim Arsan after a ridiculously blatant handball from a Chasetown defender. 'How the hell did he expect to get away with that?' asks Alan.

We come out after half-time having apparently left our resilience in the changing rooms. Within minutes Chasetown are 2-1 up, the Runcorn defence not so much capitulating as seeming to nod off. With Adam Morgan ill we're out of central strikers so we seem to be playing a false nine, though who is in the false nine role is unclear. Despite that, the rotating front three are working well and we soon get back on terms courtesy of a cool finish from Will Saxon.

That defensive resilience, however, soon goes AWOL again and, after Bayleigh Passant makes a superb double save, the defence's failure to clear despite repeated opportunities allows Chasetown to score the winner.

Walking away from the ground, my mind goes back to a game we played against Barnet at Canal Street which we also lost 3-2. For some reason, some people who inhabit the world outside non-league football had noticed the result and were winding me up about it. 'It was a great game,' I told them. 'I don't mind losing if I've seen a great game.' They didn't believe me, which is fair enough because I was lying. As a neutral you can admire a great game whatever the result but, for the invested fan, losing a five-goal thriller just leaves you feeling other people are enjoying themselves at your expense.

Attendance: 520

Saturday 9 November

APEC Taxis Stadium, Runcorn

Northern Premier League West Division

Runcorn Linnets 2 Kidsgrove Athletic 0

For an example of how football fortunes can fluctuate at ridiculous levels, look no further than Kidsgrove. In the early stages of last season they looked strong favourites to win the league, winning their first eight games, putting six past 1984 Northwich and four past Hanley Town before cruising to a 2-0 win against us. After that, for no apparently good reason, they fell apart and finished just one place above the relegation places.

Right now, they sit just above us in the table. It feels like we can beat anyone in this league and anyone can beat us so it follows that, as usual, anything could happen today.

As football is all about opinions, I suppose it's inevitable that there'll be different perspectives on what did happen. After the game, a Kidsgrove fan, amid praise for their hosts and how enjoyable this away trip was, posts online: 'Grove played well. One of those games where every bounce seemed to go their (Runcorn's) way.'

Which isn't how it seems to me, or I suspect anyone else with a green and yellow worldview. It feels like the most comfortable win I've experienced this season. In the first half goals from Naim Arsan and Jaden Jones give us a two goal lead we never look like losing and, if anything, it's surprising the margin of victory isn't greater.

Brian Howman is down from Dundee for this game, the first time he's watched Runcorn Linnets, or indeed any Runcorn team since the nineties. It doesn't take him long to build up his old head of steam, yelling abuse at the ref and Kidsgrove forwards within the first few minutes and appealing pretty much every refereeing decision. He's impressed by the ground on his first visit to the APEC, by the passion of the Runcorn crowd and by the quality of much of Runcorn's play. 'It isn't always like this,' I tell him.

'Never is. Never was,' he replies. When I show him the league table after the game, he's surprised, or perhaps horrified, to see Widnes at the top of it while sides he's familiar with from the past like Stafford Rangers and Witton Albion are struggling in the bottom half of a league that, to him, they're too big for. It's like he's woken from a thirty-year footballing coma to find himself in a world that's unrecognisable: it's not so much AI and the internet that bewilder him as the way elements of the football world have been turned upside down. He's aware of the great Northwich schism but when I tell him both sides are now in the Midland League, he just shakes his head mournfully.

If he's looking for a sign that Runcorn might one day re-establish themselves in the upper echelons of the non-league game, he's picked a good afternoon for it, seeing enough to make him determined to check us out again next time he's in England. 'I could never support another English club,' he tells me. He's a regular at Dens Park when he's back home in Scotland but in England, even after such a long sabbatical, 'Runcorn are my club.'

Attendance: 526

Sunday 10 November 2024

APEC Taxis Stadium, Runcorn

North West Women's Regional League D1 South

Runcorn Linnets 6 Wigan Athletic Ladies 3

Wigan Athletic Ladies are not affiliated with the Wigan Athletic men's team, which takes some figuring out because they wear kits that closely resemble official Athletic kids. To sow the seeds of confusion even further, the established club has now launched its own Wigan Athletic Women's team who have joined the Lancashire League this season. This team have been inexistence for 25 years and it's possible they'll have an uphill struggle now to fend off the challenge of their affiliated rivals. As with other teams in the north-west like Mancunian Unity, Wirral Phoenix and Liverpool Feds, independence can have its advantages but also significant drawbacks and the latter are likely to be more influential in scenarios like the one the Wigan Ladies now find themselves in.

This season, despite a good start, they've now slumped to a mid-table position. Runcorn start well and before long are two goals up thanks to a Molly Bennet strike and a Chelsea Gillies header. Somehow, though, a combination of terrible defending and an even more terrible refereeing decision sees them go in at the break three goals down. Alex Bellfield, looking increasingly assured as the season progresses, comes out well to save at the feet of the Wigan number 9, who looks easily their best player, before the Runcorn defence's failure to deal with a through-ball leaves her exposed and unable to prevent the same player from getting the visitors back into the game,

Within minutes they're level. The forward is easily five yards offside when she collects the ball before calmly finishing. There are no liners at this level of the women's game, otherwise it would have been disallowed immediately. The ref, however, is explaining to the protesting Runcorn players that the ball had been played by a home defender, which it clearly wasn't. I'm outraged and start yelling protests in both the direction of the ref and the guy next to me, both of us apparently overlooking the fact that we both agree it's a shocking decision to shout meaninglessly in each other's faces. It's the sort of futile behaviour only a refereeing error can instigate.

Runcorn look understandably rattled and it's no surprise when Wigan score a third to take them into a scarcely deserved half-time lead. Thankfully the home side regain their composure to take control in the second half and run out comfortable winners. They're helped by a bizarre own goal, the keeper's clearance striking the backside of a defender to trundle back past her into the net. Chelsea Gillies gets her second from the penalty spot and Mollie Bennett secures her brace with a delightful chip before Chloe Fairclough adds Runcorn's sixth.

It's an impressive second half display. Sometimes in football you've got to put a perceived injustice behind you – and in this case the injustice was very real – and just reassert your dominance over opponents you ought to be beat. It's probably taking it too far to say that every game provides a learning experience, but they come along frequently in football and today's instalment was along the lines of: Do you want to feel happy at the end of the game rather than pissed off and hard-done-by? If the former, here's what to do...

Tuesday 12 November

Rivacre Road, Ellesmere Port

Northern Premier League West Division

Vauxhall Motors 2 Chasetown 0

As their name suggests, Vauxhall Motors were formed, in 1963, as the works side of the local car plant established just a few years earlier. They moved to Rivacre Road in 1987, at which point they were admitted into the North West Counties League. Administrative pressures forced them to return to the West Cheshire League just five years later but they eventually bounced back and experienced some success in the early years of the 21st century, rising as high as the Northern Premier League Premier Division and famously knocking Queens Park Rangers out of the FA Cup.

They then spent several years in National League North but struggled to sustain operations at that level and, for the second time in their existence, opted to return to the West Cheshire League. Some may be tempted to view this yo-yo existence as evidence of a club in perpetual crisis but that couldn't be further from the truth. On both occasions, the decision to return to county-level football was on their own terms and with the longer-term picture in mind. David Proudlove is right when he congratulates the club for 'vision, foresight, perseverance, good planning and hard work.' Though it must have been frustrating for the supporters at the time, on both occasions the club were able to make swift and significant progress. Many of football's problems stem from the involvement of people with deep pockets but only short-term interests: Vauxhall Motors are the antithesis of that and, as such, deserve great credit.

They don't get big crowds here and even now, second in the league and looking good enough at least for a play-off place, the punters aren't coming in any sort of numbers. I wasn't present, of course, when Runcorn won here earlier in the season but those fans who were here say we outnumbered the home support easily. I can well believe it.

We'll soon be locking horns with them again in the Cheshire Senior Cup but tonight the Motormen are playing the latest team to have victory handed to them at the APEC. A win tonight would take Vauxhall top, and it does.

Against a rampant Motors, the Staffordshire side's physicality has no chance. With 45-year-old Kevin Ellison up front and the huge Josh Quarless in behind, a casual onlooker might anticipate Route One Plus but this is fluid, dynamic football played by footballers who know their teammates' strengths and play to them. The standout player is midfielder Jawad Jebrin who, at 22, has already passed through several clubs at this level but in this set-up he's flourishing, finding space where for others it's at a premium, creating it for teammates and frequently leaving beleaguered opponents trailing in his wake. The Chasetown defenders can't get close enough even to foul him, though that doesn't stop them trying.

It's no surprise when Jebrin scores the opening goal and no surprise either that the killer pass comes from Quarless, who has always had a fine touch for such a big player. This one's inch-perfect and releases Jebrin on the left to fire his shot across the keeper and into the far corner. At that point the golden goal ticket I have in my pocket is burning a hole: 41 minutes, it says, and I reckon the goal came around that time. '39' says the stadium announcer, leaving me rueing that the big defender who'd been closing in on Jebrin hadn't clattered him and conceded a penalty which may well have made up the time gap.

I'd have given the money back to the club anyway. A footballing side as good as this deserve it and certainly deserve an audience bigger than the one around me. This is well worth ten quid of anyone's money. Kevin Ellison, inevitably, heads a second and Vauxhall should really go on to rack up four or five but an equally devastating second half performance produces no further goals. The fans around me are giddily looking forward to Boxing Day and their game against Widnes as a potential title-decider. I think they're probably jumping the gun a bit but, based on what I've just seen, I can't blame them.

I also ponder a scenario where Motors gain promotion and their board decide they don't fancy it and opt for the homely environs of the West Cheshire League again.

Attendance: 187

Saturday 16 November

Bower Field, Stalybridge

Northern Premier League West Division

Stalybridge Celtic 2 Runcorn Linnets 3

Remember that Runcorn v Chasetown game? This time we get a five-goal thriller we can enjoy.

It's about an hour's drive to reach Stalybridge, a town where the fields of East Cheshire begin to morph into the valleys of the Peak District. Celtic were briefly a football league club in the 1920s but, like Northwich Vics before them, decided they couldn't sustain the necessary attendances and opted for a future outside the football league. They've reached the heights of Conference North in the more recent past and are equipped with a ground fit to rise again. Unlike most of the grounds in this league, it's got seated areas on both sides and covered standing at both ends. There's atmosphere too, a buzz augmented by the droves of visiting Runcorn fans. As at Atherton, we make the kind of racket that should be the soundtrack for any football game, on this occasion creating a suitable sonic backdrop for the best one I've seen so far this season.

It's surely Anthony Kay's finest moment as Runcorn manager too. After getting a pasting for the first half hour, we find ourselves two-nil down and looking likely to ship more. That's when Kaysey decides to introduce the cheat code that is Adam Moseley from the bench. James Short leaves the pitch and Naim Arsan drops in at left back to accommodate Adam further forward: within two minutes we've got a goal back, Moseley's sublime pass putting Will Saxon through to round the keeper and score.

In the second half we're a different team, constantly threatening the Celtic defence with devastating attacking forays, the fluent interchanges of Saxon and Moseley something they find it increasingly difficult to deal with. The equaliser, were it scored in the Premier League, would have the pundits purring as they replay it on Match of the Day. Arsan's deft pass finds Saxon, now marauding on the left, who swiftly changes direction, cuts into the box and plays it into the danger area where Moseley slides in between two defenders to prod home. It's a passing move of the kind of delicacy and subtlety many people believe you don't see at this level and, to be fair to them, you rarely do.

Saxon is clearly in a mood to go for the kill and he does, again drifting in from the left side to shoot for goal himself: it takes a deflection off the leg of a bemused defender and Runcorn are ahead. The players fall into a celebratory huddle near us and I find myself yelling 'Come on boys, we go again,' over and over, like the fucking idiot I am. And we do, again and again, until a Celtic defender is dismissed for hauling down Luke Wall as he advances on goal. We don't add to the goals tally and don't need to: Celtic are beaten.

We applaud the Runcorn players down the tunnel and a nearby groundhopper, a Blackpool supporter, tells me it's the most impressive performance he's seen all season.

Attendance: 630

Tuesday 19 November

Spare a thought, if you will, for the volunteers labouring in Murdishaw to try to get tonight's game on. It's snowed heavily overnight and the rest of us are reaching for our social media feeds hoping that their work is not in vain and eventually we'll receive news that the ground is match-ready and all's right with the world: while the rest of the north-west of England freezes, the Cheshire Senior Cup tie between Runcorn Linnets v Vauxhall Motors will go ahead as planned.

I'm in online work meetings all day so inevitably that means I'm constantly peeking at updates whenever I get the chance. News of the fallen begins coming through by late morning. Atherton LR's Lancashire Cup game against Ashton Athletic bites the dust before 11am is even upon us. Just after midday Winsford's game against Glossop in the Macron Cup loses the battle against a snow-covered pitch. An hour or so later we get news from the west that Cammell Laird v Warrington Town's Cheshire Senior Cup game is also off. The clock ticks past 2.30 and the Macron Cup tie between FC St Helens and Lower Breck gives up the ghost.

Finally, news comes through that there's a pitch inspection at Runcorn at 4pm then, fifteen minutes later, we get confirmation that the match has been postponed.

In retrospect, it was always going to be called off but, as a football fan, we get a lot of practice in the art of blindly hoping in the face of insurmountable odds. My wife thinks I should be happy not having to go out in the freezing cold but I'm sulking like a kid who's been told Christmas has been cancelled. She's been through this so many times with me down the years that she's aware of how it is, but still can't fathom why, which is understandable.

It'll be scheduled in the future though, won't it?

Not the point.

I sympathise with your wife.

So do I.

Saturday 23 November

This time a postponement comes as welcome news. Because of work commitments, the Runcorn v Stafford Rangers game today is likely to be the only home league game I can't get to this season. Thankfully, the thaw comes too late and the mischievously named Storm Bert is following on its heels, so the game is off. I've got a smile as wide as a 3-0 away win. My wife just shakes her head.

Saturday 30 November

Bucket Hat FM

Tim's gone on the coach to Clitheroe today but the workload's still heavy so I can't make it. Instead, I'm tuning in to Bucket Hat FM hoping we can continue our recent away form. For some reason, there are certain grounds I seem to miss visiting on a regular basis and Clitheroe is one of them: I'm told it's one of the best away trips, a claim I'm still sadly unable to verify.

Clitheroe suffered an 8-1 walloping at the hands of Hednesford in their last game. League form is so up and down for so many teams in this league that the most likely thing to happen today is they bounce back at our expense and, indeed, it takes less than three minutes for the home side to take the lead from a Potts header, apparently with the Runcorn defence waiting for an offside call that doesn't come.

'It's been a bit long ball,' says Sam as we approach half-time, which seems a questionable tactic as it's not a game plan that's likely to get the best out of our players. Clitheroe have some very tall players, for one thing. For another, Adam Moseley, a player who prefers the ball to his feet, is playing in a central attacking role.

Soon after, Luke Wall's drag-back puts in Adam for a tap-in through the keeper's legs and a lacklustre Linnets find themselves level. The celebrations are barely over, however, when the mercurial Sefton Gonzalez sets up Poilly to restore the home team's lead.

Jack is questioning whether Bayleigh could have done better with both goals but there's general agreement he can do nothing to prevent Clitheroe's third, which comes just after half-time. The Corn are faced for the second consecutive game with having to come from two behind. Wracking my brains since Stalybridge, I've still not been able to recall another time when we managed to do that so a repeat occurrence seems unlikely. When Clitheroe score their fourth, Poilly squeezing the ball in at Passant's near post, we find ourselves 'faced with a mountain to climb' as the pundits would have it. From where I'm sitting it feels like Kilimanjaro.

'It feels like, in the two weeks we haven't played, they forgot each other,' says Jack.

'Sloppy,' says Sam of the second half performance.

'Diabolical,' suggests Jack.

'Rusty,' adds Sam.

Many people will assume I'll be glad I didn't go, but they couldn't be more wrong. It's always better to be at the match for a heavy defeat. Even though the experience can hardly be called enjoyable, the disappointment is communal and you feel less isolated in your despair. Even the taunts of the home fans feel easier to take that way than when you just hear them as background noise behind Sam's commentary. It still feels shit but the shared burden means the shit is spread more evenly. Or something.

December 2024

Tuesday 3 December

APEC Taxis Stadium, Runcorn

Liverpool Senior Cup Round Two

Runcorn Linnets 1 Ashton Town 1 (Runcorn won 2-1 on pens)

An early Jacques Welsh goal direct from a free kick seems to confirm pre-match expectations that this is a night for us to pile up the goals. Following Saturday's heavy defeat, what could be better than an easy game against a team fighting to survive two leagues below us?

As it turns, out we only swerve an exit from out the Liverpool Senior Cup by taking marginally better penalties than them.

We fail to build on that early goal and Ashton begin to cause us problems, deservedly equalising before half-time. In the second half, Runcorn have the better of the possession but struggle to carve out anything meaningful and it's the visitors who have the better of the chances, repeatedly squandering them as the cold of an icy December night begins to bite with increasing ferocity: around the ground, pints of Madris are sunk quickly lest they freeze in gloved hands.

It seems, over the years, penalty shoot outs have gone from being regarded as a necessary evil to the main event. That surely only applies if you're the kind of casual observer whose attention only really focuses on football during international tournaments. I hate them. Football games are to be lived through, and if necessary endured: they aren't, or shouldn't be, a prelude to this kind of manufactured entertainment, which is football with the best bits taken out, designed to appeal to people who don't really like it.

Like everything in football, though, it feels better if you win. Ashton go first, plonking what looks like an attempt at a Panenka onto the top of the bar. Ryan Brooke, making his return after injury, then sees his penalty saved before Tom Myles saves for Runcorn, only for Jacques Welsh also to have his attempt parried. Gloves are being returned to blue fingers with the realisation we could be here all night. But after Tom saves again, the always reliable Niam Arsan steps up with an assured finish to give Runcorn the lead. Ashton's next effort goes in but Peter Wylie restores the advantage before the final Ashton penalty sails over the bar to give Runcorn the squeakiest of passages into the next round.

Runcorn players don't seem inclined, thankfully, to go for one of those ridiculous pile-ons that have become customary during shoot out celebrations. Instead, the warmth of the dressing room evidently beckons and the pitch clears quickly. Frankly, they look a bit embarrassed, as they should. We applaud off the Ashton players: it's the least they deserve after performing so well in the footballing section of the evening, only to lose in the bit that belongs more to the world of Ant and Dec.

Attendance: 243

Saturday 7 December

Shaw View, Urmston

Northern Premier League West Division

Trafford 1 Runcorn Linnets 1

I've got my feet up, watching a bad Christmas film while Storm Darragh wreaks havoc outside, roof slates falling as regularly as the Northern Premier League and North-West Counties League fixtures as social media pages become peppered with the words 'off' and 'postponed'. There are likely to be few, if any, alternatives should the game at Trafford fall victim to the weather, which begins to look inevitable. When it's announced that even the Everton v Liverpool game has been cancelled due to safety considerations, the 11am pitch inspection seems no more than a formality.

To my amazement, the match goes ahead and, much as I'm not looking forward to a drive eastward up the M62 in Darragh's gale force winds, Trafford's Shaw View ground remains one I haven't visited this year (though I've been in the past). Many won't understand that this takes priority over my personal safety, but nonetheless it does.

There's the option of the train. Urmston Station is less than 20 minutes' walk to the ground and, though we would need to get an earlyish one to make sure (train services are dropping like recently sprayed flies too), there's the prospect of a warm pub not far from the station to wait around in. Soon, however, only one train service from Widnes is left standing, and that requires a change at Warrington, not in itself a huge problem but it means there's an additional train that could be cancelled on what is, at the best of times, a weekend service prone to such hazards. I can't risk its cancellation preventing me from getting to a game that has survived against such hefty odds so into the car we get, battling motorway side-winds in the pursuit of footballing nirvana.

Not that Shaw View on a blustery afternoon gives a very passable impression of a state of bliss resulting from the extinction of the soul, or at least not the first part anyway. In addition to the winds, it's freezing cold and raining hard, so we immediately head to the covered area at one end of the ground where much of the small crowd – home fans and travelling Linnets alike – are gathered.

Shawe View is just 16 minutes' drive from Manchester United's ground and the songs and chants here have a distinct Stretford End vibe to them. They even have their own version of 'Take Me Home Country Road', the lyrics of which work far better than those in the United version. Celebrated member of the United Soccerati Andy Mitten is involved with the club and his *United We Stand* fanzine sponsors an advertising hoarding here, generating much-needed funds for a club whose crowds rarely approach what we'd consider to be levels acceptable at the APEC even on more pleasant afternoons.

The wind's blowing in our faces as Runcorn defend the goal in front of us. It's obvious that corners at this end are going to be a nightmare to defend and, sure enough, the home side take the lead via that very route, Norris's far-post header sneaking over the line as Tom Myles paws at it in a forlorn attempt to push it away. I check the 'golden goal' ticket I picked up on the way in. A Trafford goal after 21 minutes is what I need and I think I may have it. The official time turns out to be 22. As at Vauxhall, I feel cheated, violated even. Footballing fortune keeps on conjuring new ways to mock me, it seems.

We go in one down but have the benefit of the wind in the second half. It duly obliges when a gust catches Naim Arsan's corner and pulls it into the net. Any burgeoning optimism at the prosect of a late winner is dispelled, however, when Jack Grundy gets a straight red for something he does at the other end of the pitch – I'm not entirely clear what and don't even see the card being hoisted as I'm shielding my face against an onslaught of icy rain mingled with dead leaves. I just see Jack walking towards the dressing room with his head down, which is all you need to tell you that (a) he's been sent off and (b) he deserved it.

We hold out against both Trafford and the increasingly intense Storm Darragh winds to leave Urmston with a point.

Attendance: 216

Tuesday 10 December

APEC Taxis Stadium, Runcorn

Cheshire Senior Cup Round Two

Runcorn Linnets 2 Vauxhall Motors 1

Vauxhall's win over Chasetown was probably the most accomplished team performance I've witnessed this season and anything resembling the limp effort against Ashton will surely see us entering the new year with just the LSC to play for.

Thankfully, a very different kind of challenge meets a very different response from Runcorn. After the recent bad weather the pitch at the APEC is looking a bit threadbare but neither side lets that prevent them from playing their natural passing game and the result is one of the most entertaining matches I've seen this year. There's no Kevin Ellison for Vauxhall tonight but Josh Quarless again proves a handful and Jawad Jebrin is causing us the kind of problems Chasetown had no answer to.

Thankfully the Runcorn defence prove able to withstand the early pressure from Vauxhall and we grow into the game, eventually taking the lead through Karl Clair just before half-time. 'One goal won't be enough,' I mumble to Tim during the interval and that proves to be the case as, just after the restart, a sweeping Vauxhall moves ends with Jebrin bringing them level.

The game could go either way at this point but excellent work from Arsan down the left sets up an opportunity for Doyle, on as a half-time sub, to turn and fire home to give us the lead. From that point, Runcorn are the better side and should make things comfortable by adding another. Being Runcorn, we don't but a one-goal lead proves to be enough.

The CSC draw is shaping up well. R

Having beaten our old rivals Witton in the last round, we've now removed the obstacle of high-flying Vauxhall Motors, conquerors of Altrincham. The draw in the quarter-finals looks a kind one – the winners of 1874 Northwich and Cheadle Town – prompting those of us of a certain age to start dreaming of a night to rank alongside those heady eighties memories forged at Moss Lane, Gresty Road and the Drill Field...

Attendance: 197

Saturday 14 December

APEC Taxis Stadium, Runcorn

Northern Premier League West Division

Runcorn Linnets 2 Hanley Town 1

There comes a point in every season when the realisation dawns that it is no longer 'early days' and hasn't been for some time. This game marks the mid-point of Runcorn's league season – match 21. Nantwich Town face Vauxhall Motors today in a match-up between two teams who can now be said to have designs on the play-offs at least: a six-pointer, if you will. And Widnes, top of the league, must, extraordinary as it may seem, be taken seriously as potential champions.

Hanley Town, meanwhile, are very much at the wrong end of the table and, along with City of Liverpool, are beginning to look doomed. In their case, the Midland League presumably awaits. As for CoL, who knows? One of their supporters recently told me he wasn't sure whether the club would survive relegation, given the continuing uncertainties about a potential ground.

The Purps, you won't need reminding, did pretty well last season so the reversal of fortunes this time round has been dramatic. Hanley, it must be said, have struggled ever since their promotion in 2022, yet have somehow managed to come away with a draw and a win on their two previous visits to the APEC, secured via a combination of their dogged resistance and our inability to hit a bull's arse with a banjo. On their first visit here, they gave a generous donation to the local Halton Haven charity. We have a good relationship with them and will be sorry to see them go, though of course that doesn't mean we want Runcorn to go easy on them this afternoon.

We look easily the better team, but experience tells us that might not be enough. Runcorn take the lead in the first half, Wylie's excellent ball into the box being met with a superb first-time finish from Doyle, and we're well worth it. But despite the many opportunities that fall our way, we can't add to it and, when Hanley grab an equaliser, there's a hint of déjà vu in the air. Not only that but Runcorn's bad start and subsequent inconsistency leaves us only six points above the relegation zone ourselves going into this game and there's still an uneasy feeling in my gut about us potentially being dragged into the bunfight that looks set to ensue.

Or maybe it's just the mince pies. There's certainly a festive feel to the ground today, with cheesy Xmas tunes booming from the PA at half-time and a guy wearing a turkey on his head, provoking the entertaining if somewhat predictable chant of 'He's got a turkey on 'is 'ead' in the Shed.

Festive spirits are enhanced further when Will Saxon makes a surging run to latch onto a ball into the box and, getting ahead of his marker, deftly connects to send his shot into the far corner. Mayhem in the Shed. Flags are wrenched off the back wall and held aloft. The head-

turkey bobbles in a surreal celebratory jig. In the APEC, we're forging an early Christmas celebration while our friends from Hanley troop off looking like kids who've found wrapped up dog turds in their stockings.

Attendance: 409

Tuesday 17 December

Edge Green Street, Ashton

North West Counties Division One North

Ashton Town 4 Maine Road 3

The town of Ashton-on-Makerfield, which lies to the south of Wigan, is home to both Ashton Athletic and Ashton Town. The latter, of course, gave Runcorn a fright in that Liverpool Senior Cup tie. Their shootout nightmare recurred at the weekend when they lost in a similar fashion to Atherton LR in the FA Vase.

I mention the Runcorn game to the guy at the turnstiles as we go in. He appears to have no knowledge of the game even taking place. It's a reminder that not everybody, even among those dedicated enough to give up their free time for their clubs, takes the senior cups seriously. In truth, they come quite far down the list of priorities for many fans, as attendances even at the APEC frequently demonstrate.

And unlike Runcorn, Ashton Town don't have any kind of history of success in any senior cups. As inhabitants of a town close to the border of Greater Manchester and Merseyside, they're possibly not even sure which ones they're supposed to be in. They were founded in 1953, though an earlier club of the same name existed in the early years of the twentieth century, folding in 1911. Tim comments on the unusually high number of advertising boards around the ground: despite attendances that struggle to get much above the 100 mark, there's clearly an impressive level of support from local businesses and community organisations and you can bet someone within the club is doing a lot of work to make that happen. Sadly, it doesn't appear to be helping performances in the league. Although they reached the play-offs last season, Ashton Town now sit just above the relegation places, which is perhaps another reason why senior cups aren't the first thing on the minds of many of their fans.

Maine Road, in contrast, are knocking on the door of the play-off places and we're standing near a bunch of their fans in the receding drizzle. Although they're mostly discussing the recent decline in form of Manchester City, they sound confident that Maine Road will take home the three points, particularly when they open the scoring after a dominant display in the early stages. Ashton, however, find their way into the game when a clumsy challenge gifts them a penalty. 'Don't try the Panenka,' I think, recalling their opening gambit in the APEC shoot-out. Leon Wright steps up, tries the Panenka and executes it perfectly to level the scores.

It's a thrilling encounter in which the momentum shifts suddenly and decisively at different points throughout the game. Although the sides go in level at half-time, that equaliser has given a much-needed boost to the home team and Wright, from right-back, gets his second early in the second half, lobbing the keeper with a shot that catches the wind and plants itself in the top corner. The home side are now well on top while Maine Road's defence suddenly looks uncertain and jittery, unable to pick up the runs pouring forth from the Ashton midfield and it seems only a matter of time before they go further behind. So it proves. Wright's cross finds the head of George Lomax, who extends the lead, then adds another to make it 4-1.

Town's last league game was a 4-3 thriller they lost in injury time to Charnock Richard. Understandably, a tangible sense of relief takes hold of the small crowd when that fourth goal goes in. They might well need it, you feel, and it turns out they do.

Hope is suddenly and dramatically restored among the visiting fans when Maine Road pull back two late goals. They're on the front foot again, taking the game to their suddenly nervous hosts and twice coming close to adding another and sharing the points.

The game has so many twists it could have ended anything from a comfortable away win to a comfortable home one to a draw. Alongside the goals there's plenty of clumsy defending, misplaced passes, heavy mistimed challenges and players gasping like spent fish long before the end. No doubt this kind of thing isn't everyone's idea of football at its most enjoyable, but it's mine.

Attendance: 113

Saturday 21 December

APEC Taxis Stadium, Runcorn

Northern Premier League West Division

Runcorn Linnets 3 Wythenshawe 1

Brian's back down for this one. Dundee are away at Rangers – 'We never get anything there' – and he's visiting his mum, who lives in Northwich. After that one-off visit to the APEC a few weeks ago he's hooked again, planning to time his forays south of the border for when we're at home. It means he's on hand to witness another of Runcorn's better performances.

We're on it from the first minute, the only concern a failure to turn our dominance into goals. That's until Ryan Brooke, still edging towards the top of the Linnets' all-time top scorer list – steers the ball goalwards from outside the area after a defensive mix-up by the visitors.

We go in at the break knowing we need at least another to feel comfortable. I tell Brian about what happened against Chasetown and I know we've got it in us to capitulate like that again. I needn't have worried: Runcorn's dominance continues after the break and get a second when a dangerous cross is headed into his own net by Ben Mail. We've not quite got Trafford-like conditions here, but the wind has picked up and that's enough to make it an almost impossible task for Mail to clear the ball. The resulting header is one Brookie would be proud of.

Lewis Nolan grabs a third before Wythenshawe's Adam Owen pulls one back four minutes from time. Other than that, it's an unblemished performance from the 'Corn, the kind that has you thinking, 'If we can just sustain this into the new year...'. Which of course we won't but we're now just three places and four points off the play-off places.

Brian asks me if I think we can make the play-offs and I tell him about our play-off adventures of the last three seasons, including an expanded account of the debacle against City of Liverpool last season, a club who, Brian is aware, now sit adrift at the bottom of the league. 'Maybe it's better this way,' I add optimistically. 'Maybe if we build up momentum and go into the play-offs on a run of form...'

There's a Peter Pan-like element to being a football supporter. It seems you're never quite old enough to know better.

Attendance: 461

Thursday 26 December

Berry Street Garage Stadium, Bootle

Northern Premier League West Division

Bootle 0 Runcorn Linnets 1

'Boxing Day games were brilliant,' recalls Brian Howman. 'You'd go home smelling of cigar smoke rather than cigarette smoke.' That was a long time ago, of course. You'll see the odd fan sucking on a vape these days, but the days of smoke-filled stadia are long gone. At this level of the game, though, the tradition of local games over the Christmas period persists. While the TV companies are happy for fans of Premier League club to travel the length of the country for Boxing Day games, at NPL level you can expect, if not a local derby, then at least an encounter close enough to ensure you're back home in time for whatever it is people do on Boxing Day evening. This year we've got a trip up a largely deserted M57 to Bootle.

Just before Christmas, the club confirmed the rumour that has been swirling around the APEC that Will Saxon will be leaving the club. It's a huge blow: Will has been a great player for us since joining from Kidsgrove in the summer of 2023 and we've seen some of his best form of late. He's on his way to Australia but leaves on good terms: he's playing this last game for us before heading off to the Antipodes and, in a great gesture from the club, wears the captain's armband, leading the team out into the gathering fog.

Will isn't at his best today but many of his teammates are, in the first half anyway. We should have the match in the bag but go into half-time narrowly ahead through Ryan Brooke's excellent header. Soon after, Saxon is put through on goal, set up by the head of Brooke: a finish like his first goal at Stalybridge would be an ideal parting gift but he blasts it over the bar. It should give us the cushion we deserve at half-time but doesn't, and nor does Sam Barratt's audacious lob from the half-way line after seeing the keeper off his line.

At half-time our biggest worry is the fog. South of the Mersey estuary, Tranmere's game has already been called off and the mist enveloping the ground here is thickening. Thoughts of an abandonment are foremost in our minds, and perhaps in the minds of some Bootle supporters too. 'Why do you think we'll be able to do it in the second half when we can't do it now?' I hear one home supporter tetchily asking his evidently more optimistic mate. 'We were crap and we'll still be crap.'

His mate's prediction turns out not to be unreasonable, though as Bootle take the game to us after the break. They might not need the fog to save them after all. It's still carrying a threat, gradually obscuring both corner flags on the other side of the pitch from where we've standing. For the bulk of the second half, my neck is straining to the left: the game becomes a series of prolonged and sustained raids into the Runcorn area.

Runcorn need a combination of last ditch defending and several important interventions from Tom Myles to secure a hard-earned three points to move us closer to those play-off places. We leapfrog Trafford, whose game against Avro has been abandoned late on with them leading 2-0. Even the fog, it seems, was on our side today.

Attendance: 623

January 2025

Wednesday 1 January

APEC Taxis Stadium, Runcorn

Northern Premier League West Division

Runcorn Linnets 0 Witton Albion 4

Witton visit the APEC with both sides on something of a roll. They've won their last three, while Runcorn have now won four on the trot and I head to game with a confidence I'm aware is precarious and possibly misplaced.

Last time we had such a run was in the autumn of 2022, when only a defeat at Spennymoor in the cup interrupted a run of seven victories, if you include a win on pens against Chester in the Cheshire Senior Cup. We then entered a winter period which saw only one win in eight that effectively ended any thoughts that we might challenge Macclesfield for the title that season.

During that run there was a visit to our guests today where we shipped four goals, something we managed to emulate on that dark Bank Holiday Monday. We're a different side now, though, aren't we?

It's New Year's Day, there's no Premier League programme and not much else to do, all conditions that ensure the travelling support is the largest we've seen at the APEC this season. I kind of wish the visitors had a sufficiently flexible songbook to accommodate references to Will Saxon's departure: 'Where's your Willy gone?' would surely be a worthy addition to the pantheon of 'Chirpy Chirpy Cheep Cheep' inspired terrace anthems.

I'm not sure whether this thought occurs to them or not, but they certainly enjoy themselves. The bar is certainly benefiting from it and even before the game high spirits are in evidence. I suspect there may even be some here who've just continued from last night. With the game barely twenty minutes old one Witton fan wobbles up to me, holding on to the perimeter fencing, to ask me the way to the toilet. I'm stewarding at the end they've occupied and at one point go over to ask them to stop messing with the goal nets. I wonder if there's a record for how many times a Manchester United supporter has been called a 'scouse prick' because I think it may just have been beaten.

By this point, Witton are two goals to the good and we just haven't turned up. A classic NYD hangover or simply another of those performances we've seen far too often this season? In the second half, we go close on a few occasions but we're wide open at the back and Albion exploit this with two goals to emulate that scoreline in August, a game we've been kidding ourselves belonged very much to the past.

Sam Barrett goes off injured in the first half, the kind of defensive injury we also hoped we'd put behind us and, because Peter Wylie has already replaced the withdrawn Harvey Washington at this point, the ever-willing Eden Gumbs is forced to fill in at right-back. It doesn't help our cause but the increasingly boisterous songs from the Witton end are mainly focused on their ex-player Callum Grogan who, like the rest of the Runcorn defence, has a torrid afternoon.

Kelly Jones wanders by with her camera. The rain is now beating down but not enough, despite hopeful speculation from some of the home fans, to get the match abandoned. 'It's just as bad from this angle,' I tell her.

Just as Runcorn has given Sam Phillips an outlet for his passion for commentating, so Kelly was able to discover a vehicle for her love for photography. 'I've always loved photography,' she says. 'I'd basically seen the camera in the office one day, and I'd asked whose it was and they said it's the club camera. Who uses it? They said "nobody" so I literally took it and I've never returned it since.' She later clarifies this. 'I'm using my own camera now. I've given the club camera over to Gabby Evans. She does all the social media and everything admin-wise for the Ladies' team.' She takes hundreds of photos a game and every now and again, you get that special photograph that says more than thousands of words ever can. Handy, perhaps, on a day like to day when frankly words fail me when it comes to describing Runcorn's performance.

After the game, it's announced that Tom Myles has had his loan spell ended by Manchester United. We've lost both Will Saxon and an excellent keeper during a holiday period which, right now, feels anything but festive.

Attendance: 761

Saturday 4 January

DCBL Stadium, Widnes

Northern Premier League West Division

Widnes 1 Runcorn Linnets 1

Last night, Luke 'The Nuke' Littler was crowned World Darts Champion. In the semi-final, he beat Steve Bunting of St Helens. More evidence, it seems, that darts is muscling in on traditional rugby league territories.

Luke is a Manchester United fan, while Steve supports Liverpool. Presumably the attention of both this weekend, along with that of much of the rest of the world, will be on tomorrow's Liverpool v Manchester United clash. Before the game, both sets of fans will be forming an unlikely alliance to protest ticket price increases, anticipated in the case of Liverpool but very much a reality for United fans, whose owners have, in the middle of the season, raised the ticket price for remaining applicants – senior citizens and children included – to £66.

From the Liverpool side, AFC Liverpool founder Alun Parry put it in stark terms as long ago as 2008 when he told the Daily Telegraph: 'A season ticket in the Kop cost £45. Today it's £650...in inflation terms eighties prices should equate to £98 today.' In real terms, that means season tickets have more than doubled in price. John Coleman, a Liverpool fan who played semi-professionally for the likes of Burscough, Rhyl and Accrington Stanley, recalls paying 40p to get into Anfield as a teenager. He told Simon Hughes, 'At that time, my dad was earning 40 quid a week, which is one hundred times what I was paying to go to the match. Now, instead of it being a hundredth of your dad's salary, it's a tenth. If you think of how that has impacted upon the common man, football has become like opera.'

Although recent years have seen a slowing down of the rate of increase – clubs at the very top, after all, bring in a far greater proportion of their income through sponsorship, TV money and merchandise – the economic logic is, for club owners, compelling. Occasional fans with deep pockets, labelled 'Commodores' by Half Man Half Biscuit's Nigel Blackwell ('Once, twice, three times a season') are targeted: they descend on Old Trafford or Anfield, spend heavily on merchandise and hospitality, their only concession to the unofficial merch sellers the abomination that is the half and half scarf around their necks.

It's not that I don't enjoy watching Premier League football, even given United's woeful performances of late, but for me the penny dropped some time ago: the club's owners don't want me there. 'They've forgotten it's a working-class game,' said a fellow United fan to me after the ticketing news broke. I disagree. It's not that they've forgotten: they'd just rather turn top level football into something different and have been successfully doing so for decades now. And United know that, even during the bad period they're going through now, they'll have no problem filling the seat I'm leaving vacant.

In the NPL, however, I'm wanted, as is everybody else who walks through the turnstiles at Runcorn or any of the other clubs I've featured in this book. In my stewarding capacity, I patrol the turnstiles pre-game these days and see Peter Cartledge welcoming fans, often by name. Their presence as supporters is valued and, though non-league football isn't immune to many of the problems at higher levels (as the cases of clubs like Chester and Northwich Vics adequately demonstrate), as a support you don't feel expandable in the way that supporters of big teams, whether they admit it or not, unquestionably are.

I'll still watch the Liverpool v United game on the telly because, despite all the above, I'm an addict. But the derby game I'm at this weekend is a very different kind of derby, and one taking place in unfamiliar circumstances. While Runcorn forage for scraps from the play-off table, Widnes are living the dream of a six-point lead at the top.

Despite this, Widnes fans at the DCBL are still rattling around like peas in a very big tin. But Runcorn are in town again and that means a decent crowd, if not one that will come close to filling this large but characterless venue.

Although they've been doing well on the pitch, Widnes have had some problems off it of late with the activities of some of their younger fans. They've now introduced a policy of only admitting children who are accompanied by an adult, something which is a shame for the many teenage Runcorn fans, the majority of whom cause no trouble at all. Outside the ground, one guy is arguing with stewards about the refusal to allow unsupervised children into the ground. As he evidently isn't a child, this can presumably only mean that he's brought one with him but doesn't want the kid anywhere near him while he's watching the match. 'Why doesn't this happen when City of Liverpool are here?' he asks a steward, who simply replies, 'Their kids don't cause trouble.'

We're saved from the large queues because Tim has the presence of mind to bring some paper money with him, allowing us to use the shorter 'cash entrance'. Not being blessed with Tim's foresight, Widnes FC somehow haven't anticipated hundreds of Runcorn fans converging on the ground, even though we do it every year. The length of the queues means people are still coming in 20 minutes after kick-off.

Admittedly, the attendance is bigger than last season's El Clasitol, but only slightly, so there's no excuse for Widnes not to get their act together. Runcorn usually operate on a single turnstile and manage to get bigger crowds than this one into the ground without any problems. We have a separate gate for season ticket holders, for one thing, and keep in reserve an option of opening a separate 'correct cash only' entrance if the size of the crowd warrants it, depending of course on having enough volunteers on the day. A scenario like this illustrates again how, despite their success on the field this season, Widnes don't seem well prepared off it. If they're promoted, I wouldn't fancy the chances of an operation like this managing to accommodate FC United coming to town.

Widnes have won every game this season when they've scored first so there are fears that a repeat of the start we made against Witton will result in a similarly severe hammering. We start better but still manage to concede first, an excellent save by Bayleigh Passant, now restored to goalkeeping duties, unfortunately bouncing off the post and falling to the prolific McGowan, who taps in from close range. To get anything out of the game we'll need to do something other sides haven't managed to do against Widnes this season, either home or away, and we do, brilliant work from Luke Wall on the right leading to Naim Arsan's decisive finish, which restores parity just two minutes later.

It's a frantic and entertaining encounter and both sides have chances to win, though even Ello, unusually restrained on the sidelines, admits later that Runcorn deserve a draw. Something of a derby atmosphere begins to crackle, especially after a Widnes sub who bears a passing resemblance to Robbie Savage appears to apply a stray elbow to the cheek of Karl Clair. The ref doesn't see it that way, or perhaps just doesn't see it, and gives him a yellow.

We come close to squandering a well-earned point in the final seconds of injury time as the Runcorn defence play statues during a Widnes attack, resulting in the ball bouncing around the area only eventually to roll harmlessly out of play, with players on both sides gesticulating to each other, presumably asking why the hell somebody didn't do what they didn't do and kick the bloody thing.

It's a good away point for Runcorn. Widnes' lead in the table, meanwhile, has been narrowed as the two clubs immediately behind them in the league – Congleton and Vauxhall – win, as do the wealthy Hednesford, who move menacingly into fourth place.

Attendance: 633

Tuesday 7 January

Heavy snow brings the cancellation of the game against Stafford Rangers for the second time.

Saturday 11 January

Not unexpectedly, the continued freeze across the north-west of England means the Wythenshawe Town game is of. It's a second successive postponed home game for Runcorn and already the financial knock-on effects of that are threatening to bite.

Runcorn have opened the clubhouse and are inviting fans to watch the Liverpool v Accrington Stanley FA Cup game there, a match that's unlikely to be a nail-biter but, as many Runcorn supporters also double as Liverpool fans, it's an opportunity for the club to generate some revenue and for fans to mingle as they normally would on a Saturday afternoon. Despite my earlier rant about the trajectory of big-time football, at times like this the 'two worlds' of football coming together in this way can be helpful.

With the Runcorn Linnets Ladies game called off last Sunday, the pitch hasn't been used since New Year's Day and the next scheduled home game for the men's team isn't until 25 January. Unless the weather allows for some of the fixture backlog to be accommodated before then, it'll be almost a month between games and, while the above schemes might might make up some of the shortfall, it's certainly not an ideal scenario, either for clubs like Runcorn or fans like me who build much of our lives around them.

Tuesday 14 January

Ericstan Park, Wythenshawe

Northern Premier League West Division

Wythenshawe Town 0 Clitheroe 2

The snow has melted, which is good news, or would be if melted snow didn't turn to water and leave many pitches in the region waterlogged. I'd been hoping to see 1874 Northwich play Cheadle Town in the Cheshire Senior Cup – the winners will play Runcorn in the next round – but Vicki England informs me the Townfield Lane pitch is 'completely sodden,' and the game has been called off.

I grasp in desperation for football-related activities that aren't weather dependent. The draw for the Liverpool Senior Cup Quarter-Finals takes place and there's a live stream for it. This lasts just over one and a half minutes. There's no faffing around and no celebrity ball-pullers, which is how it should be. Runcorn draw Tranmere Rovers, which could be good or bad depending on the side Tranmere choose to put out.

I saw them at Rylands last year, of course, and there's another opportunity to visit Gorsey Lane tonight, where South Liverpool are the visitors in the LSC, the winners now knowing they'll face Southport in the quarter-finals. Although Warrington Town's Cheshire Senior cup tie against Stockport is called off due to a waterlogged pitch, somehow Rylands have managed to get their game on. I hate going there though and I decide that, if it's a choice, between that and Eastenders I'll stay in and watch Eastenders, even though I never watch it and don't even know if it's on. Staring at a blank screen would be preferable to going to Rylands, I decide, even given my current state of deprivation.

Thankfully there's another option, a game between two teams who've handed us our arses this season but now sit well below us in the table. We head down the M56, waving a cheery two fingers in the direction of Warrington as we pass the A49 turn-off, arriving at Ericstan Park in time for the warm-up. Normally the first figure I recognise when Clitheroe are playing is, naturally, the living legend that is Sefton Gonzalez, but he doesn't appear to be out there.

I ask a nearby fan about his absence, only to realise he is wearing a Trafford FC bobble hat and isn't any wiser than us. It's clear we're not the only ones in the ground tonight who have been experiencing withdrawal symptoms and just had to get to a football ground, any ground. Or, in my case, almost any ground.

Fortunately, a nearby Clitheroe fan is on hand to explain he's injured. The ice has been broken with the Trafford fan, though, and he turns out to be very chatty. Except he's not actually a Trafford fan, he explains. He's an Oldham Athletic fan but pops along to watch Trafford when he's got nowhere else to go. He's a groundsman by trade and is impressed with the quality of the Town pitch after the recent bad weather. He also expounds, in elaborate detail, on his passion for Greek cheese, before asking me who I support.

'Runcorn Linnets,' I tell him.

'Runcorn Linnets, eh?' he puzzles, nodding with a faraway look on his face, like he's trying to figure out the answer to some conundrum I've unintentionally posed.

Though it seems almost heretical to claim it, Clitheroe look better in Sefton's absence. Before this game, they'd only won once away from home this season but the fluidity of the youngsters up front causes headaches in the Town defence from the first minute. In contrast, Town look one-dimensional, bereft of ideas, far from the side who tore Runcorn apart here in the FA Cup.

After a while, the chairman of Ashton United joins us, a friend of the bobble hatted groundsman who, apparently, sorted his pitch out for him after it had been left in a bit of a state: he shows us some 'before and after' pictures and it seems it went from something akin to the trenches of the Somme to what now looks a perfect playing service. Of course, I only have the groundsman's word for it that these two pictures are of the same ground. The two of them talk shop, issues familiar to those all clubs at this level face such recruiting, retaining and managing volunteers, some of whom carry an enormous burden which, the chairman says, comes with a risk both to their health and to the club's long-term prospects: who replaces them when they decide to call it a day or, worse, their health decides it for them? The Oldham fan in the Trafford FC hat just shakes his head.

Soon after, Clitheroe deservedly take the lead from the spot.

'Was it a penalty?' asks the groundsman.

'Clear pen,' I tell him.

'My eyesight's fucked.' He's struggling with the brightness of the Wythenshawe floodlights, which do seem notably brighter than on previous visits. There's something different about the ground every time we come, it seems, with a scoreboard now going up at the end which last year resembled an especially messy builder's yard. The quality of the pre-match music has nosedived though: faceless pop where once we got Madchester classics.

The groundsman reckons the player taking the penalty will miss because he's left footed. He can see that much, apparently. 'I don't like left-footed penalty takers.' He crashes it firmly into the corner.

They're both impressed with the Clitheroe number 11 – a 19-year-old called Luke Gill – and the chairman says he's made notes on him and will investigate further. The Clitheroe fan, who still hovers close by in the first half before joining his fellows at the other end of the pitch after half-time, tells us he normally plays in a central attacking role, which only seems to pique their curiosity further. 'We got him from the Cheshire League,' he tells us. It turns out he was previously with Vulcan, based in Newton-le-Willows and I point out he's up against Sam Sheridan, a veteran midfielder who's playing out of position at right back, which may be exaggerating Gill's qualities somewhat. I almost venture to suggest he's not a patch on Adam Moseley, which he isn't, but I don't want them putting any feelers out in that direction so I keep my thoughts to myself.

Sheridan's the nephew of John Sheridan, I inform the groundsman, who remembers him as Oldham manager on six separate occasions. 'A record,' he tells me. 'Family of fruitcakes,' he adds.

The player who catches my eye is Emerich Poilly, who scored against Runcorn earlier in the season. His runs from deep into the heart of the Town defence cause problems all night and it's Poilly who eventually secures this rare away win for Clitheroe, scoring their second just after the hour mark.

The groundsman leaves before the end to continue a life spent roaming the M60 in search of football to watch and grounds to tend. He's talked affectionately of visits to Mossley, Stalybridge, Hyde and pretty much every other ground hanging on to the outskirts of Greater Manchester. I tell him to come and say hello if he ever ventures as far west as Runcorn. He seems grateful, probably not for the invitation but because he's been wracking his brains about where the hell Runcorn is.

Attendance: 215

Saturday 18 January

Seel Park, Mossley

Northern Premier League West Division

Mossley 2 Runcorn Linnets 0

Mossley, on the east side of Greater Manchester, illustrates the Manc/Scouse divide possibly better than any other geographical location, at least in a phonetic sense. For a start, if you say 'Mossley' to someone from Liverpool, they're likely to think you're referring to the leafy Scouse suburb of Mossley Hill. More to the point, they'll emphasise the double-s in pronouncing it as it's written. For those in Greater Manchester, the place is 'Mozley', a town that clings to the side of the Pennines as if hanging on for dear life.

We've had a good run against them recently, convincingly winning here last season and pretty outplaying them in our two most recent home games. This worries me probably more than it should.

Runcorn have brought in a new forward, Dean Adekoya, on loan from Stoke City Under-21s. It's certainly been a problem position for us this season. The promising Taylor Bowen shone before getting injured, Adam Morgan looked the part before disappearing and Ryan Brooke is injured again.

On a terrible Mossley pitch, we start with three central defenders, a baffling choice as we have enough players available to play our normal formation. Although Runcorn start well, the usual problem with three at the back - space behind the wing-backs - allows Mossley to take the lead, Mugalula entering said space behind Peter Wylie and scoring with a low drive. Soon after, Harvey Washington is dismissed for a professional foul and it all unravels from there. The three at the back trial can hopefully be consigned to the dustbin where it belongs but it's a damaging experiment all the same and I've no idea why Kaysey thought it was a good idea.

The ten men make a decent go of it in the second half, but Mugalula secures the points with his second and we have that feeling at the end that, in normal circumstances, this is a team we should have beaten. That they've now leapfrogged us in the league makes the feeling that Runcorn are under-achieving this season still more acute. Even before the sending off, the defence looked vulnerable enough to ship goals, we only got a chance to play our normal game after one of the back three had been red carded and if Adekoya is the answer to our central striker problem, we're not asking the right question. He looks a capable athlete with good technique but, if there's a natural goalscorer in there, it's not on show today. A quick search on my phone tells me he's mostly known as a left-winger, which figures.

The cold Pennines afternoon is giving way to an even colder Pennines evening as we leave the ground. Someone's brought a megaphone today and some fans are using it to call for Tony Kay's sacking. Kay tells Sam Phillips after the game that he's aware of the danger of drifting away from the play-off chase. 'We need points,' he says, 'and quickly.' He comes across as desperate rather than reassuring. The desperation of a man, perhaps, who suddenly pulls a three-man defence out of nowhere and takes a punt on a young left-winger in a central attacking role.

Widnes, Congleton and Vauxhall Motors now occupy the top three places in the league, with a gap of five points over fourth place. That means two of the four clubs with the smallest average home attendances last season and one of the promoted clubs could be slugging it out for the title. To put that in perspective, it would roughly be the equivalent of Brentford, Fulham and Ipswich Town filling those positions in the Premier League.

Attendance: 521

Friday 24 January

APEC Taxis Stadium, Runcorn

Northern Premier League West Division

Runcorn Linnets 2 Atherton Collieries 1

Following our victory at Atherton earlier in the season, I pronounced Colls likely relegation candidates. Since then, their prospects have improved. Of the four relegation places available this season, City of Liverpool and Hanley Town now look likely to occupy two of them. Above them, Atherton are one of a number of sides who still have the threat of relegation having over them, but currently they're hovering just above the danger zone.

On this evidence, they'll still struggle. It's one of those games we seem comfortably in control of yet still find ourselves hanging on at the end. The game's been switched to a Friday night. If we're hoping to maximise attendance by avoiding a clash with Liverpool's home game tomorrow, that doesn't materialise and the crowd is once again under 500, better than most games in this league will attract this weekend but, for Runcorn, part of a worrying recent pattern.

Although Runcorn remain one of the best supported clubs in the league, a failure to maintain the upward momentum of recent years always carries with it the threat of declining attendances. There are fans at any club who will continue to attend matches no matter what but, outside this hardcore element, others will vote with their feet or find something else to do on a Tuesday evening or Saturday afternoon. It appears many of them can think of better ways to spend a Friday night too.

Kelly Jones, in the fan engagement role she's recently taken on, believes part of the answer to keeping feet on the terraces lies with better communication between club and fans. She's keen to begin holding fan forums. 'It's just keeping people involved really. There's so much going on,' says Kelly, 'and fans don't see that...but then, no one tells them. How do they know? Things like signings, or people leaving the club.'

Although social media sites are updated regularly and fans are informed about high-profile departures like that of Will Saxon, it's true that some happenings at the club go under the radar. What happened to Adam Morgan after his arrival earlier in the season, for example? He went to Clitheroe as assistant manager but, speaking to fans around the ground, many seem unaware of this. I didn't know until I carried out a google search. It may be that the club posted this information somewhere, but I didn't see it and it appears many others didn't either. Even with the communication advantages of social media, much still relies on an old-fashioned terrace grapevine to get around. And when fans stop attending games, what then?

Tonight, anyway, turns out to be a good night for those present. We take a first half lead with a fine finish from Luke Wall. Colls have rarely troubled the Runcorn defence and look unlikely to when, in the second half, Kielen Adams is shown a red card. Few in my vicinity of the ground appear to know what's happened though one supporter enlightens us, explaining 'He took Doyley out.' I assume he's referring to violent conduct rather than a candlelit dinner for two.

Whatever it means, Doyle hangs around long enough to double Runcorn's lead with a sweetly struck shot into the roof of the net.

It turns out we need it because in injury time Dwyer halves the Runcorn lead, ensuring we get a couple of nervous minutes at the end. It would be good if we could see off opponents without this kind of drama but it appears that just isn't how we do things. As the players leave the field, there's a scuffle with Colls players surrounding Doyle, presumably in relation to the sending off. Or perhaps they all fancy a romantic evening with him.

Attendance: 483

Saturday 25 January

Brocstedes Park, Ashton-in-Makerfield

North West Counties League Division One North

Ashton Athletic 2 Thornton Cleveleys 4

Runcorn's Friday night switch gives me an opportunity to visit the one remaining ground on my list. Ashton Athletic and Ashton Town may theoretically share the territory of Ashton-in-Makerfield but my drive takes me well beyond the town and towards the countryside, down a narrow road and into a small car park that services a ground that, despite its rustic surroundings, is small and neat. Brocstedes Park lies to the west of Town's ground, on the edge of a large rural area on the other side of which sits the Merseyside boundary. There's none of Mossley's hanging-off-the-side-of-a-hill charm, nor the rugged grandeur of Stalybridge Celtic. It's the sort of stadium you'd find enclosing an artificial pitch, but thankfully there's grass.

Ashton Athletic were formed in 1968 and have played their home matches here ever since. Starting out as a Sunday League team, they've variously competed in the Warrington & District League, Cheshire League, Lancashire Combination and Manchester League, enjoying a brief period in the North West Counties in the eighties before being thrown out for having a shite ground. Having carried out the improvements to turn Brocstedes Park into what it is today, they eventually rejoined the NWCL in 2006 and were promoted to the Premier Division two years later. There they remained until relegation in 2002 saw them drop into this division.

'I think we'll win this one,' says the Thornton Cleveleys manager to a small group of visiting fans standing near the dugout. It's a bold claim. Thornton, who are based near Blackpool, are only just above the relegation zone or, to put it more accurately, just above the line below which your fate lies in the mercy of committees and their calculators. Yet his team justify his faith and produce a performance that belies their lowly position, despite the pitch bearing the scars of the recent bad weather and not being exactly conducive to the flowing football they produce. They look the more likely to score first but manage to concede a goal from perhaps the worst corner I've ever seen (and I've seen Phil Jones taking them). The corner taker appears to stub his toe and the ball bobbles towards the near post, inexplicably finding its way into the net via the leg of a hapless defender.

The Athletic keeper appears in too charitable a mood to allow his teammates to bask in that narrow lead for long. A dreadful attempt at a clearance lands at the feet of Aspinall, who finds the empty net to give Thornton their equaliser.

The visitors deservedly take the lead when Aspinall grabs his second early in the second half but the more direct football of Ashton brings its reward when Hill thumps home a loose ball inside the area to get them back on terms.

At this point it could go either way but it's Thorton who finish more strongly, re-taking the lead with ten minutes remaining through Lang and finally securing the points via the same player's injury time penalty. The Thorton fans tell me he's missed his last five: I'm not sure whether they're being serious or not, but he makes no mistake this time, capping a performance that's more than justified the boss's earlier confidence to take all three points back up the M6.

Attendance: 75

Tuesday 28 January

APEC Taxis Stadium, Runcorn

Northern Premier League West Division

Runcorn Linnets 1 Stafford Rangers 3

I have some fond and not-so-fond memories of encounters with Stafford Rangers, a side we regularly met in the old Conference days. In the first half, I'm standing near a group of Stafford fans and sharing some of them with them. They're also Stoke City fan love non-league football because they can have a drink while watching the match. That's why they hate going to Widnes. 'I've been to watch rugby league at Widnes with 8000 fans in there,' one of them says, 'and you can have a drink. When we went to watch Stafford there were about 200 and most of them were our fans, but we couldn't take a drink in.'

They all shake their heads at this manifestly appalling scenario. They weren't aware, until I tell them, that City of Liverpool are sharing the stadium now. 'So we've got another game we can't drink at?' There's mass exasperation and even more shaking of heads. Then they drink some more beer.

I tell them I recall a defeat at their place when Ray McBride saved a Stafford penalty and Runcorn fans were baiting the Stafford keeper with taunts like, 'Bet you couldn't do that, y' fat bastard.' Then the inevitable happened: Runcorn were awarded a penalty and a chance to get something from the game and he saved it, grinning to himself for the rest of the match.

There's some banter between the Shed and the Stafford keeper tonight too, who at one point in the second half goes down in a whingeing heap and the ref, taken in by his antics, awards a free kick. The score is 1-1 at that point, Stafford having taken the lead after comedy defending from Runcorn in the closing stages of the first half. The scorer is Zidane Sutherland, on loan from Hednesford for whom he scored here earlier in the season. 'A great player, but a lazy bastard,' one of the Stafford fans tells me. It comes at the end of a manic first period after which the score could easily have been 3-3. It's such an open game that I'm confident Runcorn can get back into it and we do, Luke Wall equalising early in the second half.

What happens after that quickly erodes any confidence another worryingly small Runcorn crowd have as Stafford take control of the game. The Runcorn performance begins to bear comparison with some of our very worst showings earlier in the season. Stafford score another and never look like sacrificing their lead, adding a further goal late on to secure a deserved win. By that point the Shed has become increasingly restless, many calling vociferously for Tony Kay's sacking and quite a few leaving well before the final whistle.

Before the game, Runcorn announced the loan signing of Leslie Adekoya, brother of Dean, from Warrington Rylands. Leslie is, I'm reliably informed, a real centre forward. He comes on in the second half but, to be fair to him, has such limited service it's difficult for him to make any kind of impact. With Ryan Brooke also coming on, our formation looks confused: it's difficult to detect a coherent plan, or at least anything the players can respond to. We look bereft of ideas, belief passion or any of the other things that a football team needs to function. While our recent form has been erratic rather than continuously bad, there have been enough performances like this through the season to feel there's now a huge question mark hovering over the whole Anthony Kay project.

I can't remember a smaller number of fans left to applaud the team off at the end, and I'm struggling to recall a time when the players looked so embarrassed to receive it.

Attendance: 431

February 2025

About as comfortable as a couple of ginger toms in Battersea Dogs' Home...

Saturday 1 February

Bucket Hat FM

Anthony Kay's departure was announced on Thursday. Tuesday night's display against a relegation-threatened team was, apparently, the kind of performance that changes the question from 'Do we stick with the plan and hope things get better?' to 'Are we really just going to do nothing while our play-off chances get flushed down the shitter?'

I'm often sceptical of the 'sack the manager' solution to a club's problems: on many occasions it smacks of a desire to placate disgruntled fans and does nothing to address deep-rooted issues within a club. However, there are times when the relationship between manager and board or between manager and players has broken down to such a degree that a parting of the ways turns out to be the best thing for everybody. Leaving aside the way things ended for Ello at Runcorn, his sacking at City of Liverpool led to an improvement in the club's fortunes; he went to Widnes, where his appointment has been an unqualified success.

For today's match at Newcastle Town, Ryan Brooke is taking temporary charge with Karl Clair as his assistant. I can't get there so I tune in to Halton FM to hear what the guys say about the game and, inevitably, recent events.

With not entirely convincing optimism, Jack breaks into a rendition of *Start of Something New* from *High School Musical* before kick-off. Brookie and Karl Clair have named themselves in the starting line-up and the Adekoya brothers are nowhere to be seen: will they forever be viewed in Runcorn circles as Kay's final folly? It was coming to the end of Dean's 28-day loan but it sounds like Leslie must have copped a lift from him: 'just drive, chief'. After a long absence through illness, club captain James Short is helping Brooke and Clair in the dugout today.

Runcorn are 'gritty' says Jack; 'dogged' adds Sam. It's level at half-time but you sense optimism is beginning to build. It builds further when Ryan Brooke strikes in the second half to give Runcorn the lead which they hold on to until the final whistle.

Sam announces that both members of the temporary management team will be doing the post-match interview with him. 'What, like, finishing each other's sentences and stuff like that?' says Jack. In the end, Shorty joins them to give his thoughts too. We know these three won't be a permanent solution but for now the arrangement feels like one we can enjoy.

Tuesday 4 February

APEC Taxis Stadium, Runcorn

Northern Premier League West Division

Runcorn Linnets 2 Wythenshawe Town 2

Groundhog Day. Another Tuesday night chance to enter the play-off places if results go our way. It feels slightly strange that we can screw up as often as we have this season and still not be out of the running.

Standing outside the turnstiles, it feels busier but this turns out to be illusory, or perhaps just wishful thinking on my behalf. For the second home game running, the attendance figure needs the presence of a few dozen away supporters to limp past the 400 mark.

The three amigos are in charge again tonight, but a new manager has been appointed: Brad Clarke, who managed Atherton Collieries during a good period for the club. Brad's new charges demonstrate there's plenty for him to get his teeth into. The first half is a defensive shambles: the Town attackers are allowed far too much space and Grogan and Washington in the Runcorn defence give the impression of having only recently been introduced. With some inevitability, the visitors take the lead and only a couple of fine interventions from Bayleigh Passant prevent them from giving Runcorn the proverbial mountain to climb at half time.

In the second half, Runcorn produce some fight of their own and, when Naim Arsan is felled in the area, he converts the penalty that gets us back in the game. The better chances are falling to Runcorn now and, though sometimes we're as wasteful as our opponents were before the break, Ryan Brooke eventually puts us into the lead.

Sadly, the Runcorn defence are still performing some kind of 'gentleman's excuse me' and it's no surprise when Town equalise with a headed goal from a right wing cross. After it, the visitors scurry quickly back to the centre circle for the restart. Realistically, both sides will feel they need more than a single point from this but, ultimately, that's what they get.

There's some bemusement among the Runcorn faithful when the Bucket Hat FM presenters announce their Man of the Match as Callum Grogan. Looking up at the media platform, one Runcorn fan shouts, 'Are you on the fuckin' ale up there, or what?' Tonight, both Callum and Harvey have looked about as comfortable at the back as a couple of ginger toms in Battersea Dogs' Home.

A draw feels like a fair result, even though both sides will be rueing missed chances. From a broader perspective, though, it means we've played Town four times this season and not come out on top once. Remembering how uncomfortable they looked on their right side against Clitheroe, I regret us not probing that weak area enough. I remember the torrid evening that young striker gave Sam Sheridan and, with Sheridan filling in at right back again today, I do wonder if the earlier introduction of Adam Moseley might have helped swing it our way.

At the end of the game, I applaud the ref off, telling him he's the best we've had this season. Tim says he probably thinks I'm being sarcastic. I'm not, and the fact that no one is shouting abuse at him at full-time tells its own story. It shouldn't be that difficult to find refs who let the game flow and don't produce petty cards for no reason, but apparently it is so I'm going to give credit to one who manages it.

Somehow, the play-offs are still in our sights, just. Over to you, Brad.

Attendance: 440

Saturday 8 February

APEC Taxis Stadium, Runcorn

Northern Premier League West Division

Runcorn Linnets 1 Vauxhall Motors 1

Brad Clarke's first game in charge comes against a high-flying Motors side who have emerged as Widnes' main rivals for the title this season. I can't believe I'm writing that.

Despite this, Runcorn are seeking a hat-trick of victories over the Ellesmere Port side this afternoon, which, if it happens, would be both impressive and kind of annoying.

Until a questionable penalty decision in the second half, we never look like losing this one. There are over 500 in the ground, a welcome improvement that may have something to do with the arrival of the new boss: it's more likely a combination of that, the absence of a Liverpool or Manchester United game today and an above average turnout of Vauxhall fans. Paul Non-League Rover the well-known groundhopper is here: balancing two half-time pints (not very well – he's tipping lager everywhere) he lavishes praise on the club, the ground, the chairman, the town of Runcorn...he may well go on to include Run Corn, the tea bar snacks and the Vets4Pets across the road, but by that point I've resumed my post at the far end of the ground where, due to some complaints from Wythenshawe Town on Tuesday, I've volunteered to keep an eye on some allegedly wayward youngsters.

Maybe these are different youngsters, because they look fairly angelic to me – but then, wayward kids, when they know they're being watched, often do – and don't even have any latent delinquency pricked when a fight breaks out 16 minutes from time in the Runcorn area. It results in Peter Wylie being given his marching orders and, eventually, the ref deciding, after long consultation with the liner, to award a penalty.

No question about the sending off: it's a clear retaliation from Peter and certainly warrants a second yellow. However, to be punished for retaliation means you must have something to retaliate against and it seems to me – standing at eye level from the incident – that the initial foul was committed by the Vauxhall player. The ref clearly didn't see what happened, unless of course the conversation with the liner, which takes place behind furtive hands, is a discussion about whether it's going to be safe to have a post-match pint.

Anyway, there's a heavy feeling of injustice as Vauxhall's Rankin dispatches the penalty to give the visitors the lead.

And that, I assume, will be it. But I reckon without the fighting spirit of a wounded Runcorn side who, unexpectedly, produce their best football while down to ten men and, following a sustained barrage of the Vauxhall area deep in injury time, a corner finds its way to Jacques Welsh who fires home from close range in front of a delirious Shed.

Vauxhall fans can be heard thanking the liner at the end, which tells you everything you need to know about the penalty decision. Another Vauxhall fan, who I'm sure I've met before, concedes to me that Runcorn deserved a point. It's a justified but nonetheless honourable response to the events of the day, given the disappointment their fans must feel at conceding so late on. Widnes have unexpectedly lost at home to Atherton Collieries and, although Vauxhall have closed the gap by a point, they'll be frustrated not to be breathing down their necks by 5 o'clock today. We've done Widnes a favour, unquestionably, but, as the players leave the pitch behind a 'By Fans 4 The Fans' flag, it's all about the 'Corn.

Alternative review from Paul the Non-League Rover's Travelogue:

Today, I'm off to a club I've wanted to visit for ages and it's FINALLY happening.

2nd and final train of the morning, next stop Runcorn!

Do I have to wait for an escort, Murdishaw Massive, or have I got the clearance needed?

This HAD to be done, the Archer as we know it from 2 Pints! Tony, who's part of the Buddhist Temple, showed me around, a very lovely chap.

After gaining clearance to enter the estate from the Murdishaw Massive, I've been treated like royalty up here. Everyone is so friendly and welcoming. Absolutely love it.

Goal! Vauxhall Motors Connor Rankin pen.

Wow what just happened!!! One minute I'm singing Derby songs on a megaphone, then Runcorn Linnets equalise, then I'm in Joanne's car. Bloody hell football hey! OK, so back at station, waiting train south, Murdishaw Massive have let me out, but what a day. Thanks to EVERYONE!

Thanks Kelly Jones and Joanne for the lift to the station. I love you all and the very best for the rest of the season. Those last minute limbs were special. What a club and what a day out!

Attendance: 535

Tuesday 11 February

APEC Taxis Stadium, Runcorn

Cheshire Senior Cup Quarter-Final

Runcorn Linnets 6 1874 Northwich 1

I don't think I need to repeat my declarations of affection for the Cheshire Senior Cup, but there's extra love in the APEC tonight because '74 are back at the APEC. Not so great for them, perhaps, because we deliver the kind of walloping that has visiting fans counting down to the whistle, simply hoping the margin of defeat doesn't grow even more embarrassing.

I'm catching up again with Vicki England as the first two goals go in – both from Karl Clair – which leaves me in that awkward situation of celebrating goals among away fans while their hopes of an upset are disintegrating before their eyes. Despite this, Vicki is happy to talk about their experiences in the Midland League this year.

'We're having adventures,' she confirms. 'It's nice to go around different grounds, going on the coaches and everything. It's a very different experience, going to places where I'd not even heard of the clubs. But whether I'd want to do it long term, I'm not sure.'

She's been surprised by the quality of the league. 'It's a tougher league than I would have guessed. People said to me that, if we're going to get promoted, this will be the best route but it's a tough league. There are five or six really good teams but even teams at the bottom of the league will come and give you a game. Lichfield are top: they're very consistent, but they've had four years of getting used to this. They lost out in the play-offs last season.'

Although the 74 are taking fans south on a regular basis – apart from Vics, all the other clubs lie in that direction – they aren't getting a lot of visitors. 'We went down on Saturday to Stourport Swifts and we must have had about 70 there, which is not bad. We're making good away days of it. They're making quite a bit of money out of us all and we're enjoying the experience. But we don't get that at home. They don't come. Even some of the teams at the top, you get ten and that's it.'

Despite this, they're currently recording the best average attendance in the league. 'I'd say the home crowds have stood up well to what they were last year: our home support has been steady. We're just not getting the away support.'

Despite the relatively low numbers of visitors, she's finding a lot of people know about the club's history going back to the Vics days. 'Wherever we go, we get asked about it: tell us about you and tell us about Vics. Northwich Vics is a grand old name in football. There's 150 years of history there.'

I keep the celebrations muted but when Ryan Brooke hammers home the third just after the half-hour mark I'm back among the home fans and can comfortably register my appreciation of what already looks a job well done by Runcorn.

The 74 get something to grasp onto when Joel Jones applies an exquisite finish to the excellent ball that sets him free on their right just before half-time, but just after the hour mark it's game over when Luke Wall, from a similar position, restores the three-goal cushion. In the dying minutes two graduates from the Linnets academy, Adam Moseley and Jorge Dwyer, both find their way through a tiring 74 defence. While Adam strikes his shot cleanly and powerfully to find the net, Jorge dinks a delicate chip over the advancing keeper.

We're into the semi-finals of the CSC and we face holders Hyde United next. For me, that means a score to settle that's lingered for 36 years.

Attendance: 338

Saturday 15 February

Swansway Stadium, Nantwich

Northern Premier League West Division

Nantwich Town 1 Runcorn Linnets 1

Runcorn fans are 'a credit to the club' are the gratifying words posted on the Nantwich Town Twitter account when the Linnets roll into town and, in a tight match, come away with a hard-earned point.

It could have been more, with Runcorn having the better of the second half chances, drawing a couple of fine saves from the Nantwich keeper. Ryan Brooke also narrowly fails to head home an excellent Luke Wall cross at the far post.

Before all that, it was Nantwich who'd taken a first half lead, the Runcorn defence failing to deal with an excursion down the left that leads to an excellent curling shot at the edge of the area which finds the far corner. I recall the 1-0 defeat to Nantwich at the APEC and how we struggled to get back into it, so there's some relief when we're back on terms before half-time. It's long been my contention that, if you can't put a decent corner in, you should put in a bloody awful one. This one is reminiscent of the one Ashton Athletic scored from against Thornton Cleveleys, except it's the leg of Ryan Brooke that diverts it home rather than a hapless defender. taking him level with Kyle Hamid in the all-time Runcorn Linnets goalscorers list, now only five points from equalling Mark Houghton's record total.

Despite those squandered second half chances, it's an even contest between two well-matched teams. In our situation, a draw has to be seen as points dropped and we've had three in a row now. There's some satisfaction that in all three we've come from behind to get something out of the game, but that doesn't bring the play-off pack any closer.

Attendance: 573

Saturday 22 February 2025

Runcorn are away at Chasetown, a team on the edge of the play-off pack who we can't afford to lose any more ground to. Disappointingly, I can't make it down there and, also disappointingly, there's no Bucket Hat FM commentary. Subsequent reports speak of a great day out, during which Linnets manage to reverse the 3-2 scoreline we went down to earlier in the season.

There's no need to come from behind in this one. Instead, Runcorn take the lead twice only to be pegged back quickly but, with one minute of normal time left, Joe Ferguson, an impressive right back recently signed from FC United, finds enough space on the right to put in a peach of a cross for academy graduate Lewis Crane to finish and send the Runcorn fans behind the goal wild. Thankfully, there's a recording of all this to savour for those of us who couldn't be part of what looks one hell of an away day. Wish I'd been there but, in the absence of that, three points to close the gap on the play-off places will do nicely.

At the top, Vauxhall win 1-0 to close the gap on Widnes who are unexpectedly hammered 4-0 at Clitheroe.

Wednesday 26 February 2025

It's rare Runcorn play on Wednesdays so I've been caught out on this one and, having made prior arrangements, I can't make it to the Liverpool Senior Cup Quarter Final against Tranmere Rovers at the APEC tonight. Rovers send a youth team so it's an easy night for the Corn, who run out 4-0 winners to secure a place in the semi-final of the LSC to add to the one we've already booked in the Cheshire Senior Cup.

March 2025

I see envy in his eyes and I don't think it's just because of the result…

Saturday 1 March

APEC Taxis Stadium, Runcorn

Northern Premier League West Division

Runcorn Linnets 2 City of Liverpool 0

The first day of March could, in theory, bring the first confirmed relegation of the season. It's unlikely though. Even if City of Liverpool lose at Runcorn today, they'll only go down if four clubs floating above the relegation trapdoor all win. Even so, they're clearly doomed. An 8-2 demolition at Nantwich last Saturday has surely set up a scenario where a buoyant Linnets push them further towards, if not through, that trapdoor today.

In the end a series of wasted chances means it's late in the game when Ryan Brooke heads his second goal to make the result secure. I manage to miss the first one because I'm stewarding on the gate near the clubhouse and struggling with the lock mechanism because someone wants to go and get something out of his car. I turn round to see the ball entering the net but have no idea how it got there.

Because we're so wasteful in front of goal, a late scramble in our area evokes fears that Purps will somehow snatch a point so there's relief when Brooke, who has looked back to something like his best recently, eventually settles what has been a massively one-sided contest. He's deservedly named Man of the Match by Bucket Hat FM, though for me Naim Arsan deserves a lot of credit, as he so often does, for the constant threat he provides on the left.

With Congleton Town losing and now occupying the last of the play-off places, we're just three points behind them but have a massive -18 goal difference deficit. We could still come to regret our failure to pile up the goals on days like today to make up for the goals we shipped in those hammerings earlier in the season.

At the end, it's good to see a lot of kids, many from Linnets junior teams, lined up as a guard of honour for all the players, coaching teams and officials, as they leave the pitch. There's been a deliberate attempt of late to find ways of making sure children feel part of things here and it, including the return of Ron Corn as a fixture of all home games. 'It sounds daft, but kids love seeing a mascot,' says Kelly Jones. She's right. You can be a purist about it and expect 8 or 9-

year-old kids to do what I did and simply go to football grounds to watch football. There are more competing pressures on a Saturday afternoon now though and, if you're a kid, getting a high five from someone dressed up as a novelty ear of corn can make a difference. Getting one from Ryan Brooke as he leaves the pitch can, inevitably, mean even more.

Attendance: 566

Wednesday 5 March

Barton Stadium, Winsford

Midland League Premier Division

Northwich Victoria 1 Shifnal Town 2

There have been rumours circulating for months that Vics' tenancy at Winsford will be terminated at the end of this season. Now we know the outcome: next season Vics will leave Barton Stadium and share the APEC with us. I managed to grab a few words with 'Corn chairman Peter Cartledge on Saturday. He knows there are mixed feelings among the Runcorn support, with some concerned about over-use of the pitch, but he believes these concerns will be assuaged when the groundshare begins. 'It's a win-win,' he says. The ground will no longer be made available for Sunday League games and, with the clubhouse in use every weekend, there'll be financial benefits for the club that outweigh any other considerations. 'They won't be using it for training, just on match-days, and Runcorn will always have priority.

'And they're nice people,' he adds. 'They came to us about it and we came to a quick agreement. We want to help them.'

This expression of solidarity in the non-league game is arguably the best reason of all for helping Vics to get through yet another difficult period in their existence, putting to rest any concerns that they'll be groundless next season.

'They have a long and proud history,' Peter says in his statement, 'and we could not countenance the prospect of a club with such tradition being left without a home. We also remember that Northwich Victoria were among those clubs who supported our predecessors Runcorn AFC by offering them a temporary home in their final season.'

Vics' chairman Ian Egerton says the termination of the tenancy at Winsford has come about 'due to subletting concerns raised by Winsford Town Council.' There's no sense of any animosity between the two clubs. 'The help and support in recent seasons from Witton Albion, Winsford United and now Runcorn Linnets will be forever a part of our history and our gratitude will always be remembered for the support shown.'

Tonight, Vics are facing a Shifnal Town side who are second in the league and the only realistic challengers Lichfield have for the Midland League Premier Division title. They've brought a small group of extremely drunk fans with them. I like a few pints but this is a level of drunkenness where inhibitions haven't just lessened but seem to have disappeared completely. As the game enters the second half they begin to goad some Vics fans, labelling Northwich a 'shithole' (they seem unaware that they aren't in Northwich) and referring to them as 'paedos'. The Vics fans deal with it in the best way, minimising the potential for confrontation by moving away, after which they receive taunts of 'you're pissing yourselves', something which there's a fair chance some of the Shifnal fans did a while ago.

Shifnal go into half-time two goals up. For both goals, there's the kind of delayed reaction from their supporters that confirms they aren't fully in tune with what's going on in the real world. One has just eaten a pie out of a pizza box. I saw some discarded pizza boxes in the rubbish outside the turnstiles and it seems that, in his inebriated state, he's commandeered one as a makeshift plate.

On the field, although Vics look lively and inventive, the visitors' defence is solid and they carry a threat every time they venture forward. At half-time it looks like it could turn into a pasting for Vics but they respond well and look the better side after the break, Lloyd halving the deficit just before the hour mark. There are other chances to equalise as a flowing game becomes more and more open and Shifnal also squander chances to add to their lead. As Vics press, there's a bad challenge from a Shifnal player which, from where I'm standing, looks like a red card offence but the ref is convinced it's a yellow, as are the group of staggering drunks to my right though I'm not sure they saw what happened. Indeed, whether they can still see at all is probably questionable.

When the final whistle blows, it takes a while for the travelling supporters to realise and begin to indulge in whatever celebrations their addled conditions allow them to, which is basically a silly, stumbling dance with fingers waving in the direction of the field.

Overall, Shifnal were the better side but Vics deserve credit for making a contest of it. They look like a club for whom a few pieces of fortune going their way might just tilt them towards the business end of the table in this league and, from there, who knows? That'll need to be next season now, of course: we're too far into this one for Vics to make any sort of surge into the play-offs. After a 5-1 hammering at Atherstone last night, 1874 are by no means certain of being in them either.

Attendance: 105

Saturday 8 March

Anfield Sports Community Centre, Liverpool

North West Counties League Premier Division

Lower Breck 5 FC St Helens 1

Hopes for a repetition of Bury's promotion nosedive of last year seem remote but if anyone can catch them, it's the team we're visiting again today. On Thursday Breck beat West Didsbury & Chorlton, leaving them nine points adrift of the leaders with two games in hand. Having been impressed by them when we visited earlier in the season, it's no surprise that Breck, at the very least, the very least look certainties for the play-offs.

Whether they'll be allowed to progress in the longer term is another matter. The ground here is only open to spectators on three sides and there's minimal seating. However, three years ago, when manager Gary Moore ('the man who masterminded Lower Breck's football domination' as the club's website has it) was asked by Gary Langley whether they'd promotion would ever be realistic, Moore spoke positively about discussions with the local footballing authorities about future development possibilities. 'We sat down and looked at the potential space in and around the facility and discussed what options there were for progressing and developing the facility. We are an ambitious club and are not ashamed of aiming for Step 4 football but obviously the higher we go, we need the facility to match.'

Their visitors today are also ambitious. FC St Helens have certainly made an impact since last year's promotion. The signing of former Swansea and Ecuador winger Jefferson Montero earlier in the year got them a lot of publicity, including a feature on Sky Sports. If the signing of Montero was a last attempt at an unlikely play-off slot, it's not worked. If it was designed to get the club some much-needed attention while Rugby League was still in its close-season, it's been at least a qualified success.

It's a 1pm kick off today, presumably so fans can make a quick dart to Anfield for the Liverpool match. This suspicion is confirmed when a large proportion of the crowd leaves about 20 minutes before the end, by which point Breck are already well in control.

I'm a bit surprised to find, on my arrival, that the car park that was free last time I was here is charging 12 quid. More astute readers will already have put together why this is and I do eventually but at the time it just leaves me puzzled, my argument with the car park attendant increasingly resembling the Monty Python Argument Clinic sketch.

'It was free to park last time.'

'No it wasn't.'

'Yes it was.'

'No it wasn't.'

After several rounds of this, she's not to be moved and I'm not willing to cough up such an exorbitant fee so, seething with injustice, we head off back the way we came. It's not difficult to find a side street to park in, but I only notice the 'residents' parking only' signs at the last moment by which point it's getting close to kick-off. I decide to risk a parking penalty in the interests of not missing the opening minutes of the game. It's a situation that calls for a testing of priorities and those are mine.

I arrive at the ground with minutes to spare and watch Breck dismantle St Helens with impressive ease. There's no question FC St Helens (for whom Jefferson Montero is absent) aren't a bad side. The convincing nature of this victory is all down to Breck, how well they press, close down space and attack with pace. They look well-equipped to survive at Runcorn's level. The constant pressure eventually leads to a St Helens defender turning a cross into his own net for the opener, after which the floodgates are jarred apart and, just before half-time, Hughes adds a second and Dowling a third to prise them open fully.

Their dominance continues into the second half, Burns adding a fourth and fifth before the crowd begins to peal away in the direction of Anfield. At this point, the penny finally concludes its slow journey to the floor. The car park was being used for Liverpool fans, explaining the obstinacy of the attendance and her insistence that it's never been free to park there.

If I'd made it clear I was there for the Breck game, would I have been allowed to park for nothing? As Tim says, there probably aren't many in that position: you'd assume a large majority of the home support live in the area around the ground so the issue probably only arises for casual visitors like us or away fans. It's hard to make a judgement on the latter since St Helens fans are as conspicuously absent as the celebrated Jefferson.

Their team add a late consolation through Houghton in a game that has reaffirmed Breck's credentials both for promotion and as difficult opponents for Runcorn when we arrive here for our Liverpool Senior Cup semi-final.

Attendance: 141

Sunday 9 March

APEC Taxis Stadium, Runcorn

North West Women's Regional League D1 South

Runcorn Linnets Ladies 2 Mossley Hill Ladies 2

There are over a hundred in the ground today, a healthy turnout, though for a while it's not clear we'll get to see a match. After warming up, both sets of players have returned to the changing rooms and we're already past the scheduled 2pm kick-off time.

I await the announcement that, for whatever reason, it's not going ahead. Instead, there's a different announcement: the referee is late and we'll get started as soon as he arrives. I use the term 'announcement' loosely. For the women's games there's nobody operating the tannoy so it becomes a matter of listening in to what the coaching staff are saying to the players and to each other. An unexpected presence on the bench, however, is the Mossley Hill manager, who I assumed would be suspended after he received a red card in Mossley's game against FC St Helens recently after going berserk on the touchline and sending a slew of foul-mouthed abuse in the direction of the ref. It's a popular misconception that there's no swearing in women's football. Anyway, apparently he's appealed the decision and will be able to retain his place on the bench pending the result.

The game eventually kicks off at 2.25. Runcorn's squad is depleted, Jack Slater tells me, due to a variety of factors: injuries, personal circumstances and pre-booked holidays among them. The team look well-placed to achieve his objective of improving on last year's fifth place so this raised his expectations: it looks like it will be a battle between us and our visitors today for third place.

Despite circumstances not being in their favour and having to defend for much of the first half, Runcorn take the lead when Lile Ashley latches onto a superb ball through midfield to chip the keeper. Mossley are a very good side, though, and we don't hold on to the lead for long. There's a suspicion of offside when they draw level through Rhoden, but the ref – who at least gives explanations for his occasionally contentious decisions – sees nothing amiss and the goal stands.

Runcorn survive further pressure with some robust defending to re-take the lead just before half-time. This time Ashley's shot misses the target but Mollie Bennett is on hand to finish at the far post. Again, the lead isn't retained for long: Mossley Hill go up the other end and level almost immediately through Howard.

It's been an entertaining first half but I'm concerned we'll struggle to contain the lively Rhoden up front for the full ninety minutes. I mention to Jack how impressed I've been with her and he agrees but says he's more concerned about the number 10 Mortimer, who's pulling all the strings in behind the front line. After he's pointed her out to me, I see what he means; Mortimer's constantly finding space behind the forwards, ensuring attacks are quickly recycled after they break down and setting up Rhoden for multiple chances which Runcorn keeper Alex Bellfield is doing well to deal with.

There's a discussion among the Runcorn coaching staff about whether to bring Chelsea Gillies into the back line to cope with the frequent attacks but Jack is concerned about taking her out of midfield. 'She's the only available player we've got who can play there,' he explains to me, reeling off a list of missing personnel.

Despite all this, we come out with a creditable draw against very good opponents. It's a game that, in the past, Runcorn would probably have lost. I think back to that defeat at St Helens at the end of last season. It's been hard work for the players out there today, but when that hard work ends in a draw rather than a narrow defeat, that's a very different feeling.

Tuesday 11 March

APEC Taxis Stadium, Runcorn

Cheshire Senior Cup Semi-Final

Runcorn Linnets 2 Hyde United 1

Last time I saw Hyde United was in a Cheshire Senior Cup semi-final in 1990. Runcorn hadn't lost a game in the competition since the 1984 final. We'd won every CSC in between but, after Hyde's late winner that night, we've never won it since.

We thought we'd reached the final in 2019 only to be expelled from the competition for fielding a player in the semi-final whose registration documents hadn't gone through in time. But it's that night at Hyde I remember as the time our long and successful relationship with the CSC came to an end. Back then Hyde were below us in the pyramid – NPL to our Conference – but now they're a league above us. They went on to win it after beating us in 1990 and are the reigning holders now.

We know it will be tough and it is, but this Runcorn side now look capable of going toe to toe with anyone and we take the game to Hyde from the first miute, squandering some good chances and drawing one excellent save from the Hyde keeper before Adam Moseley strikes to give us a deserved lead. We hold on until half-time, well worth the advantage but feeling we might have made more of opportunities to extend it. You feel there'll be a point in the match when a good Hyde side will come back at us.

We need a second goal and, in the second half, we get it. Hyde's defenders make the fatal error of not only appealing for offside but apparently stopping in the expectation that they'll get it, only for Ryan Brooke to sneak in and score from close range. For the record, he's clearly onside. The Hyde protests are futile but perhaps a perceived sense of injustice is what fuels their best period of play so far. They bombard the Runcorn goal and just after the hour mark halve the deficit through Fearnley.

It feels like a real cup tie. Would it be too much to compare it with those nights in the FA Cup under John King when Runcorn FC gave league teams the fright of their lives and, occasionally, beat them? Maybe, but it's nights like those I'm reminded of tonight: every yellow shirt standing firm against a team from a higher level. We've taken our chances when we've been on top and you sense that the players out there are filled with a belief that they'll see this out.

There's trepidation in the air around the APEC: whatever the players think, many of us in the crowd are not sure we can hold on now that Hyde have the scent of an equaliser in their nostrils. But we do, meeting the onslaught defiantly and carving out a few chances ourselves which might, if they'd gone in, make the closing minutes easier to live through. Ultimately, though, we hang on. I'm counting the players off the pitch to ease my concerns that there might be an unregistered one in there again but, finally confident that they're all legit, Runcorn

Linnets can look forward to their first ever Cheshire Senior Cup Final, the first for any Runcorn side since we lost the 1998 final to Macclesfield.

27 years. It's been far, far too long.

Attendance: 389

Saturday 15 March

Hollinwood Road, Kidsgrove

Northern Premier League West Division

Kidsgrove Athletic 1 Runcorn Linnets 1

'The most warm-hearted and respectful thing I've ever seen by a set of football supporters,' says Kidsgrove fan Neil after the game, labelling Runcorn's away support 'a class act and superb set of fans'. We knew that anyway, of course, but he's speaking of the fifth minute applause for Bobby Holmes on what would have been his fifth birthday: a young man taken from his family at the kind of young age it's difficult to imagine the horror of. But imagine it we do, responding to the request to honour his memory in a way that you'd like to think anyone with the smallest amount of decency would.

If you want to experience non-league football at its very best, it's on display in Staffordshire today. I'm not so much talking about what's happening on the pitch, though it's a pretty good game too, as the atmosphere created by two sets of fans who desperately need the win for different reasons: while Runcorn's eyes are still on catching up on the play-off pack, Kidsgrove have slid into the relegation zone. City of Liverpool are already down, Hanley Town are certain to join them and Wythenshawe would need a minor miracle to stay up, but that fourth relegation place is still up for grabs and our hosts today currently occupy it.

We get the train down and call into the wonderful Blue Bell Inn near the canal for a couple of pre-game pints. It's one of those great pubs you still find scattered up and down England, small and friendly with a range of ales that are all well-kept, delivered by bar staff who know how to handle a hand-pump.

From there we walk towards the ground in the Staffordshire sunshine, getting in around ten minutes before kick-off to see the enormous flag display Runcorn have laid on at one end of the ground. It looks spectacular and becomes even more so when the players come out and it's embellished with the kind of pyrotechnic display that's frowned upon by the authorities but, in truth, is nothing more than a vigorous demonstration of footballing passion. The playfulness continues, with Runcorn mascot Ron Corn conducting the display from the pitch before being kidnapped by Kidsgrove fans and branded with a 'Grove sticker to walk around for the rest of the day in.

On the pitch, Runcorn start slowly and Kidsgrove deservedly take the lead. The response is quick, though, as Linnets shift up a gear and are soon level through a Lewis Nolan goal. We're struggling for personnel out there today, though. The influential Karl Clair has been added to a growing injury list and Luke Wall is missing too. The bench is packed with youngsters: very promising youngsters, admittedly, but it would be good not to have to rely on them at the stage of the season we're at now, where you sense the experience of Clair will be missed.

Despite his absence in midfield, Runcorn begin to control the game, Lewis Doyle is particularly impressive, winning 50-50 challenges and laying off simple, quick passes to maintain the pace of our attacks. In the second half we're the better team but a rare Kidsgrove attack results in the ref awarding a penalty and we're beginning to think a game we really need to win, and should win, has slipped away from us. The penalty is fired down the middle of the goal, though, and a diving Bayleigh Passant sticks out a foot and saves it. There's the kind of delirium among the Runcorn fans that only a penalty save can bring and we who now see the team go up a further gear. There are howls for a penalty at the other end when a Kidsgrove defender seems, surely, to have blocked a shot with his hand: if so, it's not just a penalty but a red and the kind of incident important games like this can hinge on. The ref waves away the protest though and we're forced to settle for a draw.

Our train's delayed so we nip into the Blue Bell for another one, chatting with a Stoke City fan who's been to the Kidsgrove game today out of curiosity and is hugely impressed by the standard of football and passion of both sets of fans. He's surprised when I inform him of the low league position 'Grove currently occupy.

I tell him I hope they don't go down and I mean it. He asks me if that's because of this pub. I admit it's a contributory factor.

Attendance: 377

Saturday 22 March

APEC Taxis Stadium, Runcorn

Northern Premier League West Division

Runcorn Linnets 3 Stalybridge Celtic 2

It's non-league weekend again and I'm doing what I'd be doing anyway. Stalybridge are another of the sides chasing the play-off pack. We can't afford to drop any points today but neither can they and a combination of a lack of Premier League action, some nice spring weather and many away fans means an improved attendance at the APEC today.

Many of those present on both sides will, of course, have attended the away thriller at Celtic earlier in the season, when we saw Runcorn come from 2-0 down to grab that incredible win. Perhaps the footballing gods felt those who couldn't be at that game deserved to see something just as astonishing today.

At half-time it's still goalless despite a frenetic first half. If it goes on like this though, it isn't likely to finish 0-0 and that prediction turns out to be correct, though I doubt anyone in the ground anticipates what's about to happen.

Which is that Stalybridge race to a two-goal lead, revisiting a script from the autumn that they'll be aware doesn't end well. Nonetheless, there's delirium in the away end, the blue and white of the away side mingling with the green and white of another Celtic (the Glasgow one) in the traditional multi-coloured display they put on when things are going well. Some Celtic fans protest to me later that Sam Phillips doesn't give the name of their goalscorers over the Tannoy ('They even do that at Avro,' he says, 'and Avro are bastards'), so, in case they're reading, I'll do that here: Lewis Ramsthorn opens the scoring after 54 minutes and Jack Irlam adds a second ten minutes later.

OK now? Still isn't going to change what happens next, boys. 2-0 down with 20 minutes to go, Runcorn have brought on Reece Daly – a former player now returning on loan from Chester – for Adam Moseley. Normally, taking Adam off isn't something I approve of but something positive happens to the shape of the side when Reece enters the pitch and what we get, including injury time, is the best 24 minutes of football played by Runcorn this season.

Ryan Brooke's glancing far-post header halves the deficit and equals Mark Houghton's long—standing goalscoring record. Perhaps Stalybridge remember what happened last time we got a goal back in these circumstances because they're all over the place, chasing shadows, half-clearing balls into to the feet of another yellow and green shirt. It's a candidate for goal of the season that brings us level. I'm mentally entreating Joe Ferguson not to try it when I see him shaping for an overhead kick but thankfully telepathy isn't one of his many attributes and he meets it cleanly in midair, sending the ball into the roof of the net as the Celtic keeper watches helplessly on.

There's only one way this should end and that's what happens. With six minutes left, yet another ball into the box finds the foot of Brooke to give Runcorn the lead and leave him out on his own as Runcorn Linnets' record goalscorer.

We see it out and, as is our way, applaud both teams off at the end. A small group of Celtic fans are continuing to moan around me as we do what Runcorn fans have been doing of late, giving the players – both sides - a kids' guard of honour and applauding them off the pitch. 'Acting like you've won the cup,' says one. I simply point out that this is what always happens here: we've a community club and we celebrate that identity, win, lose or draw. Some of his mates around him are nodding – 'fair enough', I hear – but I see envy in his eyes and I don't think it's just because of the result.

Attendance: 689

Saturday 29 March

Marston Road, Stafford,

Northern Premier League West Division

Stafford Rangers 2 Runcorn Linnets 2

Following their victory at Warrington Town on Tuesday night, we now know we'll be facing Stalybridge Celtic in the final of the Cheshire Senior Cup. Another five-goal thriller? 'They'll probably beat us 3-2 this time,' muses Tim. At the time of writing Runcorn have got three coaches going and Tim will be on one of them.

For me, despite waiting for so many years for it, it seems there will be no Cheshire Senior Cup Final. The game has been scheduled for 6 May at the Deva Stadium. On 5 May I head to Cambridge for a week of work meetings I can't get out of. I'm usually fortunate that my most intensive period of work for me lands in May and June, when the football season is coming to an end. This year, unless I can figure out a way of getting from Cambridge to Chester in time, which seems extremely unlikely, I'm going to be absent for this historic occasion.

For now, I'm putting it to the back of my mind and heading for Marston Road. I've not been here for over thirty years but every time I came to see the old Runcorn play, we lost. I've still got that atrocious performance against them at the APEC in my mind, though Duncan, a Stafford fan, tells me they tend to be better away from home. 'I think it'll be close,' he tells me.

He turns out to be correct. As at Kidsgrove, we start slowly, though there's the mitigating presence of a cold wind blowing towards our goal for us to deal with. I tell Tim I fancy our chances if we go in level at half-time, with this wind at our backs in the second half. We manage to, only to go behind to a Wara goal early in the second half. As has been the way of things of late, adversity sparks us into action and we equalise through Doyle's superbly placed shot which evades the keeper's reach to squirm in at the far post.

Runcorn are well on top now but almost hand the hosts a lead when Bayleigh Passant performs an Andre Onana tribute act high in his own half, dribbling past one forward then almost losing possession when he tries it with another. But in his head Bayleigh is now playing central midfield and, casting logic to the wind, he continues to forge forward, the rest of the team piling into Stafford's final third ahead of him. The wave proves impossible for the hosts to resist and Gumbs eventually bundles the ball into the net to give Runcorn the lead with ten minutes to go.

Several sides above us are losing, including Chasetown who now occupy the final play-off place. There's a golden opportunity to revive our play-off push here. We look in control and should see it out. We think we have. The ref indicated five minutes of injury time and we've had six minutes when a Stafford corner finds the head of Anderson who nods home to give them a scarcely believable share of the points.

It's an example of how the football supporter's mood can change in a split-second. I'm looking forward to the prospect of heading down the M6 to a Half Man Half Biscuit soundtrack, buoyed by a massive three points, our promotion prospects still alive. A single moment at the end turns that on its head. It's a miserable drive back, accompanied by Dylan at his most sombre: 'Ballad of a Thin Man', 'A Hard Rain's A-Gonna Fall', 'It's All Over Now, Baby Blue'...

Tim's on his phone confirming that Chasetown did lose in the end and that Widnes managed to get beat at home to Witton, allowing Vauxhall Motors to close the gap to six points. It's Avro and Stalybridge who are the main beneficiaries of the Chasetown defeat, keeping their play-off hopes alive while Runcorn's keep dying the same death over and over again.

Attendance: 836

April 2025

Tuesday 1 April

Barton Stadium, Winsford

North West Counties League South Division

Winsford United 4 Cheadle Heath Nomads 0

I'd long ago pencilled in today as an important date for someone in the NWCL divisions; I just wasn't sure who. As it turns out, Atherton LR will move close to the NWCL North Division title if they beat Droylsden tonight but will not clinch the trophy yet. Winsford, in the South Division, can win the championship tonight, which is why I find myself at Barton Stadium one more time.

For Winsford this represents a truly remarkable turnaround. This time last season, fingernails were being bitten to the elbows as the prospect of relegation to the county leagues loomed. This season, they're storming to the title. Even if they lose tonight, they'll still have three games in which to gather the two points necessary to secure promotion to the Premier Division.

The recruitment of the management team of Dom Johnson and Dean Jones from Alsager Town last year turned out to be a masterstroke, especially so as they brought 13 Alsager players with them. Jones, on his appointment, called Winsford a 'sleeping giant'. It wasn't an exaggerated claim by any means. Winsford should be too good for this level, so the very real possibility of dropping even lower was a timely wake-up call for the club.

When visiting for the pre-season game with Northwich Vics, I was impressed by what I saw from Winsford and thought they probably had enough to avoid any flirtation with relegation this season. I never expected anything like this, though, and I suspect most Winsford fans, if they're honest, will admit the same. The start of the season offered little indication of what was to come. The first game resulted in a loss to Alsager and you suspect more than a few fans were wondering if they'd brought in the wrong players. This was followed shortly after by defeat at Eccleshall. Since then, Winsford haven't lost a league game.

While the celebratory champagne – or whatever they drink round here – is on ice, there remains a question mark about what happens when (there's no evidence of any 'ifs' within the large crowd) promotion is confirmed. Two years ago, Winsford took voluntary relegation from the Premier Division to avoid having to join Vics in the Midland League. Would promotion take them back into the Premier Division or will the geographical lines be drawn in a way that offers them the prospect of the Midland League again, something which the board at the time deemed to be 'unsustainable'?

'It'll be the Midland,' says a fan standing nearby and he isn't fazed by the idea. 'You've got Vics and 74 in there now so there are some local clubs and it'll be good to see some new teams.'

He's worried, though, that some of the players might not fancy the longer trips. 'A few are based in Manchester and work there, but we'll see.'

It's an interesting sub-plot but one that doesn't seem to be engaging the minds of many of the home fans tonight. They're entirely focused on getting their hands on the trophy, which they'll achieve if they beat Cheadle Heath Nomads or if Stafford Town, in second place, fail to win.

Understandably, the fans near me would prefer the former. There's a feeling of impending celebration hanging in the air around the ground and it would be a huge anti-climax if it didn't culminate in a trophy presentation. Nomads, for their part, are on the edge of the play-off pack and need the points for different reasons but never look likely to get them.

In a dull first half, Winsford take the lead after just seven minutes when Birchall receives the ball on the right of the area, sees the keeper advancing and loops the ball over him. It lands just inside the far post, puncturing any remaining doubts among the home support.

Cheadle's main hope of avoiding defeat seems to lie with the stadium's electrics. As the teams are heading off at half-time the floodlights fail and we're plunged into darkness for nearly half an hour, at the end of which we're beginning to fear the worst. 'It's the third time it's happened this season,' says a Winsford fan. Perhaps one day, with more nights like this, Winsford will be able to afford a new set and not have to rely on these enormous beasts, dishing out enough power to light up the gardens of the council estate to the back of the ground and beyond. Eventually, one set suddenly blinks into life to enormous cheers around the ground and the rest gradually follow. There's a small warm-up and we're off again.

Winsford deliver a second half performance worthy of champions. Birchall flicks on a near-post corner to double the lead. There are bouncing kids behind the goal now, chanting 'highlighter' at the pink-clad Nomads keeper, though this soon becomes to the somewhat less original 'Who's the wanker in the pink?' He's standing between the home side and a hammering, making several smart saves before parrying a shot into the path of Pope, who scores the third. Jenyons adds a fourth after 75 minutes.

We leave to the sound of celebrations on the pitch and around the ground. This time last season the regular fans here were fearing removal from the league: now, the worst that can happen is a few long trips to the Birmingham area next season.

'A crazy season,' club secretary Mike Dawson says after the match, clearly metaphorically pinching himself after carving a dream season from the remains of a nightmare one. 'It's been full of highs, and beyond our expectations. Coming into 2024/25, we just wanted to stabilize the club.'

Among other things, Winsford certainly look stable. Enough for them to face Midland League exile with less trepidation this time? It doesn't seem that such pragmatic concerns are troubling anyone in the ground tonight.

Attendance: 481

Saturday 5 April

APEC Taxis Stadium, Runcorn

Northern Premier League West Division

Runcorn Linnets 0 Clitheroe 3

It's generally accepted by most Runcorn fans I've spoken to that the last-minute goal conceded at Stafford was the final nail in the coffin of our play-off hopes. Perhaps deep down the players think so too because the performance here is by some distance the worst since Brad Cooke took over as manager.

It's a sunny afternoon in Runcorn but the Clitheroe fans generally turn up in coats and jumpers, meaning either that the weather isn't as pleasant in their part of the world or they somehow expected it to get worse as they headed south.

Whatever the reason, they soon remove their winter clothing and any fun to be had in the sun is all theirs. The Runcorn defence looks as wide open as it did in those early weeks of the season and the visitors have several chances to take the lead before Danny Wilkins eventually takes one just before the half-way mark. Second half goals from Creech and Windass give them the resounding victory they deserve.

Afternoons like this have been all too familiar this season and the truth is we haven't done enough to deserve a place in the play-offs. Reasons for that can be speculated on but the failure to replace Molloy in the close season, meaning no back-up for Ryan Brooke up front, followed by the early problems of settling in a new defence, then Will Saxon's departure at Christmas, all helped contribute to a season of underachievement. I'd also add losing Karl Clair in these final months too: his experience fortified the midfield after our early bad start and his presence in the middle of the park is once again missed today.

With the game gone, I'm spending much of the closing stages talking to manager of the women's team Jack Slater about the big plans he has for the summer. Tomorrow they'll be playing at Mossley Hill Athletic, one of the teams with whom they're involved in a tussle for third place. Jack believes they have a good platform from which to aim for the championship next season. He shows me his phone, which has the contact details for about 15 players he's looking at as potential summer signings. I recognise a few of them.

Otherwise, optimism in short supply today. There's a fear that Bury will be up next season and could, given their resources, dominate the league. Will the prospect of making the play-offs next season prove just as illusory as it has this time? Many are leaving early today with some muttering the kind of dissatisfied comments that indicate Brad Cooke's honeymoon period is now over.

Elsewhere, Widnes are beginning to wobble at the top with a draw at Newcastle Town that allows Hednesford, Congleton and Chasetown all to close the gap. Atherton LR's coronation as NWCL Division One North champions is complete with a 6-0 victory over Bacup Borough.

Defeat for Warrington Town in National League North means they'll be back in the NPL Premier Division next season.

Attendance: 544

Thursday 10 April

Anfield Sports & Community Centre, Liverpool

Liverpool Senior Cup Semi-Final

Lower Breck 3 Runcorn Linnets 1

Nothing in football feels quite as bad as losing a semi-final. Obviously losing any game feels terrible, but going out of a cup competition in the early rounds means at least it's out of the way and you can concentrate on other things. Losing in a final spoils a good day out but I still retain fond memories, at least, of the journeys to and from those three Runcorn FC FA Trophy defeats at Wembley, and even the defeat to Marine on penalties in the Liverpool Senior Cup. Losing in a semi-final just feels like a lot of wasted time, of failure on the precipice of something memorable. There are other kinds of football-related misery, but none quite have the hollowness of a semi-final defeat.

I head to 'The Anny' expecting we'll be up against it tonight. On paper, NWCL opposition might seem like a testing proposition. However, having seen Breck twice already this season, I'd say they present more challenging opponents than most in the NPL. The home side have already amassed a remarkable 100 points in the league, exceeding the total achieved by champions Wythenshawe last season with two games left. They've won their last eleven matches in all competitions, including a 4-1 demolition of Prescot Cables in the quarter-final of this competition.

It starts positively enough, Ryan Brooke nodding down a high ball to put Adam Moseley clear. Adam finishes calmly to give Runcorn the lead after three minutes but that's as good as it gets. Even before that, Breck had caused panic in the Runcorn area and they cause a lot more, swarming all over a makeshift Linnets defence. Eventually they equalise from a free kick, Millington's shot finding a gap in a poorly assembled wall. I begin chatting to the Lower Breck supporter standing next to me. He tells me he's a Liverpool fan who lives locally and only comes here occasionally. He isn't aware Runcorn play a level above the home team and, frankly, what's happening on the pitch isn't likely to convince him.

Runcorn have chances in the second half and at one point force Breck to clear off the line, but the home side manage to hit the woodwork three times before Barrow's header gives them a lead they never look like losing. In injury time, Buckley adds a third.

There's no doubt Runcorn's shortcomings are evident on the night, but Breck have assembled a very good side here and, if they don't manage to go up from the play-offs, I wonder, not for the first time this season, if any of them would fancy turning out in the NPL in yellow and green.

Attendance: 354

Saturday 12 April

APEC Taxis Stadium, Runcorn

Northern Premier League West Division

Runcorn Linnets 1 Avro 0

It's something we've not experienced for a long time at this club: four games remaining at the end of the league season and nothing to play for.

There is, of course, something else to play for, and following two defeats Brad Cooke has made it clear shirts are up for grabs ahead of the Cheshire Senior Cup Final. He fields a young team today, giving starts to Jorge Dwyer, Jay Lee and Lewis Crane which, along with Adam Moseley and the returning Harvey Washington, means that half the outfield players who start this one are under 21.

Avro need a win today to keep their play-off hopes alive but you wouldn't know it from their approach which makes Runcorn's display against Clitheroe seem almost respectable. Admittedly, they've had an interesting few weeks, and not in a good way. The management team who'd taken them to this position announced they'd be leaving at the end of the season, only for the board to dismiss them on the spot. This was after a run of six consecutive wins. It's perhaps understandable that the team looks confused and rudderless, far from the outfit that hammered us at their place earlier in the season.

The first half has a distinct end-of-season feel to it. Runcorn's youngsters use the time they're allowed to bed in and, in the second half, the home side begin to control the game. Lewis Crane gets free on the right and, although his initial shot is blocked, he picks up the ball again and floats a sumptuous cross to the far post, where Adam Moseley is on hand to finish. From there we manage the game effectively, each youngster getting an appreciative round of applause from the APEC crowd as he's subbed off for a more experienced replacement, who if nothing else knows he's now got competition for his place in at the Deva.

Attendance: 485

Wednesday 16 April

APEC Taxis Stadium, Runcorn

North-West Development League Division B

Runcorn Linnets U21s 4 Vulcan FC U21s 2

Sadly, it's often been difficult to fit Runcorn's Under 21 matches into what's become an intensive football-watching schedule this season. They usually play home matches at midday on a Sunday and I've sometimes caught five or ten minutes at the end of a game but that, of course, doesn't count.

Fortunately, this is the time of the year where teams are playing catch-up on fixtures that, for one reason or another were postponed earlier in the season and fortunately, the U21s have a match on a Wednesday night when I've nowhere else to be.

Runcorn currently sit third in Division B of the North West Under 21 Development League. They've got games in hand on the three teams above them, however, and have been on a run of eight wins since their defeat at top of the table Nantwich Town in February.

In recent years, the Linnets academy has been thriving, bringing through both Eden Gumbs and Adam Moseley. Recently, the new management team have shown a willingness to blood more new talent, with Lewis Crane and Jorge Dwyer getting frequently getting minutes off the bench and young left-back Jay Lee also getting game-time: all featured in the starting line-up on Saturday.

Kelly Jones began her day-to-day involvement with Runcorn as an admin assistant for the Under 21s and it's clear this is where her true passions lie. Kelly is a rare example of somehow who got involved with Runcorn and then became a football fan, rather than the reverse. 'I like watching England in the World Cup and the Euros, but I was never that into it. But it was something me and my partner started to do together, come up here and watch the football and then it just went from there.'

Involvement with the club is, for Kelly, more important than the results. 'I come here and I have a good time because I'm here, not because of the scoreline. I wouldn't say I feel just as happy...I feel disheartened but it's nothing to do with the scoreline. It upsets me that the team are upset.'

It's a refreshing perspective when contrasted with the blame and finger-pointing that are more frequently encountered reactions to adversity on the football terraces. Perhaps this nurturing approach is what leads Kelly to find her natural environment among the youth set-up where, although a winning mindset is very much encouraged, the main objective is to nurture and promote young talent.

I caught the last ten minutes of the crucial 1-0 win against Southport recently. At end Kelly strode across the pitch to the players she calls 'her lads', beaming like a proud parent.

'I want the Under 21s to go as big as they can,' says Kelly. She's conscious of the need to make Runcorn fans more aware of the good work going on at this level. 'We want to make the website more inclusive for all the teams, so that it's not just about the first team.' While Kelly makes a massive contribution across the club, promoting the Under 21s and seeing the players progress seems akin to a personal mission.

Unlike other teams in their league, the youth players regularly get to play on the main pitch at the APEC. 'Every team we play have a first team and we're yet to play away games on any first team pitch. They have to hire elsewhere, or they play on a training ground.'

It's important to recognise what clubs like Runcorn Linnets are achieving in a youth system dominated by the academies of the big clubs. Kids who sign up to Manchester United and Liverpool at a young age are offered a dream that rarely materialises, with only a small proportion of the thousands of boys between the ages of six and eight who join their academies retained even into their teens.

At Runcorn, there's the admittedly humbler dream of achieving the more achievable aim of pulling on that green and yellow shirt, feeling a part of a set-up that's smaller but less likely to end in rejection. For the club, it's not just about unearthing the next Eden Gumbs or Adam Moseley, this is part of their wider community vision.

After several weeks of sunshine, this match is played in driving rain. We stand under cover, a yard back from the fence because it's slanting down into our side of the ground. Vulcan FC are based in Newton-Le-Willows and their Under 21s occupy a healthy mid-table position. They've got a couple of big lads out there but rarely get an opportunity to get a cross in to them as Runcorn dominate the first half. Despite Lewis Crane missing a penalty, we run up a four-goal lead with goals from Schofield, Crane, Parker and Eden's brother Eneil Gumbs, who impresses in midfield.

I'm expecting more of the same in the second half but Runcorn go down to ten when Prince is sent off. It gives Vulcan an opportunity to get back in the game and they pull a couple of goals back but Runcorn manage the closing stages well and come away with a deserved three points, leaving us two points behind the leaders with four games in hand.

Friday 18 April

Vauxhall Motors Radio

Good Friday at home. I've watched *King of Kings* on BBC2 this morning and had a couple of hot cross buns. How to spend the afternoon?

A choice, really between radio commentaries of Bootle v Wythenshawe Town or Vauxhall Motors v Stalybridge Celtic. I opt for the latter, keen to do whatever I can (which is, essentially, nothing) to will the Motormen to win and continue to press Widnes and Hednesford for the title.

Is it as good as listening to Jack and Sam? No. Although the commentator brings in a nearby female fan on occasions, there's no real double act here and the experience is lacking because of it. But he does a good job of keeping us updated with the action, 'us' at the start being a total of six listeners, which rises to a maximum of 18 in the game's later stages.

But let's be clear: this is great. When I was a kid listening to radio commentary was the only way you could keep up with almost any football match, unless you were there, so to have commentary of games in the NPL now is fantastic and those who put the effort in, whether it's Runcorn, Vauxhall, Bootle or any other fans, deserve enormous thanks.

I'm hearing numerous familiar names. Tyler Hill, who played for Runcorn earlier in the season, is at Vauxhall now. There's Josh Quarless, of course, the 6'9" striker who turned out briefly for Runcorn under Dave Wild before very publicly flouncing out, and the evergreen Kevin Ellison, who has recently announced he's still got no plans to retire anytime soon.

It's Ellison who gives Vauxhall the lead eight minutes before the break. I find myself punching the air. With Runcorn out of the equation, I realise how much I'd like them to have a chance of promotion and a win today will secure at least a play-off place. I also realise how much I don't want Celtic to make the play-offs. The childish whinging of some of their fans at Runcorn has really got to me on some irrational level and here the commentator tells me they're singing 'Have you ever won the treble?' on account of the three-trophy season they had 24 years ago. Worth remembering that the promotion that followed that glorious campaign was followed by relegation a year later.

The commentator is also keeping us informed on what's happening in the two other games being played today. By half-time, Hednesford are also one-nil up: a win will take them top of the league ahead of the Widnes game tomorrow. There's a part of me – a very small part, I admit – that is enjoying viewing all this from afar this season, after three seasons of play-off disappointment.

Soon after half-time, though, Celtic equalise with what the commentator calls a 'pea-roller'. The cheers when it goes in are far louder than when the home side scored, confirming that, as expected the travelling Celtic fans far outnumber their hosts. Some of them will no doubt be nodding with self-righteous satisfaction that the Vauxhall PA does announce the name of their scorer.

Five minutes from time, Vauxhall find themselves in trouble as Tyler Hill is shown a red card. They'll have to play the last few minutes with ten men, focused on holding onto a draw, enough to secure that play-off place.

And that's how it finishes. Vauxhall now have a huge game on Easter Monday against Widnes, needing the points to grab third place in the league, which would mean a home game in the play-offs. Meanwhile, Bootle beat Wythenshawe Town 1-0, meaning the home team are safe from relegation while Town languish in that fourth relegation position. Hednesford score a second in the second half, leaving them top ahead of Widnes' game tomorrow.

Saturday 19 April

Halton Stadium

Northern Premier League West Division

Widnes 0 Nantwich Town 0

The option of going to watch Runcorn at Congleton today isn't realistic, sadly. I'd have less than an hour to get to the ground and Google Maps is telling me it'll take 56 minutes.

Instead, I have a choice of a couple of games closer to home. My real preference would be South Liverpool v AFC Liverpool. So why do I end up in the soulless environs of the DCBL again? Because Widnes, against the odds and despite a poor run of late, are on the verge of winning the league and I feel impelled to experience that in some way.

They want to get out of the DCBL. Not only is the ground far too big for them, it's costing them a bomb to play there. The club have identified as site on the King George V Playing Fields more of less across the road from it but getting approval proving to be a long process. There's been no apparent movement since last May when several members of the local community raised concerns about public fields being taken over by a private company and essentially removed from community use. The playing fields in question currently contain several football pitches used at the weekends by grassroots clubs.

As I've said before, there's a kind of cartoon rivalry between Runcorn Linnets and Widnes, something I don't, as a Widnes resident, feel much part of anyway. As a Runcorn fan, it's disappointing that a team with such a pitifully small fanbase seem to be heading for the NPL Premier Division while Runcorn can't even manage the play-offs. However, it would be churlish in the extreme to deny Ello and his team the praise they've earned this season.

They don't perform today, though, unless you count their contribution to the headcount of yellow cards, which finishes 6-5 to Nantwich, though the haul of Widnes captain Irwin is more significant as he picks up two, leaving the home side to play the last half hour with ten men.

In such circumstances, it may seem a draw is a good result: it keeps Widnes one point ahead of Hednesford Town going into the last two games. They're on a bad run of form, though, and look nervous throughout. The first-half penalty they're awarded should help to ease those nerves, but not when you crash it against the bar.

On the plus side, the good season they've had seems to have overseen some emergence of an atmosphere here. The size of the crowd – more than double what they often got last season – can't be explained solely by the sizeable Nantwich contingent. The signs forbidding entry to unaccompanied children seem to have gone and a large group of them make a noise throughout. Perhaps Widnes can become a convincing football town after all – we'll see.

At Congleton, Runcorn pick up two red cards on the way to getting hammered 6-0.

Attendance: 352

Sunday 20 April

Great Sankey Neighbourhood Hub, Warrington

North West Regional League D1 South

Warrington T. Women 2 Runcorn Linnets Ladies 1

Runcorn Linnets Ladies are closing in on the final week of their season, visiting a Warrington Town side who must win today to avoid relegation to the Cheshire League. In normal circumstances that shouldn't happen, but these are not normal circumstances. Runcorn lost unexpectedly at home to Ellesmere Port last weekend and now they're heavily impacted by injuries and players who've gone away for Easter. Unable to field eleven players, they go into the with just ten players.

Player availability is a major issue for women's football at this level. The Warrington fan next to me tells me it's the main reason for their disappointing season, with the frequent absence of forward players a particular issue. Without this problem, they'd be a mid-table side, he believes. I saw them at Wigan earlier in the season, where their win belied their low position in the table. They certainly looked a far better side than their mid-table hosts. Today, there's no doubt a depleted Runcorn side gives them an opportunity to avoid the relegation that at one stage looked almost inevitable.

I'm impressed with their number 10, clearly an experienced player who looks a constant threat on the left of the attack. 'She's 41,' the Warrington fan tells me. 'Only just got back from an ACL injury. We thought she'd never play again.' She's the standout player today and, when she begins to push forward alongside the central striker, Warrington have the numbers to cause us problems, despite a defiant performance by the Runcorn central defenders and a few excellent interventions by Alex Bellfield in goal. Warrington are soon two goals up and, though Runcorn pull one back before half-time through a Chelsea Gillies penalty, the home side secure the points they need to retain their status in this league next season, sending MSB Woolton down on goal difference. It's tough on MSB, who were only promoted last year and must have felt they'd done enough to be safe for another season.

Runcorn have two rearranged games at Wigan and St Helens left. All things being equal, they should get the points to finish above last season's fifth place, but those fixtures are coming up quickly and the problem of having enough available and fit players may prevent them from meeting that target. You feel the long list of player contacts Jack Slater showed me a few weeks ago may be vital if he's to avoid similar problems holding us back next season.

Monday 21 April

APEC Taxis Stadium, Runcorn

Northern premier League West Division

Runcorn Linnets 1 Bootle 3

It's a very different Easter Monday feeling to that of last year, where we headed off to Prescot Cables to spar for play-off positions. This season, a bad campaign seems to be finding new ways to disappoint as it enters its final stages. Jay Lee and Harvey Washington were both sent off in the massacre at Congleton last week. Next Saturday, we'll end the season at high-flying Hednesford where we could face the interesting prospect of helping Widnes to secure the title. Based on recent performances, that seems unlikely, whether we have the will to do so or not.

Today's visitors secured safety from relegation on Saturday so neither of these teams, both of whom were in the play-offs last season and have had disappointing seasons, have much riding on this contest. Runcorn, of course, are still looking ahead to that Cheshire Senior Cup Final, though, and there's a feeling we need to build up whatever momentum we can ahead of it. I'm still trying to figure out a way of getting to the game, although it seems impossible: I've worked out I can get a train from Cambridge to Chester if I can get away from my meeting for 3 O'clock, leaving me just enough time to get from Chester Station to the Deva. Realistically, there seems no chance of this happening.

So, having already decided not to go to Hednesford next week, this is likely to be my last chance to see the Runcorn men's side this season.

And it's not the kind of performance to fill me with optimism for the next one. I didn't think there was any chance the misery of August Bank Holiday Weekend could be repeated but here we are on Easter Monday following a 6-0 routing with defeat to a Bootle team whose fans are enjoying themselves after the threat of relegation was lifted on Friday. They score first through the excellent Ben Hodgkinson, who's a constant threat to a disjointed Linnets defence. Although Naim Arsan equalises with a fine free kick, Bootle score two more in the second half after Runcorn have failed to capitalise on a good spell after half-time.

I suggest to chairman Peter Cartledge that at least he can plan for next season with a manager already in place. It's a situation he's not known in three years as chairman, he says. Although Billy Paynter replaced Dave Wild in the spring two years ago, it was closer to the end of the season and, although Peter doesn't say this, frankly there was probably less to put right.

Widnes win at Vauxhall Motors. They're now three points ahead of Hednesford, who draw at Stafford in front of over 2000 fans to keep the title race going to the last weekend, when Widnes will only need a point against Trafford to become champions.

Attendance: 548

Wednesday 23 April

APEC Taxis Stadium, Runcorn

North West Development League B

Runcorn Linnets U21s 1 AFC Liverpool U21s 2

It's a final opportunity for me to visit the APEC this season and an opportunity to see a Runcorn side getting nearer to lifting a trophy. Following Fleetwood's inability to field a team on Sunday, Linnets U21s were awarded a walkover and go into this match effectively needing two wins from the last three games to secure the title.

I've won something too – a bottle of brandy in the supporters' Easter raffle – so I pick that up before the game and go to my usual place near the dugouts to watch the game. Due to stewarding responsibility when the senior side are playing, I haven't stood here much this season.

It's been a tough baptism in the first team for players like Lewis Crane and Jay Lee recently, but tonight they're back with their mates and an opportunity to experience the success their performances this season have deserved.

But things don't go to plan. Although they're well down the table, AFC Liverpool are well-organised and tough to break down. Going into half-time goalless, Runcorn know something will have to change in the second half and it does, in all the wrong ways. A ball into the area is blocked by a Runcorn hand and the result is a penalty and a red card. AFC dispatch the penalty and Runcorn suddenly have an uphill struggle on their hands.

But the home side suddenly look invigorated and are soon level when Zack Parker crashes the ball into the roof of the net. Parker deservedly gets the Man of the Match award but his mazy, slaloming runs are frequently ended by a well-placed AFC boot. It's a frenzied second half now and soon the sides' numbers are level when two of those boots crash into a Runcorn shin: again, the ref has no option but to give a red card. The AFC keeper, who's been annoyingly mouthing off at the ref all game, is suddenly the voice of reason: 'they tell us all the time at fuckin' trainin' we can't make them fuckin' tackles' he yells in the direction of his protesting teammates.

It's an opportunity, you'd think, for Runcorn to take the game to AFC yet, perversely, we played our best football when a man down and it's AFC who grab a late winner. They should have a third when Ellams, the Runcorn keeper, is caught up field at a set piece. The AFC player rolls the ball towards the empty goal and is reeling away to celebrate as it narrowly passes the outside of the post.

Soon they're celebrating for real, though, and Runcorn have missed a huge opportunity to strengthen their lead at the top. We've got two away games left and probably need to win both to prevent the league title from heading to Kidsgrove.

Saturday 26 April

Acoustafoam Stadium, Shifnal

Midland League Premier Division Play-Off Final

Shifnal Town 2 1874 Northwich 0

I know I should be at Hednesford watching Runcorn's last game of the league season but I'm looking for a feel-good story or at least one with the prospect of a happy ending, so instead of heading south to Hednesford I'm heading in a southward direction to Shifnal where 1874 Northwich find themselves in the final of the Midland League Premier Division play-offs.

74 finished fourth in the league but overcame Atherstone United with a goal deep in injury time last week to set up this game. I saw Shifnal at Vics earlier in the season – in the game of the drunken pie eater – and, although they were the better side that day, Vics might easily have got something from the game so I think there's a real chance for the visitors today.

I have a confusing dream the night before that Snifnal win 2-0. That's not especially confusing until you factor in that during the dream I wander around the ground searching for 1874 fans and all I can find are Runcorn Linnets supporters. Perhaps it's my subconscious chiding me for not being there to support my team. Or maybe it was just all that beer I drank.

Speaking of which, for its size Shifnal has a remarkable number of good pubs. We call in the Kings Yard after getting off the train. At Shifnal station, the other platforms are filled with hordes of replica Wolves shirts heading out of the town and in the direction of Molineux. Snifnal's remarkable pubs have been left to us, it seems, and we're more than happy to fill the tables they've vacated. Dozens of 1874 fans are on the same train as us and heading to the same place, while others peel off in the direction of some of the other boozers.

'They came in earlier in the season,' the landlord says. 'Fantastic bunch. Today they phoned ahead and said there'd be about 25 coming down. They asked if I could open up early, which I can't do, but I told them they'd be welcome from noon.'

It's clear Shifnal Town aren't familiar with hosting large groups of away supporters, something which becomes apparent when we eventually get to the turnstile. For now, though, there's time to have a few here and at the White Hart, which takes us a bit out of our way but turns out to be worth it. We get in there just in time before a large coach party turns up, part of a Black Country pub crawl, apparently. Among them is one of the Hairy Bikers – the one who's still alive – and it surprises me when he settles in a corner of the pub with a companion sipping a half. They're in this for the long haul, I suppose, but still, there are reputations that need upholding.

We eventually reach the ground to find a large queue and the game is delayed by 17 minutes to get everybody in. This is a ground where the average attendance is around 180 and there are going to be over a thousand here today. The early morning clouds have dispersed and the sun shines over a ground which looks remarkably like the one in my dream, aside from the absence of those masses of Runcorn fans. There's an impressive stand on one side and grass slopes around the ground suggest the potential for banked terracing. There's potential here to develop an already very good ground into an even better one should they come up.

And they are, it seems, coming up. The 74 performance is too reminiscent of our display against City of Liverpool last season for me not to share in the anguish of the hundreds of visiting fans. They never really get going, relying on long, predictable balls which cause the Snifnal defence few problems. The home side take the lead from a penalty after a handball and, just before half-time, score the killer second: the shot from Shifnal's number 7 looks set to be cleared by the 74 defender, but he can only deflect it into his own net.

Northwich's agony is prolonged by a serious injury to one of the home players which means a large amount of injury time and it's about 20 past 5 when the game eventually ends. By that point we've heard that Widnes have been confirmed as Northern Premier League West Division champions after a 1-0 win against Trafford, while Runcorn have conceded late in injury time to lose at Hednesford by the same scoreline. We finish a hugely disappointing 11th in the league. Wythenshawe Town lose at Newcastle Town and are confirmed in the fourth relegation place.

We've got an hour to kill before the next train so decide to spend some of it in the Anvil, where the black country ale trail has now landed so it's packed. The arrival of a large group of 74 fans packs it even more. Many are sanguine about the defeat today. 'Think back to this time last season,' one of them says. 'We were worried we were going into long-term decline. We'd have taken the play-offs.'

There are various murmurs, some of agreement, some mildly demurring while others just look like football has been dealing them shitty blow after shitty blow for so long it's become part of life. Which, I suppose, it has.

Attendance: 1067

Sunday 27 April

Hopes that the men's Under 21 side may give Runcorn fans something to cheer about at the end of the season remain alive, with a 2-1 victory at Southport meaning a win in their final game at Northwich will, barring some frankly unlikely goal difference gymnastics from Kidsgrove, secure the league title. Although Adam Moseley fell short of the Murdishaw

Massive's predicted total of 15 goals for the senior team this season, scoring 10, he turns out for the Under 21s today and adds another.

Meanwhile, a disappointing end to the season for Runcorn Linnets Ladies manages to get even worse with a 9-1 thrashing at St Helens. Chester have now leapfrogged both Runcorn and Mossley Hill to sit in third and this means we'll again finish fifth in the NWWRL this season.

Tuesday 29 April

It's rare I feel any love towards Warrington Rylands but tonight they've entered my affections. Their Under 21 team defeat Kidsgrove, handing the championship to Runcorn Linnets. 'Absolutely thrilled,' is the predictable, and probably understated, reaction of Kelly Jones.

May 2025

'There were tears'

Football is bound up with identity like no other sport, and like nothing else I know. No real football supporter supports a club vicariously: if they win you share the victory with them and if they lose you share that too. You may not be on the pitch but you don't celebrate from afar: it's not like watching, say, Usain Bolt and standing back and admiring it, applauding brilliance. You're part of it: in the with the mud and grass, the spitting and swearing, the gouging and tripping, the winning and the losing. It's bound up with what and who you are.

And supporting a team at this level enhances that sense of being a part of it. Speaking to people at Runcorn this season has given me an opportunity to look behind the scenes and get a sense of how much goes into making a club like this work. There's so much media attention on the manager or head coach at the top levels of the game that many fans get sucked into the idea of that being the level at which success or failure is exclusively determined. In truth, football is a team game off the pitch as well as on it.

You can add to that a level of unpredictability, something far more pronounced at this level of the game. Few would have anticipated Widnes winning the NPL West or that Winsford would have bounced back so spectacularly in the NWCL South. In the North West Women's Regional League, the issue of player availability in what is still an amateur league adds another factor that's difficult to control.

Next season, while we may look at Bury entering the NPL West and think of writing off the rest of the league as also-rans, there's no way that's a given. Bury have, after all, only just finished above those entertaining upstarts from Lower Breck this season after finishing Wythenshawe last year.

And while my levels of satisfaction will be dictated to a large degree by how well Runcorn Linnets perform next season, there are many things I'm looking forward to, including visiting the grounds of those teams who'll be coming into the league via either promotion or relegation in August, some of whom will, as always, be new to me. I'm pleased Kidsgrove Athletic stayed up in the end which means we've retained one of the league's most joyous away experiences, including but not restricted to a visit to The Blue Bell. And, although we didn't really want Bury, like other teams in the league we can look forward to a big crowd when they visit, to at least trying to put one over on them and the not inconsiderable financial benefits their presence will bring to our club and to many others.

I'm also interested to find out what Bury fans make of it all. Back in the Conference days, fans of clubs like Lincoln City and Colchester United, who were relegated from the Football League but quickly bounced back, often found themselves enjoying the non-league experiences they'd initially dreaded. Bury have had a chance to sample the North West Counties League, having been forced to endure a longer stay than they'd presumably anticipated, and I expect their fans are leaving it with some great memories and, I hope, a respect for the clubs who inhabit that territory on a more permanent basis.

Vicki England has no doubt there's a lot of respect out there for the non-league game and for supporter-run clubs. It's earned by people like her and others who do so much unseen work to make football at this level happen.

'The people I work with...they're generally United, Liverpool, city, that kind of thing,' says Vicki England. 'They'll give me a little bit of ribbing about the level we're at but there's quite a lot of respect out there for those of us at any club that do what we do – especially a fan-run club. We're in complete control. We might go down to step six, but it'll be run in the right way and I think people see that and they respect that. It's a different world than going Old Trafford or Anfield and they take an interest.'

In her book *Under the Lights and In the Dark*, Gwendolyn Oxenham looks at how football can emerge in the most unlikely places. She writes, for example, about a refugee camp in Denmark where a group of kids – boys and girls - from different parts of the world – Afghanistan, Bosnia, Iraq, Armenia – discover the joy of kicking a ball around. 'The refugees can't speak each other's languages,' she writes, 'but watching football, they don't need to – it is visual, it is physical, it is a game they reproduce once they get back to their own ramshackle field in the middle of the refugee centre.'

It's always been in football's nature to lay down roots in unlikely places for as long as the game has existed. What the clubs I've featured in this book all have in common is an indomitable spirit, borne from finding a place in an area of the world where some of the world's biggest clubs already have a stranglehold, in which they've still managed to create something meaningful, a community vision, an aura that will continue, you feel, long after the lights have gone out for the last time on the mega-clubs, pulled down, perhaps, by their own bloated greed in a world that values surface glamour over the simple pleasure of a group of players working alongside each other to kick a ball between a couple of sticks.

Thousands of players in England alone do this at weekends for little or no material reward. In a world that tries to define the pursuit of material wealth as the only worthwhile goal, there's something inspiring in that alone. That many thousands also gather to watch them tells me that football continues to have an organic power that is unknown to those who seek only to commodify it.

'We've seen examples in the Football League and Premier League of so many wealthy owners coming in and then it just doesn't work out. The number of owners who have the best interests of the club at heart are probably minimal, in my view. I've always stressed that everything we do has got to be sustainable,' says Bren Connolly.

Over the next week, while much of the footballing media's attention will be on the top five of the Premier League and qualification for next season's Champions League, I'm thinking of a cup final I can't be at, the prospect of a group of youngsters from Runcorn securing a league and cup double and a massive game at Anfield that has nothing to do with Liverpool FC...

Saturday 3 May

Anfield Sports and Community Centre, Liverpool

North West Counties Premier Play-Off Final

Lower Breck 2 Padiham 0

This always passionate footballing community is especially vibrant right now. Up the road, Liverpool have just won their 20th league title, equalling Manchester United's record. With that minor business out of the way, the field in Anfield is left to Lower Breck who, with a Liverpool Senior Cup Final still to come, are playing for promotion to the Northern Premier League West Division.

It's a different world, of course, and one I'd much rather be part of. It's no great revelation that top level football has become a commodity, a means through which the already rich can either make great sums of money or use as a mechanism for greater power and control.

It's true that a kind of football allegiance can be bought by glamour and success. This is especially so for non-league football where the enticement of success on the field must come a distant second to things such as community, camaraderie and the unquantifiable value of mutual allegiance. There's no doubt football can be about money, but that certainly isn't all it's about.

And that's the reason why football at lower levels is necessary. Because, basically, the rich don't get football. They get its glamour, its prestige, its earning potential, its commercial possibilities, but you've only got to look at the various ideas that have been floated to understand that the future is filled with threats that will endanger the sport as we know it. The breakaway European Super League, the Premier League's 39th game idea, squeezing more world cups into the calendar...all are driven by the desire, not to further the game, but to bleed as much cash out of it as possible.

Meanwhile, clubs like Lower Breck retain an identity beyond any of that. Nearby, part of the area has been bulldozed so that Anfield could have its capacity increased, to allow Liverpool FC to 'survive' in the global marketplace. Just up the road, Everton's Goodison Park – once the greatest stadium in the land and the home of a community idea long since vanquished – is soon to be demolished, the club displaced to the docklands area that itself has been concreted over, robbed of its former identity to house designer retail outlets and soulless bars.

But the presence of Lower Breck means a community club still exists and I'm delighted to have been able to witness some of the highlights of their remarkable season, even though my own club was one of the casualties. On Tuesday they'll face Everton in the Liverpool Senior Cup Final. Everton have won the competition 46 times, more than any other club. Nowadays, they enter a youth team, while 41 times winners Liverpool FC don't enter it at all. Lower Breck have never even been close to winning it. You can guess who it means more to.

But the Lower Breck fans I speak to around the ground acknowledge it's secondary to the prize on offer today: a place in the Northern Premier League West Division for the first time in the club's short history.

There was a small bump in the road last weekend, when West Didsbury & Chorlton scored first in the semi-final, meaning Breck had to come from behind to secure a 2-1 win. We'd anticipated a showdown with Ramsbottom United, who finished close behind Breck in the table, but their bump in the road proved more significant: it's their conquerors Padiham who'll contest the final at the Anny today.

Padiham, perhaps buoyed by that unexpected victory, start brightly and it takes a while for Breck to get going. At one point an old woman who looks strikingly like my nana – who's been dead for more than thirty years – squeezes in next to me, lager can in hand, shouting abuse at the opposition, who she seems to believe are Oldham Athletic. Thankfully she moves on, allowing me to have a conversation with the guy on the other side of me who is obviously excited by the prospect of Breck going up this season but is unsure whether the club can make the necessary improvements required for a longer stay in the NPL. Extending the ground on the opposite side from us, he agrees, makes sense: whether the local council will see it that way is another matter though.

It's a close game until close to the hour mark when the ball breaks for Breck in the Padiham area and the defender rugby tackles the Breck forward to the ground. It seems an insane rush of blood as the keeper looked well placed to come out and smother the ball anyway. The ref has no choice: penalty and a red card. Dowling tucks away the penalty and half a dozen excitable children run on the pitch to join the celebrations. The ref isn't impressed with the invasion and orders a Breck steward to inform the crowd that he'll abandon the match if it happens again. The steward turns out to be the guy who was standing next to me in the first half and is understandably miffed to be in the firing line of his colleagues.

'Look, I'm only telling you what the ref says. He'll abandon the game if it happens again.'

'Send the kids back on!' shouts a lone Padiham voice.

Thankfully the miniature pitch invaders manage to quell their enthusiasm until the end of the game. Even with ten men, Padiham put up a fight until, deep in injury time, they're caught upfield and Breck break for Hughes to finish off the move and send the near-capacity crowd delirious. 'We know we're going up and we won't fuck it up' is the predictable refrain accompanied by a few rounds of 'Oh when the Breck go marching in...'

I feel for Padiham who, but for a defender's rush of blood, might well have taken Breck all the way but there's no question that, over the season, the home side deserve promotion. We depart the ground, leaving the committed to celebrate their triumph. One guy in front of us is explaining to his mate the plan from here: 'Yeah, it'll be Northern Premier League West next season, then up to the Premier Division. After that, National League North, National League Premier then League Two.' Such levels of optimism are surely permitted – indeed, they're almost mandatory - on occasions like this.

Attendance: 646

Saturday 4 May

I'm not around to see it, sadly, but the Runcorn youngsters beat Kidsgrove to secure the league and cup double for the U21s, a fabulous reward for a memorable season.

'There were tears (mine),' says Kelly Jones.

Tuesday 6 May

The Cheshire Senior Cup Final

Bucket Hat FM

I'm sitting in an air-conditioned room in Cambridge gazing out at blue skies and brutal sunshine. Apparently it's a similar story in the north of England when what I really need is for a typhoon to be heading down the Dee Estuary, tearing up everything in its path. I've never longed so earnestly for a postponement and if what it takes is for the Deva Stadium to be destroyed by Typhoon Willie, or whatever, then so be it. A pile up on the M53? Loss of life? You don't want to know how far I'd be willing to go.

I look instead for fate to strike closer to home. If a disaster of some kind should befall one or more of my colleagues and I somehow escape to make the 3.20 train, I could get a taxi from Chester stadium...but my hope that one of them would slip in the shower this morning didn't yield results and no one around me looking even remotely peaky. With me in the room is a United fan, a city fan and a couple of others who occupy that strange portion of the human race that doesn't care about football. None of them is aware of my problem; possibly they don't even know there's such a thing as the Cheshire Senior Cup and presumably wouldn't care even if they did.

3.20 ticks by with agonising precision and a train leaves Cambridge station without me on it. If Runcorn win the Cheshire Senior Cup tonight, I won't be there to see it happen. Accepting defeat, I head out with the others for a couple of pints and a curry, both of which normally come high on my list of favourite things to do. Some way behind football though.

I'm getting updates from Tim, who's gone on the coach. We exchange a concern that, having come from behind to beat Stalybridge twice this season, striking a third such blow will be beyond us. As it turns out, we don't need to. We're two up at half-time thanks to two Adam Moseley goals. The hissed 'yes' that escapes my lips on both occasions isn't ignored by my colleagues, especially as it's accompanied by a spray of biryani, but they're kind of used to this...me taking a curious interest in events that to them seem as remote as events on a far-off world.

Further beer is proposed after the curry but I'm heading back to my hotel. Because kick off was slightly delayed, it gives me a chance to listen to the second half on Bucket Hat FM. I turn it on to hear Sam announcing that Adam Moseley has his hat trick, that Runcorn are 3-0 up and are heading, surely, for victory. I feel a strange mixture of exhilaration and regret.

Sam Phillips is already sounding hoarse with the emotion of it all. 'This is the day when the boy becomes a man,' he yells as Moseley's third goes in.

Jack is, uncharacteristically, more measured in his assessment. 'Runcorn have been clinical in the moments that mattered,' he observes, sagely.

Tim's still sharing his observations by text. He's 25, a year older than I was the last time I saw Runcorn do this: see the Cheshire Senior Cup bedecked in yellow and green ribbons, a competition which, more than any other, is bound up with the club's identity and this with my own.

Eight minutes left and the sound's gone all weird. Someone on the chat says Sam sounds like Norman Collier, but, if so, it's Norman Collier while he's having a stroke.

I worry that communication will break down fully before I get to hear the triumphant roar that will no doubt escape Sam's throat when the full-time whistle goes. But fortunately this historic occasion is taking place in the 21st century and the guys get the YouTube site functioning so we can hear the rest of the commentary through that. We get a couple of minutes of breathless anticipation then see the Runcorn bench flood onto the pitch in the kind of outpouring of communal joy that is unique to football.

Sam is on the pitch too, looking for players and staff to interview, which is easy. More difficult is getting them to heed his plea not to swear while they're on air.

'James Short...how does it feel?'

'Fuckin' great, innit?'

Brad Cooke offers a bit more detail: 'I'm buzzing for you lot. I said before the game that I could see how much it meant, the volunteers and the stuff that you do behind the scenes that no one sees, all these unbelievable fans...I'm proud as punch to be managing this football club and I'm so, so happy for you lot. This club's been starved but the world's turning now. That was unbelievable.'

I get to watch the trophy presentation live. It's better than nothing.

Actually, it's better than most things.

Epilogue - Summer 2025

The lesson of history is that even the biggest bubbles always at some point. Football at the highest levels has a look of the Roman or Mayan empires about it right now: it may continue for centuries but it's hard to avoid the conclusion that its greatest days are behind it and that its bloated size contains within it the seeds of its eventual downfall.

This summer we're treated to the 'spectacle' of the inaugural Club World Cup, crammed into the shrinking gap we once knew as the close season. It's an ego trip disguised as a football tournament, with FIFA boss Gianni Infantino having his own sticker in the official Panini sticker album and President Trump hogging the limelight when the cup is presented to eventual winners Chelsea, before deciding to keep the trophy himself and send Chelsea back to England with a replica.

Chelsea, of course, are not the best club in the world, or even in England, so their crowning as world champions in such farcical circumstances seems fitting. During the summer they've been fined for historic violations of financial regulations and have sold their women's team effectively to themselves to generate the cash necessary to avoid another penalty. Aston Villa, also fined, have followed them by doing the same thing and there are rumours of other Premier League clubs following their example. It may be the beginning of a great separation of men's and women's football at the top level, though it looks far more like yet another example of the creative accountancy that big time football is now riddled with. Football is drawing in some of the richest and most powerful people on the planet and they certainly aren't in it for the love of the game, whatever soundbites they put out.

Manchester City, already skilled in the art, have some of the finest legal and financial minds on speed-dial, allowing them to place block after block in the way of allegations that have now been swirling around them for seven years. My own club, United, have the opposite problem: the huge debt that sits in their owners' holding company, requiring the syphoning of operational profits to pay off the interest every year. When Jim Ratcliffe says the club is in danger of going bust, what he really means is there's a danger of these profits disappearing, the debt bulging, and Wall Street investors departing the scene like thieves in the night, an analogy I'll leave you to judge the appropriateness of. United still generate more income without a ball being kicked than any other Premier League team, but very little of that income stays in football, or in England.

I could go on about agents, multi-club ownership, contracts, stockpiling of assets, exploitative academies and hundreds of other things, but my attention during the summer months was far away from all this. Judging by the limited interest in the Club World Cup, I wasn't alone. Tickets originally priced at well over $400 for Chelsea's semi-final against Fluminense were being sold for just $14 the day before the match. Infantino, meanwhile, declared it the most successful club tournament ever.

One of the advantages of non-league football is its very lack of prestige. The value of community-based or supporter-run clubs is that they can, if they remain true to their vision, steer clear of the wrong kind of attention. That doesn't mean it hasn't happened at non-league level, albeit on a different scale, or that many of the other problems that affect football globally can be avoided at our level.

Barely was the ink dry on the final NPL West Division league table than it merged that champions Widnes were in big trouble. The celebrations had barely had a chance to die down when it was announced that Ello was stepping down. Hot on the heels of that news came a very public spat between the owners of Widnes FC and the club's affiliated junior sides centring around money and who was to blame for there not being any.

Reading between the lines of the lengthy statements Widnes put out, it wasn't difficult to see what the real problem was. While those running the club sought sympathy by talking about how much they'd been forced to pump into the club to keep it afloat, they pointed the finger inadvertently in the direction of the real problem. However good they were on the field (or plastic). Widnes FC never looked a sustainable proposition at this level of the game.

Of course, sympathies lie with the small support base the club has managed to build up but this was not a problem that came out of nowhere: it was a situation unfolded in plain sight over years rather than weeks. The situation was crying out for someone to take a realistic look at the scenario and make a pragmatic decision. The club sought an unrealistic and costly one – building a club from scratch on public playing fields – rather than the kind of less attractive path that many clubs have had to travel down in the past. The option of an out-of-town groundshare or a return to the county leagues may not be what Widnes FC wanted to be about, or what anyone wants to be about, but sometimes it's a choice between that or extinction.

There is, of course, the possibility of a supporter-run club rising from the ashes, as happened with Runcorn and other clubs. Chester emerged from a lengthy period of mismanagement and have used the supporter-ownership model to forge a sustainable future. Like Runcorn, they're not currently at the level they once were, but was survival in the football league really better than the end of the season they've just experienced, with a dramatic play-off semi-final victory ending in the kind of heroic defeat in the final that has further galvanised their highly invested support base?

As I write, there seems to be no prospect of that happening at Widnes, which perhaps puts the finger on the real problem here: a lack of grass roots support and the general apathy that exists in Widnes with regard to association football. The departing owners delivered several parting shots at Halton Borough Council and local MP Derek Twigg but it's hard to see what any of them could have done to retrieve a situation that frankly always looked like ending up this way.

Sorry sagas like this one raise important questions about what constitutes success at this level of football. Is success on the field worth trading long-term viability for? Along with Atherton LR (who ended the season with three trophies, and Winsford United, Widnes can be said to have enjoyed the best season of any team featured in this book. We can add to that the achievement of Lower Breck in gaining promotion and Irlam, who won the Manchester Premier Cup for the first time. The one other bit of silverware entering the area was, of course, the Cheshire Senior Cup which now sits proudly in Murdishaw.

Looking back, would Widnes FC have been willing to sacrifice that success for a period of stability? The assumption seemed to be that a more successful club would lead to a growing fan base and pay for the climb up the pyramid, but in the non-league game that's an old story and one that rarely produces a happy ending.

Runcorn Linnets, on the other hand, have consistently made financial prudence the focal point of their existence, even if that has not always found favour with some of their own supporters. Runcorn have a strong supporter base built up over generations: although the APEC's average attendance showed a decline in 2024-25, only five teams in the league enjoyed higher support levels and a consistently large travelling support boosts attendances across the league. But the shadow of our own years in the wilderness hangs heavy in the recent past and it holds a sign that points firmly in the direction of a need for stability above all else.

The new groundshare arrangement with Northwich Victoria combines the moral compunction to help other clubs in need with the pragmatic benefits of having a crowd occupying the APEC every Saturday. Groundshares, of course, are nothing new and there are other ways clubs can ensure their own survival while contributing to the wider health of the game at this level. Next season, 1874 Northwich will continue as tenants at Barnton while also entering into a mutual agreement with Winsford United that will allow anyone with a season ticket cheap entry into the other team's ground. Whether this turns out to have much impact on attendances or not, it's the kind of low-risk strategy that's worth a try.

No football club has a right to exist. That must be obvious to almost anybody. Maintaining that existence requires hard work, sacrifice, loyalty to the cause and many other factors, one of which is the willingness to face up to real world scenarios. Those I spoke to at Runcorn Linnets made no secret of the fact that they want the club to be back at the top of the pyramid, but they're also aware that many complex factors have to be negotiated for that to happen. There is no quick fix and the game at this level is littered with the corpses of clubs who thought they'd found one.

'The absolute priority is that there is a Runcorn Linnets Football Club here in 10, 15, 20, 100 years,' Bren Connolly said to me. To me, that's not a bad aim and, if you see things differently then maybe football – any football – isn't for you.

Acknowledgements

I'm grateful for the help of my son Tim, who accompanied me on most of these adventures and to Alan who got me following this club in the first place. Massive thanks to those who gave up their time for interviews, specifically Bren Connolly, Vicki England, Brian Howman, Kelly Jones, Sam Phillips, Jack Slater, Carl and Gary Gleavey and to the many people who've offered me their opinions on both Runcorn Linnets and the rest of the teams in this book, including those whose names I don't know who were willing to talk to a random stranger who turned up at their ground one day.

Bibliography

Atkins, Fred – Pyramid Schemes
Bayley, Mike – Changing Ends
Blackstone, Mike – The Brown Sauce Is Off
Goldblatt, David – The Ball is Round
Gorman, Terry – Non-League Football Grounds of Liverpool & Manchester
Hill, Dave – The Card
Hughes, Simon – On the Brink: A Journey Through English Football's North West
Keohane, John – The Non-League Football Grounds of Cheshire
Miller, Kerry – The History of Non-League Football Grounds
Moore, Aaron – Fields of Dreams and Broken Fences
Oxenham, Gwendolyn – Under the Lights and In the Dark
Proudlove, David – Work and Play

About the Author

Mark Whitby lives in Widnes with his wife Sharon. He has two grown up children, one of whom shares his passion for football and another who shares her mum's complete apathy towards the game. He's currently working as a consulting editor for educational textbooks, among other things. Before that, he wrote a football-themed novel *Balls* and the official guide to *The Festive Fifty,* the year-end chart that was an annual fixture of the John Peel show.

Printed in Dunstable, United Kingdom

65364403R00118